The Marriage Mix

How to Create
Interfaith/Interspiritual/Intercultural
Wedding Ceremonies

A STEP-BY-STEP MANUAL FOR MINISTERS

The Marriage Mix

How to Create
Interfaith/Interspiritual/Intercultural
Wedding Ceremonies

A STEP-BY-STEP MANUAL FOR MINISTERS

Reverend Lynn Gladstone, PhD

www.babypiepublishing.com

ISBN: 978-1-945446-31-3

Cover Image: iStockphoto ©1905HKN
Back Cover Image: RobertIrwinWolf.com

Dedication

*Dedicated to my mother who always wanted me to be a doctor
and to Margaret who cheered me on in this endeavor.*

Acknowledgments

*My deepest thanks to Ifaat Qureshi, my first dedicated editor and friend,
who kept me on form throughout.*

*Thanks to Heather and the editing team at Babypie Publishing
who completed my final editing with care and precision.*

Thanks to Babypie Publishing for taking my book to the finish line.

Contents

PART II
The Marriage Mix
How to Create
Interfaith/Interspiritual/Intercultural
Wedding Ceremonies
A Step-by-Step Manual for Ministers

Appendices

Foreword

I've always been profoundly interested in the world and moved by different cultures, religions, customs and rituals, and in harvesting great happiness and meaning from love, family and raising children. I explored many paths in pursuit of these interests—from social worker to entrepreneur to human resources director—before finding the one that wove them all together and unlocked my true mission in life: becoming an interfaith minister.

I consider myself an interfaith, intercultural and interspiritual minister. I believe there are innumerable ways for us to interpret the world around us. Being interfaith enables me to serve all people through their beliefs.

I'm intercultural in that I recognize our backgrounds and heritages are blending more and more in marriage, and I am here to help facilitate this cultural phenomenon.

I'm interspiritual, believing that all faiths are grounded in the idea that there exists a universal connection and oneness among all living things. While all faiths essentially embrace the values of love, hope and compassion, it is the diversity of all faith practices that ultimately adds to the richness of our lives and to the world around us.

The goal of every ceremony and service I create is to inspire joy or reflection within every person attending. This goal is why no ceremony is the same, because no couple or family, no path to love or lifetime event is ever the same. Each ceremony is customized and personalized. It's a collaboration; one designed to be enjoyable and enlightening and evolve out of our getting to know each other.

PART I

Intention, History and Research

My Intention

My endeavor here is to offer a helpful reference manual for intermarriage wedding practitioners. I specifically use the term *intermarriage* as the umbrella for interfaith/interspiritual/intercultural (I/I/I) weddings. I have designed this manual, *The Marriage Mix: How to Create Interfaith, Interspiritual, Intercultural Wedding Ceremonies, A Step-by-Step Manual for Ministers,* to be used in creating meaningful wedding ceremonies for marriage-bound couples, both heterosexual and same-sex with an emphasis on I/I/I ceremonies. I intend for it to help wedding practitioners guide couples in the process of co-creating a custom ceremony that reflects each of them, their relationship, and what they want to occur on their marital day and in their future together. As wedding practitioners, our work and time with each couple gives us a rare opportunity to help them understand and appreciate their upcoming future together. We are not just helping them create a ceremony for their wedding day; we are also guiding couples to build a foundation for an informed, shared and mutually understood relationship and marriage together.

The Marriage Mix manual is organized into chapters covering a variety of topics from the initial contact with a couple interested in marrying, to the creation and performance of the ceremony. Each chapter offers helpful *Tools* and *Sample Letters/Emails* to guide the practitioner, step-by-step, through the whole process of working with couples and creating a custom ceremony that truly speaks of them. These *Tools* and *Sample Letters/Emails* are actually used in my work with couples.

Though many of the *Tools* included in this book are those I have developed, some of the *Tools* have been built upon the hard work of others who are credited within. I have gathered materials and concepts from the works of thoughtful mentors, wedding professionals and scholars. The commentary prose is my own.

Within this book, I first examine the history of intermarriage. I then present a comprehensive manual, *The Marriage Mix*, with step-by-step instructions and *Tools*. These resources are meant for I/I/I wedding practitioners/ministers/celebrants/officiants/reverends (note, throughout this manual, "wedding practitioners", "ministers", "celebrants", "officiants" and "reverends" will be used interchangeably) to maximize the opportunity for helping couples plan their wedding ceremonies, while allowing for growth and self-examination in the process.

As for the couples mentioned in *The Marriage Mix* with whom I have worked, their names have been changed for privacy purposes.

This book assumes that the wedding minister is legally ordained and is registered with a legal license number by a state governing body for the purpose of conducting marital unions. Officiating out-of-state weddings requires other certificates depending on the state, country or territory. Information regarding this will appear later in this manual.

History of Interfaith/Interspiritual/Intercultural Marriage

When defined broadly, *marriage* is considered a cultural universal custom. However, for the purpose of this book it is limited to the definition of monogamous interfaith/interspiritual/intercultural (I/I/I) marriages in the United States.

Throughout time, populations have responded to perceptions and changes in their environments. They adapt by accepting or adopting new behaviors as social values shift with interfaith, interspiritual, intercultural and same-sex marriages. *Interfaith marriage* refers specifically to a legal union between two parties of different established religious faiths (Yinger, *Jstor.org*). The term *interspiritual marriage* is more comprehensive in that it addresses a legal union between two parties of any interior personal belief systems (Wright, *Interspirituality.com*). *Intercultural marriage* goes further in creating legal unions between people of different faiths, ethnicities, races and geographic regions (Kahlenberg, *Interfaithfamily.com*). For example, interracial marriages are defined as *intercultural marriages* today. Interracial marriages, also known as *miscegenation* or *race mixing*, were banned in the Deep South and many states until 1967, when the U. S. Supreme Court ruled that they were protected by federal law (Head, *About.com*). Until recently, state-sanctioned or religious wedlock was a socially or ritually recognized union or legal contract between a consenting man and a consenting woman that establishes rights and obligations between them ("Marriage," *merriam-webster.com*). In 2015, the U.S. Supreme Court ruled and extended the law, so that marriage between consenting parties, adult or parental and state supported, is to be recognized nationwide (Liptak, *NYTimes.com*).

Today, when we talk of the increasing number of I/I/I and same-sex marriages, we can see that these are all fast becoming part of the fabric of social mores in the United States. The Pew Research Center's "Religious Landscape Study" found that 39 percent of Americans in 2010 were in an intermarriage compared to 19 percent who married before the 1960s (Murphy, *Pewresearch.org*). "Many of these recent interfaith marriages are between Christians and the religiously unaffiliated (sometimes called 'nones')." (Murphy, *Pewresearch.org*).

Evolution of I/I/I Marriage

To gain perspective, it is helpful to look back on the evolution of I/I/I marriage. Marriage or coupling goes back to the Garden of Eden, as we understand it, either literally or figuratively. From the beginning of time, a man and a woman coupled sexually and multiplied, thus ensuring the perpetuation of humankind. Religion did not figure into the equation.

The rise and popularity of organized religions paved the way for thinking in terms of the "religious other" (us vs. them) as related to the tradition of marriage (Seamon 5). But in fact, I/I/I marriage has existed globally for tens of centuries as described in the Torah, made more widespread by the Silk Road of commercial travel and trade, the spoils of wars, colonialism and political, social and economic exigencies (Seamon 2). Over the millennia, marriage came to serve economic survival, social-financial status and political ambition.

Despite the growing trend in I/I/I marriages, there has been plenty of historical prohibition against intermarriage: marriage between people of different religions, ethnicities or racial groups, castes and tribes ("Intermarriage," *Dictionary. com*). To name some instances, in the fourth century, Constantine mandated the embracing of Christianity by his masses. The legal, theological and social prohibitions to interfaith marriages for Christians were punishable by death (Seamon 20). In the thirteenth century, converts from Judaism to Christianity for the purposes of marriage were required to eschew contact with their Jewish relatives (Seamon 21). In the sixteenth and seventeenth centuries, the powerful Church of England annulled marriages other than those between Anglicans and other Anglicans (Seamon 2). In the United States in the eighteenth century, even after the separation of church and state in marital matters, interfaith marriage and social interaction were so fully discouraged that such marriages were unusual (Seamon 2).

In the following centuries to present day, the occurrence of intermarriage unfurled at a steady and increasing rate (Seamon 3). In the U.S. Bill of Rights of 1789, we experienced disestablishment or separation of church and state. Disestablishment led the way to both social and theological acceptance of interfaith marriage and religious choice (Seamon 40–42).

People immigrated in great waves to the American shores with the hope of escaping all sorts of oppression, including religious, economic and political. In the United States, there was hope for liberty and opportunity in the land of the free and home of the brave, established by the U. S. Constitution. As the Industrial Revolution made way for more factory and office workers, people were drawn out of their homogeneous environments (Seamon 50). People of differing backgrounds began to mingle in settings of commonality. With this mindset, the rigid lines of religious, social and class distinctions began to blur (Seamon 80).

I venture to say that the land of possibility (the United States) actually paved the way for a romantic era in which people could dream, achieve and love (Seamon 80). When there is love, there is less patience for society's proscriptive rules about marriage. Let us concentrate on this phenomenon in the United States. In 2008, 27 percent of Americans married outside their own religion (Seamon 2). If we include interfaith marriage among different Protestant sects, the number rose to 37 percent (Seamon 2). So, we are talking about a groundswell that brings challenges to couples, their families, and the ministers responsible for legalizing these unions.

During the twentieth and twenty-first centuries, the matter of intermarriage has turned nearly on its head. In earlier times, the pairing of couples was very often a practical matter and not of a romantic nature (Seamon 49–50). "Husbands and wives had different roles in different spheres . . . Men sought homemakers, and women sought breadwinners" (Miller and Bui, *NYTimes.com*). But as women's roles changed in society through education and work, "marriage became more about companionship" (Miller and Bui, *NYTimes.com*). Today we witness marriage being undertaken primarily for reasons of love and compatibility (Seamon 49–50). Indeed, we are at a point in history where marriage itself, sanctioned by the state and/or church, is not even seen as a required precursor to cohabitation or to rearing children. Couples today choose love as their primary reason to marry. And, that is the arena in which I have chosen to work as a minister. Love is an essential marker for those of us who have chosen this career path.

In 2015, I was interviewed for an article published by *The Knot* (Appendix 1), and they asked what are the greatest challenges regarding faiths that my I/I/I couples face with their families when planning their wedding. I was unable to provide much material on that subject, as nearly every couple I met was undeterred about their religious divergences. There have been couples who thought long and hard about what religious practice(s) would take place in their lives together, particularly in relation to raising their future children. Not one required the other to convert, though some said they would voluntarily practice their spouse's traditions. Many have chosen to raise their future children in one of their faiths. Some said they would find a church that reflected the values of both of their religions. Others, still, expressed an intention to expose their children to both of their belief practices and offer them the chance to choose for themselves.

There was a good deal more strife in other areas of wedding planning, such as how many guests to invite and which cousins on each side to include, than the issue of mixing religions. I am not saying that families did not have objections; rather, that these couples made it clear to their parents and significant relatives that their hearts had won over any concerns about intermarriage.

Spiritual but Not Religious

In addition to the prevalence of I/I/I marriages, there is another measurable trend in America that is on the rise. I am calling this the *Faith of Spirituality*. So many of my couples introduce themselves as "spiritual but not religious."

Defining spirituality may be helpful here. *Spirituality* is a broad term referring to a set of principles that may or may not transcend religious beliefs ("Spirituality," *Psychologytoday.com*). It is about the relationship between the self and something larger in the universe (Culliford, *Psychologytoday.com*). Being spiritual means striving for answers to questions about the infinite ("Spirituality," *Psychologytoday.com*). The spiritual path is one that seeks goodness, interconnectedness and meaning in our existence.

> The falloff in traditional religious beliefs and practices coincides with changes in the religious composition of the U.S. public. A growing share of Americans are religiously unaffiliated, including some who self-identify as atheists or agnostics as well as many who describe their religion as 'nothing in particular.' Altogether, the religiously unaffiliated (also called the 'nones') now account for 23% of the adult population, up from 16% in 2007. ("U.S. Public Becoming Less Religious," *Pewforum.org*)

More and more couples of different faith backgrounds are arriving at my office door. Many are partially or totally alienated from the religions of their upbringing. They reject dogma and seek out communities with other like-minded people. They are generally a compassionate group who are interested in doing service to better the world and for the common good. And, they do feel a connection to humanity or The Divine in their own personal ways, and on their own terms. Many define this connection as their spirituality. At the same time, they maintain their individuality, holding that they can be spiritual in their own ways.

As wedding practitioners, we must take notice of this growing group of people and be prepared to help them fashion a ceremony that speaks to their personally held beliefs.

What is an Interfaith/Interspiritual/Intercultural Minister?

I was drawn to Interfaith Seminary because of my belief that we are all unique and one at the same time. Everyone is interconnected, and love, compassion and understanding are the standards that we universally hope to live by. We are each here for a purpose, and ultimately, that is to contribute to the betterment of the world (Berke 11–15).

An I/I/I practitioner accepts and embraces without judgment all faith practices and forms of spiritual practice, including agnosticism and atheism. An I/I/I practitioner sees the value in all belief systems and the beauty and commonality that lie within them. There is a recognition that all of humanity is woven together, and thereby is able to foster compassion and peace.

In philosophical terms, these are tenets I hold strongly when working with couples:

- I believe in the inner wisdom of couples and urge them to call upon their best selves when making decisions.

- My only rules are about fulfilling legal requirements, and that we do not knowingly hurt anyone in our planning.

My task as a wedding minister is to consider what is most important to a couple in my care, and work faithfully to use that knowledge to create authenticity and joy for them in their marriage ceremony and hopefully in their future together.

As in the words of Muhyiddin Ibn 'Arabi, Sufi mystic and poet: "I follow the religion of Love: whatever way Love's camels take, that is my religion and my faith." ("Muhyiddin Ibn 'Arabi," *Ibnarabisociety.org*).

My Theology

Blog: God?

In this section, I share my personal frame of reference regarding spirituality in a blog, "God," that I originally wrote in 2012 on my website, *LynnGladstone.com*. Photography above is from iStockphoto ©Brasil2.

Let me try to tackle my theology.

As an adult and parent, I became attached to and versed in Judaism, which informs my view of the world tremendously. I am extremely fond of the Torah, as literature, fable and soap opera, and as a historic jumping-off point for discussion, query and doubt. I embrace positive Jewish values deeply and find many of these same values throughout the religious spectrum.

As for God—I was never clear in the past. I certainly thought if an all-powerful God were operating, he sure didn't give me my full measure of compassion. So, it was about me.

In my early thirties, I studied with a rabbi whose hero was Bob Dylan. He always ended weekly Torah study with this, "Remember, when you look into the eyes of another human being, you are looking into the eyes of God." This concept made a great impression on me, and I carried it forward for decades, though not exactly sure what it meant. I felt there was something in it that made spiritual sense to me.

Many years later, I found myself in an interfaith seminary where we were faced with our relationship (or not) to God on a daily basis.

Through searching the collection of my life experiences, I believe today that we are each fitted with godliness, the summation of which adds up to a powerful potential and obligation for each of us to make positive change in the world—either on a one-to-one scale, in community or in the world arena.

I believe there is a Grand Spirit of Creation that places us here in this world. Whether that is born in physics, metaphysics or God no longer matters much to me, other than as an intellectual pursuit. I believe there are forces that originate nature, the life cycle, the vagaries of our lives, and the need to love.

We are all interconnected. There is tremendous commonality among all human beings and that can move us into great compassion and understanding, which is necessary for the world's survival.

I seek what is good in every religion.

Interfaith/Interspiritual/Intercultural and Same-Sex Marriages

I consider I/I/I and same-sex ceremonies to be similar. Love is love, and it is my job to make all of my couples' marital unions legal in the eyes of the government. Whenever possible and practical, I try to think of ceremonies with a gender-neutral perspective. Both I/I/I and same-sex unions have potential challenges, particularly within families. I treat them both the same in writing a ceremony. I ask my same-sex couples if they want me to make a statement about the right of people to marry whom they love. Some do, and some do not. For I/I/I marriages, I discuss with couples the idea of creating balance, so we explore how to honor the different faiths, cultures and backgrounds. Together, we find ways to recognize and include their backgrounds, interests and belief systems into their ceremony with commentary, prayers, readings and rituals. For one I/I/I wedding and a same-sex ceremony, I interjected these statements:

Sample I/I/I Ceremony

"In this couple, we have the representation of different religions and five ethnicities. In spite of these differences, they found each other because of the one element that is human and universal. They found each other through love.

When we unite in matrimony, our families become one. It matters not what our histories are; we become an extended family. The difference of experience each family may bring to this union provides a richness of expression and perception.

As we watch more and more people marrying outside of their birth faith or cultural background, the world actually is brought closer together by the blending of the beautiful in each tradition. I have yet to find a religion in which the deepest original elements are not kindness and decency. This recognition of the common values of goodness and the increasing trend toward intermarriages offers an immeasurable chance to foster greater understanding, appreciation and peace in the world."

In the photo above, I had the pleasure of marrying Joanna and William, and photograph taken by *SnapWeddings.com*.

Sample Same-Sex Ceremony

"These gentlemen are here tonight to put both a traditional and legal exclamation point on their love for one another."

It was really just a short time ago that two men, and, so many like them, who sincerely loved another of their own gender, would not have been able to express their profound intentions to one another by marrying. They did not have the legal right to be wed as they are doing here today. This is cause for applause.

I believe that some years from now, the general populous will look back and wonder how that basic and decent right to marry could have ever been denied — the right to be recognized, protected and given the benefits of wedded couples by our government, our neighbors and even ourselves.

There is really only one question that ever needs to be asked. What is really important in life? Is there anyone who can deny that love is the bottom line? The desire to love and to be loved is both irresistible and universal. When we are lucky and love's power finds us, we become vulnerable to its random influence. Authentic love is not logical and has little to do with age, race, wealth or gender.

Love is a magnificent experience that has everything to do with feelings of familiarity, loyalty, support, values and yes, physical warmth. Everyone deserves ownership to love whomever they wish!

Basically, what I'm saying is summed up well in a quote by Whoopi Goldberg. Whoopi, in her inimitable and frank style, says, "Really, darling, it's a no-brainer. You know, I understand not everybody is for gay marriage. But if you're not for gay marriage, don't marry a gay person . . . ."

Note, I have found that well-placed, mature humor always goes over well in a ceremony. In the photo above, I had the pleasure of marrying Kevin and Joseph. Photograph taken by *JessicaCastroWeddings.com.*

PART II

The Marriage Mix

How to Create

Interfaith/Interspiritual/Intercultural

Wedding Ceremonies

A Step-by-Step Manual for Ministers

Creating Meaningful Conversations and Ceremonies

In order to produce a truly authentic and moving ceremony, I believe our job as wedding practitioners is to embrace each couple's unique perspective of their love. Wedding practitioners need to make a conscious decision to build a trusting and warm relationship with the couple during the period leading up to their wedding day, to the extent that the couple is interested. This means proactive, intermittent communication and being available for ongoing contact. Every contact is a chance to show that we are fully listening to our couples and that we care.

It means that no stone is unturned in order to customize the ceremony. By the day of the wedding, I often feel for a brief moment in time that I am a friend who is attending their marriage ceremony. This effort brings me great satisfaction and makes my work meaningful.

I am generally invited to my couple's cocktail reception, giving me a chance to chat with people (the couple's families and friends), whom I have only heard about previously. It is a very pleasant opportunity to share in the festivities, and well worth my time. On the other hand, I decline invitations to their wedding reception. In fact, though I may have that moment of feeling like a family friend, I am not and know it is time to say goodbye. If I am asked to present the meal blessing, I am pleased to do so before I depart.

It is a bittersweet moment, that goodbye. During the ceremony creation process, among the three of us a lot of intimacy has occurred. In order to soften the separation, I stay in touch with a post-wedding letter and cards for the holidays and their first anniversaries (see Appendix 2), which yield heartfelt responses. I have been delightfully notified when new babies arrive. Who wouldn't want to do this work?

A wise mentor of mine, Reverend David Wallace, taught me that when ministers speak the goal is to leave their audience inspired. I think of creating and performing weddings as a chance to inspire and perhaps even to teach and foster self-examination by the community of people in attendance. It may sound presumptuous, but to have the chance to reach the guests in perhaps a significant manner motivates me deeply.

During the pre-wedding phase when the couples' hearts are wide open, my premise is that "a teaching moment" is imminent. I provide couples with *Tools* that will come in handy throughout their married years. The *Tools* I offer and the questions I raise deliberately encourage couples to think and feel thoughtfully about their ceremony and their future together in ways that will nurture their loving bond. In having them do their due diligence during the time leading up to their wedding, my hope and belief is that they will be able to pre-empt communication problems before they are united in matrimony. This process may lead some couples to seek the support of marriage counseling.

Chapter Tips

- Every contact is a chance to show that we are fully listening to our couples and that we care.

1

Communication

In the service of building a productive relationship with couples, there is nothing more effective than keeping in touch. Throughout this manual, *The Marriage Mix,* are *Tools* including *Sample Letters/Emails* and *Questionnaires* appropriate to most situations that will arise as you work together. Every letter or email you send is a chance to foster warm and crucial communication that will be reflected in the ceremony you create.

In this day of a complex and sometimes unreliable cyber space, I recommend that you ask for confirmation of receipt of all your communications and that you do the same for theirs.

Throughout all our communication, it is important to encourage and stay where the couple is in their thinking, and steer them accordingly. Allow them the honor of producing their own ideas for the ceremony, while we act as the expert advisor and guide.

Tools: Couple's First Communication

For the wedding practitioner, contact begins with a phone call or an email such as this:

> *Dear Reverend Lynn,*
>
> *My name is Alison. My fiancé and I are planning a wedding for June 3, 2016. We are an interfaith couple and are looking for someone to officiate at our ceremony. Are you available? Please provide us with details and your fee.*
>
> *Alison*

Nine times out of ten, this is how our initial communication begins with couples.

There are a growing number of interfaith wedding practitioners today, and undoubtedly this couple has sent this same email to others. My first task is to respond as quickly as possible. It demonstrates smart professionalism and makes the couple feel that their inquiry is important, which it is.

Chapter Tips

- Respond as quickly as possible to their email inquiry.
- Allow the couple the honor of producing their own ideas for the ceremony, while acting as the expert advisor and guide.

2

Responding to Inquiries

As I have mentioned, the first order of business is to respond to inquiries quickly. Our initial reply will set the tone of our engagement with the couple. This is where we can be both informative and welcoming.

I think there are varying ways to respond to an initial inquiry — simply or in great detail. I used to respond in great detail, but being aware that the younger generation is partial to sound bites and that TMI (too much information) is frowned upon, I now choose to keep my initial response direct and short. I am including one of my typical responses below that I send by email:

Tools: Celebrant's Response to Initial Inquiry

Dear Alison (and partner's name if given),

Thank you for your inquiry. I wish you both a Big Congratulations!

I am happily available to officiate on your wedding day, depending on your location, and would love to talk with you and your fiancé about your ceremony. My custom ceremony fee is _____. Extended travel would incur additional costs.

Every wedding I do is custom and personalized for the two of you, and what your wishes are, whether secular, religious, spiritual, interfaith or same-sex.

Please visit my website LynnGladstone.com (the Wedding Page) for many details including pricing, reviews, a sample wedding ceremony and wedding videos. I am happy to address any additional information you seek.

If we find we are a good fit, we would meet in person and communicate by phone and email.

Our next step would be finding a time for us to talk about any questions you may have. Please send me available times and your phone number for an appointment.

I look forward to hearing from you and would love to be your wedding officiant.

Sincerely,

Rev. Lynn

Conflict of Dates

On the occasion of my already being booked for a wedding date, I send this simple response to an inquiry:

Tools: Celebrant's Conflict of Date Response

Email 1

Dear Josie and Tim,

Thank you for your inquiry and big congratulations on your upcoming wedding!

I am unfortunately unavailable on your wedding date, however, I would be happy to provide you with some excellent referrals, if you wish.

Best regards,

Lynn

Several times in my career, multiple couples have inquired about the same wedding date and time. I notify each uncommitted couple promptly of this occurrence by email.

Email 2

Dear (Couple),

I have just received a second inquiry for your wedding date. I will have to accept the first signed contract I receive. Would you like to set up an earlier conversation to see if we are a good fit?

I look forward to hearing from you.

Sincerely,

Lynn

Referrals to Colleagues

When I am unable to accept a client due to a conflict of date or location, I make referrals to trusted colleagues. It is a good idea to give couples a few choices of wedding practitioners. I ask the couple to let the referred celebrants know that I made the referral. In addition, I will send my colleagues notes informing them about a potential couple who may contact them.

I say this cautiously as I have had some touchy referral situations.

Before making a referral, it is essential to be familiar with your colleagues' work, as what they ultimately deliver reflects on your own professional reputation. Just because you are fond of someone, that does not guarantee their high level of professionalism.

Colleague Referrals

When a colleague refers clients to you, it is very important that you acknowledge that gesture and express your gratitude.

Tools: Celebrant's Thank You to Colleague

> *Dear Mary,*
>
> *I hope all is well for you and your family.*
>
> *I heard from Bobbi Lawrence and Jim Cates, inquiring about my services. Thank you so much for referring them to me. I appreciate the confidence you have in me.*
>
> *They sound like a lovely couple and I look forward to working with them to create their custom wedding ceremony.*
>
> *Warm regards,*
>
> *Lynn*

Colleagues Matter

Colleagues matter. They know what we go through and can corroborate and elaborate our experiences. If anything new is happening in our field of work, it is most likely that we will hear it from a colleague.

Chapter Tips

- Your initial reply will set the tone of your engagement with the couple.

- Before making a referral, it is essential that you are familiar with your colleagues' work. Just because you are fond of someone, that does not guarantee their high level of professionalism.

3

Promoting Our Services

To be a successful celebrant today requires consistent strategies for promoting our services. Here are my *Top 7 Strategies* for effectively promoting your services to attract marriage-bound couples:

1. Establish a Business Email Address and Phone Number
2. Create a Professional Website
3. Order Business Cards and Stationery
4. Advertise Online
5. Network
6. Use Social Media
7. Write Blogs

Tools: Establish a Business Email and Phone Number

I check my email and phone messages quite often throughout the day and evening. It is wise to establish a separate business email address and phone number and to set up notifications to alert you to those incoming emails. The sooner you get back to an inquiring couple, the greater the chance is to secure them as clients. By responding to them promptly, you are acknowledging that their request is important, and, indeed, their wedding is important.

Tools: Create a Professional Website

In this day of cyber communication and hurried lives, I highly recommend having a well-formatted and informative website. I cannot stress enough how vital it is to have the help of an excellent web designer who can create with you and for you an attractive, well-written and easily navigated site. Young people, the bulk of my clients, are reluctant to initially converse on the phone and would rather first gather information online, then contact you by email or text. I promise you that the expense of a good website is money well spent. Above and below are screenshots of my website, *LynnGladstone.com.* ©Lynn Gladstone 2017 and Website Design by *IfaatQureshi.com.*

The following, adapted from the "Weddings" page of my website, *LynnGladstone. com,* describes my services as an officiant, and how the process of creating a wedding ceremony works:

Option 1: Custom Wedding Ceremonies

I look forward to working with people from all faiths, unique philosophies, countries and backgrounds to design *Custom Ceremonies* that weave personal beliefs and traditions seamlessly together. On my website, I make it clear that this collaboration develops through the following process:

- A complimentary thirty-minute consultation to get to know each other

- A basic fee of $_____

- A nonrefundable deposit of $_____ to hold the wedding date

- Up to two meetings to discuss the ideas and details of your ceremony, giving consideration to your wishes, values and the role of your family

- A questionnaire that is carefully designed to help me know you and learn what you want for your ceremony

- Ongoing communications over email, phone or video

- The option to review the first draft of the ceremony

- Help resolve family members' differing expectations, should they arise

- Resources for music and readings

- Vendor recommendations and coordination with your wedding professionals

- Help planning out the details of your wedding day

- Help developing your Wedding Program

- The option of holding a separate rehearsal for an additional cost of $_____

- Wedding day: ten-minute pre-ceremony meeting

- Travel expenses apply for distances over an hour in each direction

- Balance of fee paid before the ceremony

- Presentation of the ceremony

- Legalizing and filing of your marriage license

- Charitable donation: a portion of your fee is donated in your honor to a charity of your choice

Option 2: Sweet and Simple Service

A *Sweet and Simple Service* is another option for couples seeking a more modest local ceremony or elopement ceremony, which includes the following:

- A complimentary consultation

- A basic fee of $_____

- A non-refundable deposit of $_____ to hold the wedding date

- A brief questionnaire to learn more about you as a couple

- A short service with your choice to include:

  - Welcoming of your guests and God/Spirit, if appropriate

  - Presenting how you met, and your reasons for getting married

  - Introducing vows you create or I provide

  - Conducting a ring exchange and a blessing

- Witnesses provided for a fee of $_____

- Balance of fee paid before the ceremony

- Presentation of the ceremony

- Legalizing and filing of your marriage license

- Charitable donation: a portion of your fee is donated in your honor to a charity of your choice

Tools: Order Professional Business Cards and Stationery

I advise having noteworthy business cards to hand out generously in your day-to-day travels. Investment in business stationery also gives you the professional appearance you wish to present. I use both printed and digital stationery when communicating with clients.

Tools: Advertise Online

Next, budget for advertising your services and website on a major wedding site. I chose *The Knot* because it is the top wedding site at this time. If this is too costly, there are other sites you can Google that are more affordable (e.g., *WeddingWire. com*). *The Knot* is my number one source of client inquiries. To advertise on *The Knot* does require setting up a vendor storefront (with descriptions about your services, logo, contact information, photos, etc.) in the cities you choose to work in. Below is a screenshot of my New York City vendor storefront created on *TheKnot.com.*

About this Vendor

Interfaith & Same-Sex, Rev. Lynn Gladstone, Ph.D.

Life's major milestones deserve celebration. I'm happy to help you mark your wedding with a religious, civil or multi-denominational ceremony created specially for the event. Together we'll customize the ceremony to best share the love and joy you've found with the people who mean the most to you.

Details

Ceremony Types

Civil Union, Commitment Ceremony, Elopement, Interfaith Ceremony, Non-Religious Ceremony, Religious Ceremony, Same Sex Ceremony, Second Wedding, Vow Renewal Ceremony

Wedding Activities

Newlywed Life, After The Wedding, Getting Engaged, Premarital Counseling, Ceremony, Wedding

Awards

2016 PICK the knot best of weddings

2015 PICK the knot best of weddings

Religious Affiliations

Baha'i Faith, Buddhist, Adventist, Anglican/Episcopal, Baptist, Congregationalist, Holiness, Lutheran, Methodist, Nondenominational, Pentecostal, Presbyterian, Restorationist, Protestant, Quaker, Christian, Hindu, Interfaith, Conservative, Reform, Jewish, Muslim, Pagan, Secular, Sikh, Spiritual, Unitarian, Wiccan

Wedding Categories

Planning

Tools: Network, Network and Network

My other sources for acquiring clients include referrals (personal and professional), word-of-mouth, online professional listings, distributing my business cards, social networking, and people who have seen me officiate.

Tools: Use Social Media

Social media is another way to reach potential wedding clients. Under good advice, I set up a *Facebook* Business page linked to my personal page. In order to promote my business page, I wrote a post to everyone I knew online asking them to view, share and like my page. *Facebook* and *Twitter* are also where I post my wedding and happy anniversary announcements (Appendix 2), photos, news and my blogs. Below are screenshots of my "Reverend Lynn Gladstone" *Facebook* Business page and "Lynn Gladstone" *Twitter* page. Facebook © 2017. Photograph (large cover photo) taken by *VanessaMariePhotos.com* and profile photo by *RobertIrwinWolf.com*.

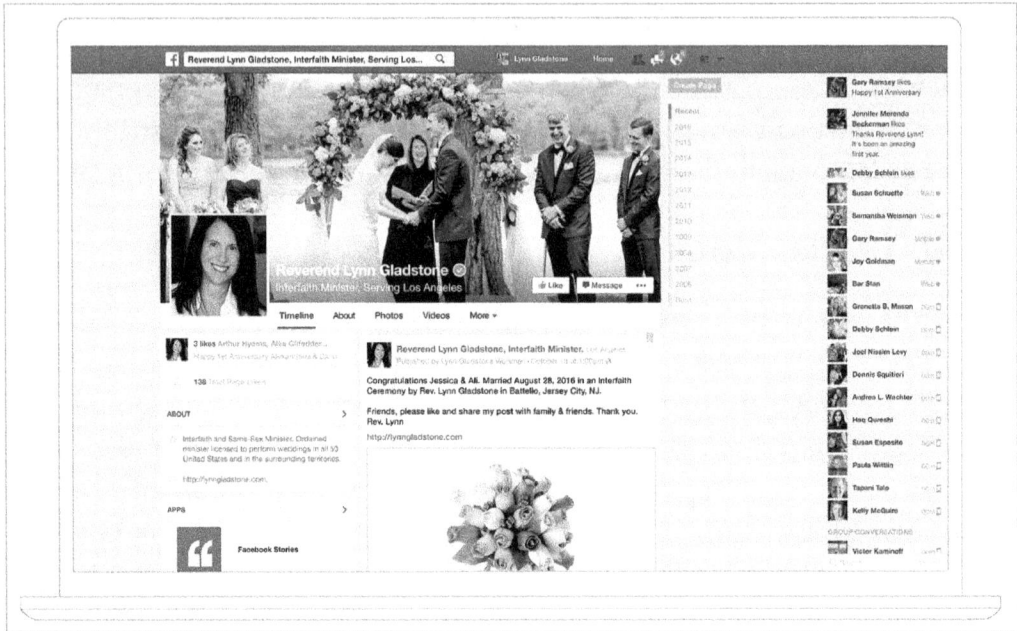

Recruit Friends/Family to Your New Facebook Business Page

Dear Friends,

Hello and best wishes to all of you who have walked into my life and were added to my address book. Many of you know that I am now an ordained Interfaith Reverend, performing a variety of ceremonies and rituals, including weddings, baby blessings, memorials and counseling.

I ask those of you who are my Facebook friends to check out "Reverend Lynn Gladstone," my new Facebook Business page, and to also review my website, LynnGladstone.com. If you like what you see, please "Like" or "Share" my business page and add a comment.

I would be most grateful.

Thank you,

Rev. Lynn

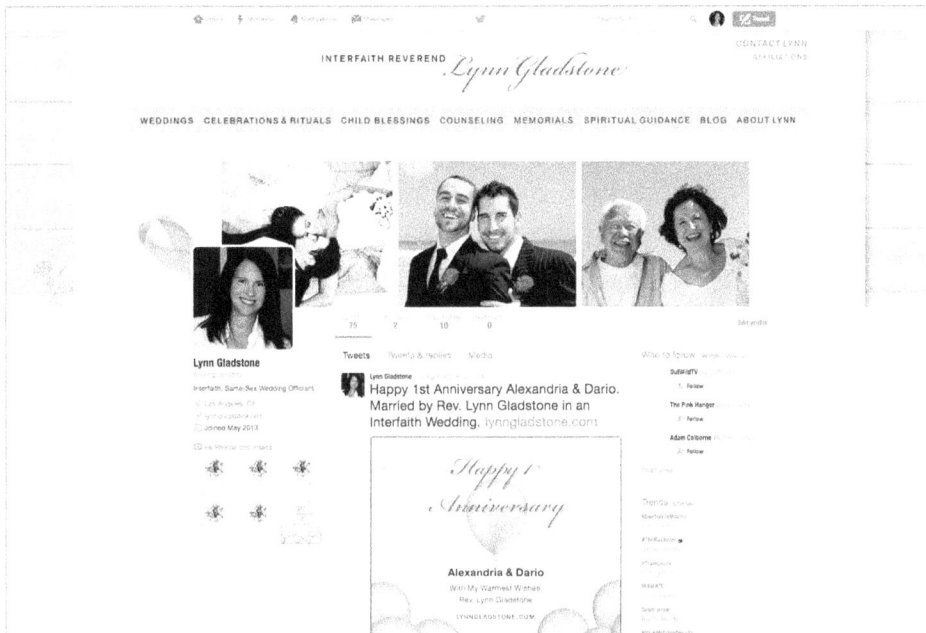

Twitter, Tweet and Twitter Bird Logo are trademarks of Twitter, Inc. or its affiliates. Photo credits include *RobertIrwinWolf.com,* iStockphoto ©1905HKN, iStockphoto ©purmar and iStockphoto ©IPGGutenbergUKLtd. Happy anniversary digital card and banner image Design by *IfaatQureshi.com.*

Tools: Write and Post Blogs

Create a blog. A blog is an easy way to connect and support couples getting married. A blog can provide background information about us and about being a celebrant ("There Are Many Ways to Bake a Cake," see below). In a blog, you can share expert advice for planning a wedding ("Tools: Planning Your Wedding?! Relax"), writing vows ("Tools: Tips for Couples Writing Their Own Vows"), dealing with family issues ("Tools: Hey! Whose Wedding Is This Anyway"), second marriages ("Tools: Love the Second Time Around" in Appendix 3), and so on. In addition, we can create and share a list of recommended wedding vendors (photographers, videographers, florists, etc.) we have worked with professionally.

When I work with couples to create their ceremony, I ask them a lot of intimate information. While I believe in the wisdom of professional boundaries, I think it is perfectly acceptable, fair and even desirable to share some of my personal experiences as they relate to the couple's situation, especially if they are curious. That idea prompted me to write my first blog, in 2012: "There Are Many Ways to Bake a Cake," below, posted on my website *LynnGladstone.com*.

Blog: *There Are Many Ways to Bake a Wedding Cake*

Hi there. I'm very excited to start this, my first blog, and I invite you to join me. *There are many ways to bake a wedding cake* whatever stage you are in your life, and all of them are delicious.

Let's flash back to 1979. My sister got married in a silver designer dress in an elegant loft with a stunning, starlit view of the Empire State Building in New York City. She and her fiancé hired a wedding consultant and caterer, a ten-piece 1920s band, invited 150 guests, were married by a rabbi with the witness of family, stepchildren and friends—and we all had a grand time.

They went on in their life together to have their own two children and worked very hard at melding the two families. This is generally a challenging endeavor, but they invested their full determination to make it work. It required having all of them facing both the importance and the stickiness of such a situation and not being discouraged by it that made them successful as a unified, supportive family.

You may hear me say often, in varying ways, that the secret ingredients to handling any difficulty among people are communication and the generosity of trying to understand. Sometimes it's really hard to get that perspective, yet it is one well worth aiming for because it makes managing life and relationships so much easier.

So their marriage carried on, and they shared great joys and managed to resolve their tribulations. My sister cherishes those many years of her life even though the marriage came to an end.

Years later, she was deeply fortunate to have met a fine man to build a new relationship with. I believe if we allow our hearts to remain open, even after painful disappointment, we hold onto the possibility of a second time around at sincere love.

In 2012, they decided to have a commitment ceremony. This time she wore a mint green dress that was purchased in a thrift shop, the ceremony took place on my small, simple deck facing the Pacific Ocean at sunset and music came from iTunes. The seven guests were their four children and their partners, and I performed the rites. Dinner was an organic meal; warmth and intimacy abounded.

My sister's experiences were meaningful. There was a great deal of joy in both services, and each ceremony reflected where my sister was at that time in life. Whenever it occurs, we each deserve to have the ceremony of our current imagination that reflects our love and commitment to one another. And, that is the kind of experience that I want to create with you.

Chapter Tips

- To be a successful celebrant today requires consistent strategies for promoting our services.

4

Arranging Our First Meeting

Please be aware that the flow of engagement may differ from couple to couple. Some couples will select you as their wedding officiant during your first phone call or video chat. Others will feel the need to meet in person before making a final decision.

Nevertheless, after preliminary communications, establish a mutually appropriate time to speak or meet in person. Maintaining flexibility, I have held meetings in my home, a couple's home, my office and even in cafés and diners, depending on mutual convenience. During the initial meeting, I make sure to get their phone numbers in case of unforeseen circumstances.

After the couple decides to hire me, and we have scheduled a time to talk, I send this email to them:

Tools: Celebrant's First Meeting Email

> *Dear Jane and Abdul,*
>
> *I am looking forward to our first meeting.*
>
> *Before we meet, in order to clarify the kind of wedding ceremony you wish to have, please consider the following:*
>
> *Types of Ceremonies**
>
> 1. *Religious (Denominational): A ceremony that includes aspects particular to one religion, faith or belief system*

2. *Interfaith (Interfaith, Ecumenical, Non-Denominational): A ceremony that includes aspects particular to more than one religion, faith or belief system*

3. *Spiritual: A ceremony that includes aspects particular to the couple's inner belief systems*

4. *Non-religious or Secular: A ceremony for legalizing your marriage without the inclusion of aspects particular to religion, faith or a belief system*

*Ceremonies may be a combination of the above.

Should you have any questions, please contact me.

Best Wishes,

Lynn

Meeting Reminder

On the day before our meeting, I send a confirmation email.

Tools: Celebrant's First Meeting Email Reminder

Dear Jane and Abdul,

This is to confirm our meeting on Saturday, May 2 at 10:30 a.m. Shall we meet at the Swiss Bakery at 168 Elm Street?

Please let me know if that location works for you, or if you have another place to suggest.

I look forward to discussing your ceremony plans with you in person.

Best wishes,

Lynn

Chapter Tips

- Make sure to get the couple's phone number in case of unforeseen circumstances.

5

Our First Meeting

At our first meeting, I welcome the couple and because we are all interviewing each other, I ask them if they have any questions about me or the wedding process before we begin.

A meeting in person or via online video chat is preferable, though not always possible. In whichever format this conversation takes place, I begin by offering the *Introductory Fun Questionnaire* below. Following that, we move onto the *First Interview Questions* below, and I take notes. As the interview moves along, we comment and expand upon their responses together.

Tools: Introductory Fun Questionnaire

Couples often arrive at our first meeting stressed about their wedding planning. In order to send the message that there is plenty of room for enjoying the whole process, I start with an icebreaker that I call *Introductory Fun Questionnaire*. Each of them fills it out separately and then shares their answers. This relaxes them and offers me some insight into their histories, personalities and interaction while offering them some thoughtful fun.

If we are not meeting in person, I send the questionnaire by email and request they email their answers back to me.

Introductory Fun Questionnaire

Instructions to the couple:

Make 2 copies to be completed by each of you and then compare!

Name:

I am (circle those that apply):

- Religious
- Not practicing but identified with one faith
- Spiritual
- Scarred from years of religious school
- Atheistic
- Agnostic
- Describe other _____

Number these 1 to 6 in order of importance regarding your ceremony
("1" is the most important to "6" is the least important):

____ Acknowledging the role of God in my life
____ Fulfilling a spiritual practice
____ Continuing the traditions of my upbringing
____ Honoring family and friends
____ Sharing our hopes and plans for the future
____ Celebrating our love
____ Other (please explain) _____

List your favorites in at least one of the following categories:

Authors _____

Books _____

Songs _____

Songwriters _____

Poets _____

Movies _____

Plays _____

Quotes _____

Jokes _____

Teams _____

You have to leave town suddenly without plans of returning. You may only bring 5 things.

List the 5 things you would pack:

1. _____

2. _____

3. _____

4. _____

5. _____

Please return to Lynn@LynnGladstone.com

Tools: Couples' First Interview Questions

Couples' First Interview

Date _____

Wedding Date/Time _____

Location   _____   Please
describe

Partner 1's name, email and phone numbers

_____

Partner 2's name, email and phone numbers

_____

Where do you live? _____

Are there any questions or comments on your mind before we continue?

_____

How did you come to contact me? _____

_____

Have you had a chance to visit my website? _____

What attracted you to me? _____

What is the significance of your getting married? _____

_____

Your occupations

1 _____ 2 _____

Your ages

1 _____ 2 _____

Who is paying for the wedding? _____

Prior marriages _____

Divorce or death documents _____

Children _____

Will you need me at a rehearsal? _____ When and where? _____

My rehearsal fee is $ _____

Microphones will be needed.

Your faiths, if any

1 _____ 2 _____

Family faiths, if any

1 _____ 2 _____

Check those that apply:

Is this a Religious _____ Interfaith _____ Spiritual _____ Secular _____ Wedding?

What is most important to you for your ceremony? _____

_____

Is God (and/or Jesus) invited to your ceremony? _____

_____

What are your families' feelings about the marriage/wedding? _____

_____

Any special needs or concerns? (To be discussed further) _____

There is something else I want you to consider. The people you are inviting are interested in you and want to hear your story, as do I. One of the ways to keep your guests engaged in the ceremony is to have me share some amusing or endearing events that have occurred since you met.

Please fill in the blank:

This is how we met _____

When we first met, I thought _____

After a while I thought _____

When I met the family _____

I knew this person could be a keeper when _____

We fell in love when _____

One of the funniest times we had together was _____

Next Steps:

My fees _____

Your names and addresses for the Marriage License (exactly as they appear on your government issued IDs) _____

_____

You will be receiving an in-depth Wedding Questionnaire. This questionnaire will enable me to understand you and help me in creating a memorable custom ceremony. Do you have any other questions or pertinent information you want to share before we conclude? Remember that you are welcome to call or email me at any time.

First Meeting Follow-Up

Tools: *Celebrant's First Meeting Follow-Up Email*

Dear Jane and Abdul,

It was so good to speak and meet with you today. From what we touched on, and if you think we are a good fit, I know we can create a most meaningful and memorable wedding ceremony for you.

In the meantime, review my blogs on my website, LynnGladstone.com: "Planning Your Wedding?! Relax," and "Lynn's Wedding Tips" at LynnGladstone.com.

I look forward to hearing from you.

Best regards,

Lynn

Tools: *Planning Your Wedding?! Relax*

The following blog, "Planning Your Wedding?! Relax" is adapted below, having originally been written in 2015 and published on my website, *LynnGladstone.com*. Photography below is from iStockphoto ©CareyHope.

Blog: Planning Your Wedding?! Relax

First things first: Congratulations!

While your wedding day will be a glorious moment in your life, try to keep your perspective. What is really important is that you and your partner have reached a new point in your loving relationship. You have decided to spend the rest of your lives together building a beautiful future. No matter what takes place before or on your wedding date, you will have a long and precious adventure to look forward to together.

Having said that, and having worked with so many couples regarding their nuptials, here are some clear steps you can take to make the planning process easier:

- *Identify what you both want*
  Take the time to speak at length together about what each of you envisions for your dream day. Prioritize what is most important for both of you. Write it down. Understand that this event process is exactly that — a process that can change along the way. Make a pact to make the process fun.

- *Define your budget*
  Be honest and realistic about your budget and agree to stick to it, even if it requires compromise.

- *Deal with family and money*
  Come up with a strategy for handling family members who may be contributing a large amount. In this common situation, express your gratitude in accepting your families' gift(s), but that you would need to maintain final word on your wedding decisions. For the family members who want to take control, I recommend you offer them the last word regarding up to three details (and only three) that are especially important to them.

- *Establish a wedding timeline*

Familiarize yourselves with a Wedding Planning Timeline and adhere to it. Such timelines are readily available online (*The Knot*) and in books or magazines. Seek advice of trusted, married friends.

- *Divide and conquer your wedding planning list*
  Look over the timeline and divvy up the tasks between you. Try to meet no more than once a week to discuss your progress. Check off completed tasks and move on.

Remember there is life beyond wedding planning to be enjoyed!

Respectfully,

Rev. Lynn

Tools: Tips for Weddings

The following is adapted from a blog, "Lynn's Tips: Tips for Weddings," I published in 2014 on my website, *LynnGladstone.com.*

Blog: Lynn's Weddings Tips

Begin Envisioning Your Wedding Ceremony: During a quiet time at home, after a home-cooked meal (or ordered in), put on some inspiring music. Turn off the phones. Get comfortable sitting next to each other. Sit in silence. Let your minds and hearts go where they will.

After two minutes, tell each other what you have experienced during the silence. Now take some time, in turn, to talk about:

- Your favorite colors
- Your favorite flower
- Your special song/lyrics
- A book you love
- A memorable quote

- An unforgettable film
- Your earliest shared memory

Jot down notes about what was said. Have a hug and enjoy the rest of your day.

Chapter Tips

- Couples often arrive at the first meeting stressed about their wedding planning. In order to send the message that there is plenty of room for enjoying the whole process, start with an icebreaker that I call *Introductory Fun Questionnaire.*

6

Making the Decision to Work Together

I encourage couples to take some time in making their decision about an officiant. To help them feel comfortable, I acknowledge that they may be interviewing with other celebrants, and I would be glad to hold their date in my calendar for up to two weeks. If I have another request for the date, I let them know that I would give them the right of first refusal. This time frame serves to avoid their obsessing on this decision for too long and protects my need to be available to other couples.

If the wedding couple decides that I am the celebrant they want to hire, I express my pleasure and reassure them that we will work together to design exactly what they want for their ceremony, and that I will be sending them materials to help ensure that end. On the other hand, if they contact me to decline my services, I simply wish them all the best in their future together.

Upon agreeing to work together, I send them a *Contract Letter*. I use one letter for my Custom Ceremonies and a different letter for my Sweet and Simple Ceremonies.

Tools: Couple Interested in Working Together

Letter 1:

Hi Lynn,

We really enjoyed chatting with you this morning and would love to have you officiate our wedding. Could you please send us a contract?

We are looking forward to working with you!

Jane and Abdul

Letter 2:

Dear Jane and Abdul,

Thank you. That's wonderful.

Attached you will find the Contract Letter. If you have any questions, call me anytime at _____.

Best wishes,

Lynn

Tools: Celebrant's Custom Ceremony Contract Letter

Date _____

Dear Jane and Abdul,

Thank you for choosing me to officiate your wedding ceremony. It will be a joy to celebrate your love with you and your closest family and friends.

This document confirms that I will write and perform your ceremony on _____ _____ a.m./p.m. at this location/venue _____ _____. We have agreed upon a *fee* of $_____. This fee includes the consulting, writing and editing of your ceremony; suggesting wedding resources, if you need them; coordinating with the professionals involved in your wedding; an additional meeting with you; ongoing emails and phone calls as needed; performing the ceremony on your wedding day and legalizing your marriage.

If you wish, I will share a first draft of the ceremony with you for your comments a week before the wedding date.

Please note, if you would like me to conduct a *rehearsal*, an additional fee of $_____ will apply. Kindly include the location, date and time of the rehearsal, if I am needed. _____

The day of your wedding, I will arrive early to meet privately with you for a few minutes in order to go over last minute details and to sign the *Marriage License that you will bring.*

A *deposit* of $_____ is required *within seven days* to reserve your wedding date. This deposit is nonrefundable. Please write a check payable to: Rev. Lynn Gladstone and mail to this address _____ _____. Alternatively, I can send you a PayPal invoice.

Please plan on paying the balance in cash or by check, prior to the start of your ceremony.

Kindly send a *photo of the two of you* (digital or hard copy) with this contract.

Just so that you know all contingencies are covered, if on your wedding day I were to become, due to unavoidable circumstances, unable to perform your ceremony (which has never happened!), I will inform you promptly. Your specially written ceremony would be given to another Interfaith Minister, a colleague of mine, and all would continue as planned and on time.

I look forward to working with you to create the wedding ceremony that you desire. Your *Custom Wedding Questionnaire* will follow-up on receipt of this *signed contract.*

Thank you for sending me:

- Signed contract ___
- Deposit payment ___
- Photo of the two of you ___
- Your wedding website address _____
- Your phone numbers _____
- Your address(es) _____

Names (exactly as they appear on your government-issued IDs to be used for your Marriage License)

_____

_____

Any questions or pertinent info you want to share before we next meet?

Signatures _____ and

_____

Date _____

Thank you. Many blessings and happy planning,

Rev. Lynn Gladstone

Tools: Celebrant's Sweet and Simple Ceremony Contract Letter

Date _____

Dear Kevin and Joseph,

Thank you for choosing me to officiate your wedding ceremony. It will be a joy to celebrate your love with you and your family and friends. This document confirms that I will write and perform your ceremony on _____ a.m./p.m. at this location/venue _____.

We have agreed upon a *fee* of $ _____ for a *Sweet and Simple Ceremony* as described on my website, *LynnGladstone.com.* Please call me should you have any questions.

A deposit of $_____ that is nonrefundable is required along with this signed contract, so that I may reserve your wedding date. Please write a check payable to: Rev. Lynn Gladstone and mail to this address _____ _____. Alternatively, I can send you a PayPal invoice.

The day of your wedding, I will arrive early before the ceremony to meet privately with you for a few minutes to sign the *Marriage License that you will bring.* Please plan on paying the balance of fee in cash or by check, prior to the start of your ceremony.

Kindly send a *photo of the two of you* (digital or hard copy) with the contract.

Just so that you know all contingencies are covered, if on your wedding day I were to become, due to unavoidable circumstances, unable to perform your ceremony (which has never happened!), I will inform you promptly. Your specially written ceremony would be given to another colleague of mine, and all would continue as planned and on time.

I look forward to working with you to create the wedding ceremony that you desire. Your *Sweet and Simple Wedding Questionnaire* will follow-up on receipt of this *signed contract.*

Thank you for sending me:

- Signed contract ___
- Deposit payment ___
- Photo of the two of you ___
- Your wedding website address _____
- Your phone numbers _____
- Your address(es) _____

Names (exactly as they appear on your government-issued IDs to be used for your Marriage License)

_____

_____

*Signatures*_____ and

_____

Date _____

Thank you. Many blessings and happy planning,

Rev. Lynn Gladstone

Chapter Tips

- Encourage couples to take some time in making the decision to work together.

7

Releases

To reach couples seeking an officiant, you must promote your services. When selecting an officiant, couples review their testimonials, wedding photographs/videos, website, etc. This is typically how a couple first begins to know you and learn about your services. Having promotional materials available for the couple to review requires getting permission for using these materials from the couples you have already married.

Tools: Celebrant's Release Form Letter for Promotional Materials

Dear Joanie and Bill,

In addition to referrals and testimonials, I have built my ministry practice with a website and other promotional materials. I ask couples if they would please sign a Release Form for the use of their wedding day photographs, video clips and testimonials. These materials allow me to share my services with other loving couples seeking an officiant. Filling in your names below in italics and emailing this form back to me will serve as your agreement.

Thank you for your participation in this process.

Rev. Lynn

Tools: Release Form for Photography, Video and Testimonial

Rev. Lynn Gladstone

- Has our permission to use our wedding photographs and video _____
_____

- Does Not have our permission to use our wedding photographs and video
_____

Rev. Lynn Gladstone

- Has our permission to use our first names _____
- Does not have our permission to use our first names _____

Rev. Lynn Gladstone

- Has our permission to use our testimonials _____
- Does not have our permission to use our testimonials _____

on her website *LynnGladstone.com,* other wedding sites (e.g., *The Knot*), in her wedding book and professional promotional materials.

Please provide the following information:

- Photographer's Name(s): _____
- Photographer's Email:_____

  Telephone: _____

- Videographer's Name(s): _____
- Videographer's Email:_____

  Telephone: _____

- Any special notes here: _____

After your wedding, I will email you a review request of my services, and I will be most grateful if you would provide one.

*Signed*_____*Signed*_____

(Type names in italics as signatures)

Date_____Date_____

Thank you,

Rev. Lynn

8

Already-Decided Couples

Some couples who contact me have already decided they want to work with me. They have seen me perform a wedding, or are amongst my family and friends or have found me through a referral. These couples require a different kind of email, like the one below.

Tools: Celebrant's First Meeting Alternate Email

Dearests Mae-Ling and Nicholas,

I am very honored to have you ask me to perform your marriage ceremony. It will be a very meaningful service emphasizing the incredible importance of your decision to expand your lives together in an ever-growing and beautiful relationship.

Here is a bit about how I work with couples: My wish is that every ceremony I create is particular and unique, reflecting both your desires. It will be your job to share yourselves with me and provide a vision we can use for your wedding day, which you can continue to adopt in your marriage.

I will design a custom ceremony that reflects the dreams that the two of you share.

That being said, I want you to relax, so that you can go deeply within. The more comfortable you are sharing your thoughts and feelings amongst the three of us, the more creative I can be. Please fill out the attached Custom Wedding Questionnaire. If there is something you do not wish to answer, that's fine. If there are things you would like to reflect on, please do so and get back to me when you are ready.

I would like to feel free to communicate with you over the next few months, in case I need clarification. By the same token, I would like you to do the same with me. Once I have the first draft of your ceremony, you will have an opportunity to review and comment on it, if you wish.

Once you have signed a Contract Letter, we can set up a meeting to explore what you would like for your ceremony. The Custom Wedding Questionnaire will be helpful to me and to you in organizing all of your thoughts. I look forward to working together.

With best wishes,

Lynn

9

Post-Meeting Summary Letter

After being engaged by a couple to officiate, it is helpful to send a *Post-Meeting Letter/Email* summarizing the ideas discussed for their ceremony. It reinforces what was talked about and serves as a reminder, down the road, of what is essential to the couple.

Below is a *Post-Meeting Letter/Email* for a couple who resided in Tokyo. Due to the time zone differences, it was difficult for us to meet in person or even to find a good time to talk on the phone. I felt it was important to put in writing what we had discussed on our first Skype meeting.

Tools: Celebrant's Post-Meeting Summary Letter/Email

Dear Abigail and Akio,

It was good to meet with you on Skype yesterday morning. We covered a lot of essential elements.

I have attached the Love and Marriage Readings that I mentioned to you. I hope they will be enjoyable, and, perhaps, that they will inspire you for your upcoming ceremony.

To review our conversation:

We spoke about the length and general contents of your ceremony (length approx. 10–15 minutes). This can be further verified when I review what you wish to incorporate.

Some of the thoughts to be included are:

Traditions and Rituals:

Honoring your ancestors is a tradition that is observed by both of your cultures. While it's important to honor the presence of both cultures, you primarily want to emphasize traditional Jewish content and rituals. "God" does not need to be included in the ceremony, as I understand it? Rituals might include a wine ceremony that Abigail's parents had in their wedding, as well as the breaking of the glass (significance previously discussed). Who will break the glass(es) is still to be determined. In acknowledging that this ritual recalls the shattering of the Jerusalem Temple and human lives in Jewish history, you mentioned the destruction caused by the recent earthquake in Japan. These parallels can be addressed in your service.

Vows:

You expressed a desire to write and deliver your own vows to your wedding guests, even though it is somewhat of a personal challenge. The Custom Wedding Questionnaire and Love and Marriage Readings may help you to organize yourselves in this endeavor. I will be happy to help you as you form your ideas. In addition, I recommend that you might refer to your favorite writers, lyrics, etc. to possibly inspire your personal vows for one another.

Participation by Others at Your Ceremony:

Abigail wants her father to walk her down the aisle. You are also not planning to have family or friends speak during your ceremony. I introduced the idea of a community blessing, which of course is yours to decide.

I have received your Fun Questionnaire responses, which are already helping me to understand your preferences and what is important to you. As you complete sections of the Custom Wedding Questionnaire please send them along to me. I am hoping the planning process will be a happy time for you.

Our next Skype meeting is scheduled for August 25th at 9 a.m., EST. Have a great month, stay cool, and contact me with any questions or concerns.

With sincere blessings,

Lynn

Chapter Tips

- After being hired by a couple to officiate, it is helpful to send a *Post-Meeting Letter/Email* summarizing the ideas discussed for their ceremony.

10

Co-Officiating

I am always happy to share the joy of conducting a ceremony with another fellow officiant chosen by the wedding couple.

To illustrate, many Catholic or half-Catholic couples seek me because they choose to get married outside of their church, opting instead for a setting and an I/I/I ceremony that has romantic meaning to them.

Tools: Co-Officiating a Ceremony

Ceremony:

Catholic doctrine requires that priests conduct wedding services within the walls of the church. One couple felt strongly about having a beloved priest involved in their outdoor ceremony and asked for my cooperation. In light of my I/I/I beliefs (*accepting and embracing all faiths without judgment*), I was delighted to co-officiate. I was pleasantly surprised that this Catholic priest had his own interspiritual point of view and was willing and grateful to be part of the union of two people he cared about. In this ceremony, he conducted the ring exchange and vows. Let's not underestimate the power of The New Spirituality, where all kinds of paradigms are shifting.

11

Creating a Custom Ceremony

The most useful tool I use in creating a ceremony is the *Custom Wedding Questionnaire.* It is designed to collect a variety of information (logistical and personal) that is used to develop a custom ceremony for a given couple's wedding. Additionally, it is constructed to encourage the partners to deeply think about who they are and what they want for their wedding service.

Tools: Celebrant's Custom Wedding Questionnaire Cover Letter (email)

Date _____

Dear Amelia and Joseph,

Please find attached my *Custom Wedding Questionnaire.* At first glance, you may find it a bit detailed. Do not fret, as the purpose of this questionnaire is multifaceted. *The more information that you share with me, the more personal, sensitive and creative I can be* in producing a wedding ceremony that reflects your relationship and your decision to marry. *However, feel no pressure, fill in only as much as you want!*

As you go through this questionnaire, it may help in organizing your wedding ideas and details. Additionally, you will be giving consideration to important matters regarding your personal beliefs and values, your relationship, your families and your wedding day. When completed, the questionnaire will also serve as a historical record for you of this precious time in your life.

May I suggest that you copy and paste it into a new document before you begin to work on it? This will end up being the completed questionnaire that you will send back to me by email at *Lynn@LynnGladstone.com no later than* _____. If you complete some sections and wish to send them to me before the whole document is completed, I would be delighted to receive them.

My intentions are to get to know who you are and for both of you to *enjoy* the process of creating your ceremony. Work at it in your own style and pace, in parts or in whole. Use as much space as you need. If you get stuck on a question move to the next one, and go back to it later. *Please indicate any answers that are confidential. If you find any question too uncomfortable to answer for any reason, skip it.* The participation of both of you in this process is essential to making your wedding ceremony authentic to you as a couple.

As to my role as the Celebrant/Officiant/Reverend/Minister/Lynn (you choose!), I look forward to working with you to create a unique ceremony based on your needs and desires for *your* wedding. Ideally, I will want to meet with you a minimum of one time. Based on your location and schedules, we will decide on how and when to accomplish that.

A week before your wedding, if you are interested, I would be happy to share with you a first draft of the ceremony so that you can make comments.

Thank you for collaborating with me in the creation of a wedding ceremony that will be most meaningful for you. It has been a pleasure so far.

Please feel free to contact me anytime at _____.

Please confirm the receipt of these documents. Thank you.

With blessings,

Rev. Lynn

Tools: Custom Wedding Questionnaire

The *Custom Wedding Questionnaire* incorporates and expands upon the works of Susan Turchin's book, *The Interfaith Wedding Manual, Creating Meaningful*

Wedding Ceremonies: A Guide for Clergy and Couples (151–157) *and* Diane Berke's book, *Interfaith Minister's Training and Reference Manual, Second Year Training Program* (67–72).

Custom Wedding Questionnaire

The Basics

Date of 1st meeting/conversation _____

Couple referred by _____

Date/Time of your wedding _____

Name and address of wedding venue _____

Number of guests _____

Main contact: with whom will I mainly be speaking during the planning period?

_____

Your wedding site address _____

What encouraged you to contact me? _____

My fee(s) _____

Partner 1 name/title _____

Date of birth _____

Phones _____ Address _____

Email _____

Vocation _____

Any hobbies or areas of special interest _____

Partner 2 name/title _____

Date of birth _____

Phones _____ Address _____

Email _____

Vocation _____

Any hobbies or areas of special interest _____

Where were you raised?

Partner 1 _____ Partner 2 _____

When, how and where did you meet? _____

_____

_____

Length of time dating _____

When were you engaged? _____

Living together? _____ How long? _____

Previously married? _____

Partner 1 _____ Partner 2 _____

(I would need a copy of the divorce or death document.)

Children? Names/Ages

Partner 1 _____

Partner 2 _____

Will this be a religious, interfaith, spiritual or civil ceremony? _____

Religious/Spiritual affiliations: What spiritual beliefs/practices do you embrace, if any?

Partner 1 _____

Partner 2 _____

With which particular ethnicities or cultures do you identify?

Partner 1 _____

Partner 2 _____

Planning the Ceremony

Who is paying for the wedding? _____

Wedding planner or venue contact name/phone/email _____

_____

Time: Ceremony _____ Time for me to arrive _____

Outdoor or Indoor? _____

What are the back-up plans, should it rain? _____

From where will guests be travelling? _____

Do you want a Co-officiate _____? Contact information _____

_____

Would you want me to conduct your wedding rehearsal? (If on a separate day, there is a $_____ fee.) When and where? _____

Will you be seeing each other before the ceremony? _____

Will the ceremony be photographed or videoed? _____

Will you want me present? _____ When/where? _____

Information you may need from me for a Wedding Program, if applicable (to be discussed) _____ _____

Processional party names, relationships, roles, order, if any, if known. Any children?

_____

_____

Flower bearer(s) _____ Age _____

Ring bearer(s) _____ Age _____

Witness's (2) names for your Marriage License, if required.

_____

_____

Who, if anyone, will be accompanying each of you down the aisle?

Partner 1 _____

Partner 2 _____

Will guests stand as the partner(s) walk down the aisle? _____

Partner 1 Parents' names _____

Are they still living? _____ Married? _____

Remarried? _____

Partner 2 Parents' names _____

Are they still living? _____ Married? _____

Remarried? _____

Any Stepparents' names _____

Please share any thoughts about your family members' roles in the ceremony.

Whom and what would you like at the altar?

Anyone who has passed to remember during the ceremony (specific or general)?

Any family issues I might need to know about that could affect the ceremony planning?

Any special needs or situations you want me to know about?

The Ceremony

Approximately how long do you envision the ceremony to be? _____

Please indicate the flavors/styles you want to project for your wedding (e.g., religious, interfaith, cultural, traditional, spiritual, intimate, theatrical, joyous, fun, meaningful, nonreligious, or humorous)?

Style of Wedding: Formal _____ Semi-formal _____ Casual_____

Other (please describe) _____

What are your wedding colors? _____

What colors are the bride, groom and wedding party wearing? _____

Will a train _____ or a veil _____ be worn?

When would you like the veil raised and by whom? _____

Any preferences for color or style of what I wear? _____

What titles would you like to be called during the ceremony (e.g., bride(s), groom(s), life partners)? _____

_____

What is the music for the ceremony (to be discussed)?

What would you like the ceremony to accomplish?

Will there be words spoken or singing during the ceremony? _____

By whom? _____

How do you feel about a guest blessing of support AND/OR a statement of gratitude for your guests?

How do you feel about a virtual toast by the guests? _____

Will you be speaking vows?

    Will you write your own marriage vows _____

    Do you prefer that I write them _____

    Or, help you write them _____

    Or, will you be speaking traditional vows _____

Will you be exchanging rings? _____

    New or heirloom rings? _____

    Using traditional, or your own ring exchange vows _____

    Who will hold your rings? _____

    Who will hold your vow cards? _____

What might you want said or not said about your relationship in this public forum?

_____

Perhaps you have observed elements of other wedding ceremonies you would like to include in yours. Please tell me about them. _____

_____

What do you especially want not to include? _____

What has been easy or hard about planning your ceremony? _____

Should you become nervous or self-conscious during the ceremony, what might you do to calm yourself? _____

Will you want to see a draft of your ceremony one week before to comment upon? _____

Spirituality, Religion, etc.

How comfortable are you talking about religion and/or spirituality?

Partner 1 _____

Partner 2 _____

How does the concept of spirituality sit with you? What role has it played in your life?

Partner 1 _____

Partner 2 _____

In what ways might you imagine your current religious or spiritual views changing?

Partner 1 _____

Partner 2 _____

If applicable, have you ever discussed conversion? _____

How do you feel about God being mentioned or not in your ceremony? Are there other words that you would prefer?

Partner 1 _____

Partner 2 _____

What words would you love to hear or not hear in the ceremony?

_____

Are there any rituals that are important to you (e.g., candles, wine, rings)? _____

_____

Are there any customs or objects to include in the ceremony from your family, ethnic background, or personal preferences? _____

Are there specific favorite readings, prayers and/or music that you want to include in your ceremony?

Or, would you prefer that I select them with or for you _____

Who will be performing these _____

Their names and relationships _____

Anything I should avoid?

Personal Info and Your Relationship

Below, please complete the "Personal Info and Your Relationship" sections individually, then share them with your partner.

Name partner 1: _____

Please tell me how you met your partner, and what initially attracted you?

Tell me about your partner. What qualities do you admire and appreciate?

Please describe your relationship with your partner.

_____

_____

_____

What would you say are the most important aspects of your relationship?

What are the strengths?

Please describe the circumstances of when you knew you were in love.

Since you first met, how has your relationship grown or changed?

Please share with me any endearing stories about your partner.

How would you feel about me sharing them during your ceremony?

Tell me about the proposal.

    How do you define love?

What does marriage mean to you?

Think about the expectations in marriage; what do you expect from one another and yourselves?

What do you want to give to your partner?

What do you want to receive from your partner?

What do you not expect from your partner?

What areas of your relationship might you want to strengthen?

How might you go about that?

What might be your theme song as a couple?

What are your favorite:

Authors/Books/Poets _____

Teams _____

Musicians/Songs _____

Movies _____

Other _____

Personal Info and Your Relationship

Below, please complete the "Personal Info and Your Relationship" sections individually, and, then share them with your partner.

Name partner 2: _____

Please tell me how you met your partner, and what initially attracted you?

Tell me about your partner. What qualities do you admire and appreciate?

Please describe your relationship with your partner.

_____

_____

_____

What would you say are the most important aspects of your relationship?

What are the strengths?

Please describe the circumstances of when you knew you were in love.

Since you first met, how has your relationship grown or changed?

Please share with me any endearing stories about your partner.

How would you feel about me sharing them during your ceremony?

Tell me about the proposal.

How do you define love?

What does marriage mean to you?

Think about the expectations in marriage; what do you expect from one another and yourselves?

What do you want to give to your partner?

What do you want to receive from your partner?

What do you not expect from your partner?

What areas of your relationship might you want to strengthen?

How might you go about that?

What might be your theme song as a couple?

What are your favorite:

Authors/Books/Poets _____

Teams _____

Musicians/Songs _____

Movies _____

Other _____

Your Marriage

Why have you decided to get married now?

Are there challenges or issues for either of you about getting married or the wedding ceremony that you would like to discuss with me?

If applicable:

Do you have children separately or together?

If yes, please tell me their roles in your lives, and, if any, in the wedding.

What do you believe are their feelings about your getting married?

What have you discussed about the 'if and when' of having children together?

What have you discussed about children's last names?

Have you discussed how your children would be raised religiously, spiritually or otherwise?

If yes, how comfortable were you both with the discussion?

What will be your last names after the wedding? _____

How would you like me to pronounce your names as a couple at the end of the ceremony?

_____

_____

Are you planning a honeymoon? If yes, may I ask when and where? _____
_____

Who's the cook? _____ Who cleans? _____

Pets, ok or not? _____

Generally, when we make the decision to marry we are planning to spend the rest of our lives together. Statistics show us that this does not always happen. Please share with me your thoughts about a pre-nuptial agreement.

What do you envision in your marriage five years from now?

_____

_____

_____

Interpersonal Matters

Tell me about the people you have attending your wedding.

Did you have a discussion with your parents or other important family members about having an interfaith (or same-sex) ceremony?

How did it go?

Describe their feelings about using elements from traditions other than their/ your own in the ceremony.

What comes up for you about using or not using elements/rituals from each of your own traditions and/or backgrounds in this ceremony?

Partner 1 _____

Partner 2 _____

Would you like me to be involved in any way with your family members regarding your wedding ceremony?

If yes, in what ways:

What names shall I call you during the ceremony (e.g., Pete or Peter, Kathy or Katherine)?

_____

I donate a portion of my fee in your honor at the end of the year. Please tell me which charitable organizations, if any, have special appeal to you.

I love to collect invitations from the couples I marry. If you have an extra invitation, would you be willing to give me one to add to my collection?

Note: I will need a hands-free microphone. You will need a separate microphone if you are speaking.

Please email the completed questionnaire to: Lynn@LynnGladstone.com no later than
_____*.*

Important, regarding your marriage license:

You are responsible for obtaining a marriage license from the City Clerk's Office (county or state depending on where you will marry). The names and addresses that appear on your government-issued IDs must be used on your marriage license application. All this information must be exactly the same on my legal documents for you.

Please include those names and addresses here

_____

_____

If you have any questions, you are welcome to contact me anytime.

Sincerely,

Rev. Lynn

Tools: Celebrant's Sweet and Simple Wedding Questionnaire Cover Letter

Date _____

Dear Kevin and Daniel,

Please find attached my *Sweet and Simple Wedding Questionnaire*. This questionnaire is designed so that the more information you share with me, the more personal I can be in creating a wedding ceremony that reflects your relationship and your desire to marry. *However, feel no pressure, fill in only as much as you want.*

May I suggest that you copy and paste it into a new document before you begin to work on it? This will end up being the completed questionnaire that you will send back to me by email at: *Lynn@LynnGladstone.com no later than* _____.

My intentions are to know who you are and for both of you to *enjoy* the ceremony creation process. The participation of the two of you in this questionnaire is essential to making your wedding ceremony authentic to you as a couple.

As to my role as the Celebrant/Officiant/Reverend/Minister/Lynn (you choose!), I look forward to creating your unique ceremony. Though not required, ideally, I will want to meet with you prior to your wedding. Based on your location and schedules, we will decide on how and when to accomplish that.

Please feel free to contact me anytime at _____ .

Please confirm the receipt of these documents. Thank you.

With blessings,

Rev. Lynn

Tools: Sweet and Simple Wedding Questionnaire

Sweet and Simple Wedding Questionnaire

Date _____

Partner 1's address, email and phone numbers _____

_____

_____

Partner 2's address, email and phone numbers _____

_____

_____

What encouraged you to contact me?

_____

Ceremony date _____ Time _____ Exact location _____

_____

Ceremony address _____

_____

Venue contact info _____

_____

Where were you each raised? _____

_____

With which particular ethnicity do you identify, if any?

Partner 1 _____

Partner 2 _____

Please tell me when and how you met and what attracted you to each other.

How quickly did each of you know this person was "the one" for you?

What are your reasons for getting married?

Your occupations and hobbies?

Partner 1 _____

Partner 2 _____

Your dates of birth

Partner 1 _____

Partner 2 _____

Prior marriages or children _____

Your wedding style: Formal ___ Semi-formal ___ Casual ___

Color theme _____

Number of Guests _____

Will your ceremony be photographed or videoed? _____

Names of wedding party, if any: _____

Any children in the wedding party? _____ Names and ages _____

_____

_____

Is your ceremony to be:

Religious_____ Interfaith _____ Spiritual _____ Non-religious/Secular _____

Your faiths, if any

Partner 1 _____

Partner 2 _____

Family faiths, if any

Partner 1 _____

Partner 2 _____

Is God, Jesus or Spirit invited to the ceremony? _____

Vows: Using yours or traditional vows? _____

Rings: New or Family Heirlooms? _____

Families' feelings about the marriage/wedding

_____

What is most important to you for your ceremony?

_____

What would you not like to have happen in your ceremony?

_____

Names of Parents:

Partner 1 _____

Partner 2 _____

May I mention your ancestors? _____

What are your favorite:

Authors/Books/Poets _____

Musicians/Songs: _____

Movies: _____

Other _____

Do you prefer choosing a Ritual/Reading in place of my Blessing? _____

_____

Any special needs or situations you want me to know?

Please tell me what you admire about your partner, and how he or she makes you feel?

Partner 1 _____

Partner 2 _____

Describe the strengths of your relationship?

Partner 1 _____

Partner 2 _____

What areas of your relationship might you want to strengthen?

How might you go about that?

What names shall I call you during the ceremony (e.g., Pete or Peter, Kathy or Katherine)?

Any other questions, wishes or pertinent information you would like to share with me?

I donate a portion of my fee in your honor at the end of the year. Please tell me which charitable organizations, if any, have special appeal to you. _____

_____

I love to collect invitations from the couples I marry. If you have an extra invitation, would you be willing to give me one to add to my collection?

Note: I may need a hands-free microphone. You will need a separate microphone if you are speaking.

Please email the completed questionnaire to: Lynn@LynnGladstone.com no later than

_____

Important, regarding your Marriage License:

You are responsible for obtaining a marriage license from the City Clerk's Office (county or state depending on where you will marry). The names and addresses as they appear on your government-issued IDs must be used on your marriage license application. All this information must be exactly the same on my legal documents for you.

Please include those names and addresses here:

_____

_____

_____

If you have any questions, you are welcome to contact me anytime.

Sincerely,

Rev. Lynn

Supplementary Tools: Celebrant's Alternate Wedding Letter and Questionnaire

Tell Me Your Story

Dear Jules and Martin,

Among the other details I will go over with you, there is something else I want you to consider. The people you have invited to your wedding are interested in you and want to hear your story. One of the ways to keep your guests engaged during the ceremony is to have me share some amusing or endearing stories that have occurred since you met. I would appreciate answers to any of the following statements. Free feel to share more if you like.

This is how we met _____

When we first met, I thought _____

After a while I thought _____

I knew this person could be a keeper when he/she _____

_____

When I first met his/her family _____

_____

We fell in love when _____

_____

One of the funniest times we had together was _____

_____

Something we did that I will never forget is _____

_____

Any charming or memorable anecdote, story:

_____

_____

_____

Paragraphs about my partner:

Write a paragraph or two about your partner and what your relationship means to you.

Thanks!

Lynn

Supplementary Tools: A Light Touch Love Game

At some point during the creation of the ceremony, I like to send this light-hearted *Love Game* to the couple:

LOVE GAME (á la Mad Libs)

From Reverend Lynn, for your amusement and relaxation.

Hold off reading the text of this story until you have first filled in all of the blanks that are prompted by the words in parentheses. Print out these pages and one of you will be the "interviewer" while the other is the "interviewee." Interviewer asks interviewee for a word described in the parentheses (e.g., nouns, adjectives, verbs). When all blanks are filled in, read the story and enjoy!

Have Fun!

For those of us who are rusty on our grammar rules, here are some tips:

Noun = a person, animal, place or thing (e.g., boy, aardvark, yoyo, swimming hole)

Adjective = describes a noun (e.g., gorgeous, goofy, odd)

Verb = action word, what nouns do (e.g., walking, thinking, being, laughing)

Title: I (verb)_____You!

My (adjective) _____ (noun) _____

is quite (adjective) _____

Today, (date) _____, this day of (noun) _____

I (verb) _____, compelled to (verb) _____ and (verb) _____.

When we first (verb, past tense) _____ at (place) _____ and we (verb, past tense) _____, I remembered (term of endearment), _____, that you were (adjective) _____ and (adjective) _____.

These (1-100) _____ years together have shown me the (adjective) _____truth about those (adjective) _____ observations I had about you — those being (3 character traits)

    1. _____

    2. _____ and

    3. _____

I so like to recall the time when you (verb, past tense) _____ me and how surprised I was when you revealed to me that you once (verb, past tense) _____. I never suspected! Not even a little bit.

And even during this past year, with all the (adjective) _____ things we have had to do to get to this moment, I (verb) _____ and (verb) _____ you to the (1-100) _____th degree.

I had no idea what to expect. Isn't our life full of (adjective) _____ (plural noun) _____ and (plural noun) _____? Now and every day I want to (verb) _____ you by sharing my most (adjectives) _____, _____, _____ and (adjective) _____ feelings with (name) _____.

My dear little (animal) _____, this is all to tell you that I (verb) _____ you with all of my (body part) _____!

The End.

Chapter Tips

- The most useful tool for creating a ceremony is the *Custom Wedding Questionnaire*.

12

The Reluctant Client

On rare occasions, I have come across clients who are reluctant to fully fill out my extensive *Custom Wedding Questionnaire*, even though I have invited them to fill out only as much as they wish. If I am unable to secure their cooperation, I do offer them some shortcuts explaining that this will limit the level of my being able to personalize their ceremony. Nevertheless, I offer them one of the shorter options I have included earlier. Please refer to the following tools:

1. *Sweet and Simple Wedding Questionnaire (3 Pages)*
2. *First Interview (2 Pages)*
3. *Tell Me Your Story* and *Paragraphs About My Partner* (1 Page)

If one of these tools is still too daunting for them, I set up a meeting to interview them and obtain the information needed to create their ceremony. Some clients just need that.

13

Going Deeper:
Marital and Wedding Counseling

The months leading up to the wedding are an important time for the officiant to work together with the marrying couple. I generally find that wedding couples exhibit a good deal of openness with me, so I see our working together as a time for potential growth in their relationship. In some cases, couples wish to go deeper in examining their relationship. For these couples, I have compiled a *Do-It-Yourself Couples' Questionnaire (DIYCQ)* that goes deep and is not for the faint of heart. Since the *DIYCQ* is rather an extensive tool, it is included in full in Appendix 4.

It invites partners to look within to answer questions about themselves as individuals and as partners.

I use discretion in offering the opportunity to use this *DIYCQ*. I present it gently, and see which couples embrace the idea of doing some emotional exploration. I explain that it is private and for their use alone, unless they seek pre- or post-marital counseling with me. I find it to be a useful tool either way. I let them know that if a sensitive area arises and they wish for my intervention, I will gladly provide it.

If this questionnaire leads couples to seek marital counseling, it should be provided by a trained, and legally sanctioned professional.

Pre- and post-marital counseling differs from wedding counseling. The former focuses on the couple's interpersonal relationship. The latter is about counseling the couple in planning their wedding and any related issues, such as dealing with their differing expectations and those of their families.

Tools: Do-It-Yourself Couples' Questionnaire

Increasingly, I have found couples to be interested in seeking counseling. I see this trend to know more deeply oneself and one's partner as an incredibly positive shift in how people go about making a commitment to one another. Completing the *DIYCQ* will foster a more understanding, accepting and evolving relationship. Below is a listing of the different areas of a relationship that it helps a couple examine.

1. About You
2. About Your Relationship
3. Sex, Intimacy and Romance
4. Political, Religious and Spiritual Beliefs
5. Your Finances
6. Career and Lifestyle
7. House and Home
8. Leisure Time and Social Life
9. Child and Family Planning
10. Your Families and the Holidays
11. Physical/Emotional Health and Medical Decisions
12. Conflict and Resolution

Tools: Tips for Couples Seeking Premarital Counseling and Wedding Counseling

The following is adapted from a blog, "Lynn's Tips: Tips for Counseling," I published in 2014 on my website, *LynnGladstone.com.*

Blog: Lynn's Tips for Counseling

First thing to do: Congratulate yourself! In planning your wedding, you have recognized that something(s) may be going off course. You have made a deliberate decision to seek professional help and that is truly to be commended. Life in the modern age is so darn complex and fast that sometimes it's hard to catch your emotional breath all by yourself. Fortunately, there are many caring and talented therapists or counselors ready to hear your story, your woes and help you find your way to what you want for yourselves.

When seeking a therapist or counselor it is most desirable to get a recommendation from a trusted friend, family member, spiritual mentor or medical professional. Try to get a few names and spend the time and money interviewing two or three professionals. Trust your intuition, your gut, to tell you which one to choose.

Deciding to go into therapy or counseling may seem a bit daunting at first. That is a normal feeling. It also may be, for you, a welcome relief. I recommend giving your therapy or counseling at least two to three sessions before you think about walking out the door.

Be patient with yourself. Subtle, slow and steady growth is what sticks. If you take one step forward and then two steps backwards, do not fret. As you do the work, make the commitment to live out what new truths you are learning about yourself, and you will find progress. It is the surest investment out there. I wish you the best!

Rev. Lynn

Chapter Tips

- In some cases, couples wish to go deeper in examining their relationship. For these couples, I have compiled a *Do- It -Yourself Couples' Questionnaire* (DIYCQ).

14

Same-Sex Marriages/Unions

Our professional aim should be to always create a unique ceremony that speaks specifically about each couple. Yet, each ceremony requires some standard elements, regardless of religious or nonreligious affiliation and regardless of gender. So often, when people hear that I am an interfaith, interspiritual and intercultural minister, they ask if I perform same-gender marriages. I answer with an enthusiastic "Yes," though I am slightly baffled by this query. As an I/I/I minister, it is an essential part of our belief system to embrace all people without prejudice or judgment.

As I see it, our role as ministers is to legalize love. Love has been around for eons, and we have been eons overdue in recognizing that love between any two people is love that cannot be denied. Whomever people love is a universal human right; it is a treasure that makes our world go round and makes it so much better, as it always has and always shall. Amen.

The following blog "Love Makes the World So Much Better" is adapted below having originally been written in 2014 and published on my website, *LynnGladstone.com.* In the photo below, I had the pleasure of marrying Danya and Holly. Photograph taken by *EricaCamilleProductions.com.*

Tools: Love Makes the World So Much Better

They were dressed to the nines.

One was clad handsomely in white tails, decorated tastefully with silver embroidery, appearing as out of a vintage fantasy. The other wore a gown sewn from endless yards of pale pastel tulle — flowing layers to the ground, resembling a most enticing, multi-tiered wedding cake.

That's what I saw when I walked into the venue to perform their wedding ceremony one hour hence.

They greeted me enthusiastically, telling each other, "Yay, Lynn is here, now we can thankfully calm down."

I was touched by this observation and happy that they felt I would help to assuage their nervousness. This, my dear colleagues, is the relationship we need to strive for.

There was, as always, last minute work to be done. We convened in the Bridal Room, an annex off the restaurant's main room where dinner would later be served to 135 hungry and celebrating guests.

I had this hour to acquaint myself with two sets of parents and to corral, meet, congratulate and direct the other members of the wedding party.

This couple had opted to not have the rehearsal the night before, rather to do it just before the ceremony and prior to any guests arriving. Then there were witnesses to locate, so that the marriage license could be legally signed.

There is nearly always a glitch or two that want to dominate a joyful occasion and in this case that rule of thumb prevailed.

The parents—who were to bring the suitcase packed with all the last minute essentials, including the required marriage license—were teeth-grindingly delayed in traffic. And, the guests were outside pouring into the courtyard.

While we waited, I offered up the mounting anxiety to a spirit of faith that all would work out fine, serving to relax the wedding twosome. I requested some moments of privacy with them, so that we could have a brief meditation with the imparting of my message of beautiful imagery and perspective. As a result, another round of calm found its way into the couple's demeanor.

Then, it was discovered their vows had been left at home, far away on the bedroom bureau, and worry returned. Having learned that an officiant, like a Girl Scout, must always be prepared, I reached into my portfolio of tricks and pulled out a copy of their vows. Enormous sighs of relief filled the room.

At last and as usual, everything began to fall into place. The parents and suitcase had finally arrived, the license was signed and witnessed, the wedding party participants had rehearsed and lined up correctly knowing their parts and guests were seated outside—*al fresco* in anticipation.

The processional music began. At the agreed cue from the DJ, one by one, we made our way down the center aisle, surrounded on both sides by the beaming smiles of those attending. Joy was in the night air.

Throughout the ceremony, this couple stood facing each other adoringly, grinning, clasping hands, their sometimes teary eyes seeing no one else. Their ceremony spoke of welcoming friends and family, remembering the departed and inviting Spirit to the altar.

The guests heard a good deal about the couple, how they met, and how their bond and love grew over years of adventures and toil. They partook in a wine-sharing ritual and presented their heartfelt personal intentions and vows. I blessed them as I always do at all marriage ceremonies and legally pronounced, "It is now my great pleasure to present you as *wife and wife.*"

Rev. Lynn

Chapter Tips

- Always create a unique ceremony that speaks specifically about each couple.
- An essential part of our belief as I/I/I ministers is a system to embrace all people without prejudice or judgment.
- Our role as ministers is to legalize love. Love between any two people is love that cannot be denied.

15

Requirements for a Legal Wedding

The Basics

Did you know that there are only four requirements to a legal marriage?

1. A legally sanctioned marriage official performs and pronounces the marriage.
2. Each partner must respond affirmatively to the question, "Are you here of your own free will to marry (name)?"
3. A marriage license must be signed by a marriage official and witnesses, if required.
4. The marriage official must mail in the marriage license by the due date.

Additional Legal Matters

- For a second marriage, the official requires a copy of a divorce or death document.
- Check with the specific City or County Clerk to determine how long before the wedding date the marriage license is valid, and if there is any waiting period after application and issuance.
- Establish with the City or County Clerk the minimum age to marry without parental consent.
- Most states prohibit marriage between close relatives.

Chapter Tips

- There are only four requirements to a legal marriage.
- Each partner must respond affirmatively to the question: "Are you here of your own free will to marry (name)?"

16

Planning and Organizing
Each Wedding

It is very helpful to use the *Wedding Worksheet* below to record the various details of each couple's upcoming ceremony. I use this helpful tool for the duration of my working relationship with the couple.

I create a folder for each couple. This is where all correspondence and documentation go. I attach the *Wedding Worksheet* with each couple's names and wedding date on the front of the folder. For future use, I also include the charity they have chosen for my donation in their honor.

Tools: Celebrant's Wedding Worksheet

Celebrant's Wedding Worksheet

Names of Partners _____

Wedding Date _____ Time _____

Location/Address _____

Rehearsal Date, Time, Location _____

How They Found Me _____

First Meeting Date _____ Comments _____

Contract Sent _____ RCVD _____ Deposit RCVD _____

RCVD:

Photo _____

Phone Numbers _____

Wedding Website _____

Legal Marriage License Names, Addresses _____

_____

_____

_____

Follow-up Letters Sent _____

Appointment Date(s) _____ Confirmed _____

Wedding Interview Package Sent _____ RCVD _____

Releases RCVD: Photo_____ Video_____ Testimonial _____

Fun Questionnaire Sent _____ RCVD _____

Gifts Ordered _____ RCVD _____

Resource Materials Sent _____

Apply for Out-of-State Clergy Certificate _____ RCVD _____

Invitation RCVD _____

Readings Selected _____

Rituals/Ritual Objects Chosen _____

Music Selected _____

Ceremony Outline Reviewed _____

Wedding Program Layout Discussed _____

Vows Selected _____

Ring Vows Selected _____

Wedding Manager Contacted _____

Microphones Arranged _____

Correspondence Reviewed _____

Details Reviewed _____

Ceremony Draft Sent _____ Comments RCVD _____

Rehearsal Outline Completed _____

Final Ceremony Draft Completed and Printed _____

Post Ceremony Contact with Couple _____

Contact Photographer and Videographer _____

Post Social Media Material _____

Send Holiday and Anniversary Cards _____

Chapter Tips

- *Wedding Worksheet:* Use this helpful tool for the duration of your working relationship with each couple.

17

Week Before the Wedding (WBTW)

Tools: Celebrant's WBTW Checklist

Review Wedding Program ⎯⎯⎯⎯⎯⎯⎯⎯⎯⎯

Final Ceremony Draft Completed and Printed ⎯⎯⎯⎯⎯⎯⎯

Prepare *ketubah*, if requested ⎯⎯⎯⎯⎯⎯⎯⎯⎯

Rehearse Ceremony ⎯⎯⎯⎯⎯⎯⎯⎯⎯⎯⎯⎯

Call Couple ⎯⎯⎯⎯⎯⎯⎯⎯⎯⎯⎯⎯⎯⎯

Pre-Wedding Letters ⎯⎯⎯⎯⎯⎯⎯⎯⎯⎯⎯⎯

Ceremony Reminder List Sent to the Couple ⎯⎯⎯⎯⎯⎯⎯

Confirm All Name Pronunciations ⎯⎯⎯⎯⎯⎯⎯⎯⎯

Put Readings and Vows on Cardstock ⎯⎯⎯⎯⎯⎯⎯⎯

Confirm Directions to Venue(s) ⎯⎯⎯⎯⎯⎯⎯⎯⎯⎯

Prepare Gifts ⎯⎯⎯⎯⎯⎯⎯⎯⎯⎯⎯⎯⎯⎯

Check My "To Bring List" ⎯⎯⎯⎯⎯⎯⎯⎯⎯⎯⎯

Conduct Rehearsal ⎯⎯⎯⎯⎯⎯⎯⎯⎯⎯⎯⎯

Tools: Couple's WBTW Ceremony Review Letter

A week before the wedding, I send a letter or email with a draft of the couple's ceremony. I ask for their comments within forty-eight hours to give me time to make any changes and to limit their time to stress. Here is an example of a letter or email I sent with the draft of their ceremony.

> *Dear Michelle and Derek,*
>
> *What a great time in your life this is. You must be excited!*
>
> *Attached you will find the draft of your ceremony. I hope you enjoy reading it, as I have enjoyed creating it with your valuable input. Please review it and add any comments you may have in RED and send it back to me. Please do not delete any of the content at this time.*
>
> *If you wish to speak about anything, give me a call anytime.*
>
> *Please send your final comments to me by this Sunday.*
>
> *Have a great weekend.*
>
> *Warmest wishes,*
>
> *Lynn*

WBTW Overview of Wedding Letter

In the days leading up to their wedding, couples have their hands full, to say the least! I take it upon myself to send them a *WBTW Ceremony List*.

Tools: Couple's WBTW Ceremony Letter and Checklist

> *Dear Fran and Gene,*
>
> *I trust you are both excited about next weekend. Though you probably have matters under control, I am including below A Week Before the Wedding Checklist of items we have discussed for your wedding service.*
>
> *As your wedding day approaches, I want you to know that it has been a sincere pleasure getting to know you. Thank you for sharing your most personal thoughts about your ceremony with me.*

Amidst the magical excitement of the day, I hope you will get a chance to connect to each of your guests, who are there to support you.

You are entering into sacred, loving matrimony, and as your future unfolds, please remember that you are individuals with dreams to pursue. Respect that and continue to be best friends. Whatever form your faith takes, rely on it.

I look forward to conducting your wedding ceremony, and I feel honored to be part of your matrimonial union.

Couple's WBTW Ceremony Checklist

- *Bring wedding rings.*
- *Bring two copies of the front of the marriage license along with the original and the stamped envelope for the Clerk's Office.*
- *Bring a copy of Gene's divorce document.*
- *Pay the balance of my fee before the ceremony in cash or by check.*
- *Bring two wine goblets.*
- *Bring white wine, vintage 2012, the year you met.*
- *Bring your vows.*
- *I will bring the Love and Marriage Readings on cardstock.*
- *Bring handkerchiefs if you think you will get teary-eyed.*
- *Are hands-free microphones confirmed for me and you?*
- *Where may I park on the wedding day?*
- *I need five to ten minutes with you before the ceremony, together or separately.*
- *Kindly forward the three attached congratulations letters to your parents.*

If you have any last minute questions or concerns, please contact me. If you wish, please stay in touch after your wedding. I would love to know how you are doing.

I have a favor to ask: I love my work and want to continue to serve other couples as an officiant. Client reviews are the biggest influence on the success of my practice. If you have been pleased with our work together, would you be so kind as to complete an online review for me after your wedding? For simplification, I will send you an email review request from The Knot. Thank you for your consideration on my behalf. Best wishes.

Rev. Lynn

Families' WBTW Congratulations Letters

Family members, especially parents, are deeply invested in the well-being of their children and the wedding process. In most cases, they have been joyfully waiting for the news of their children getting married. I like to acknowledge that.

In the week preceding the wedding, I send congratulatory notes to parents and stepparents (assuming these are positive relationships). Below are examples of what I write to them.

Tools: Families' WBTW Congratulations Letters

Family 1:

Dear Brad (father of the groom),

Please allow me to congratulate you on the marriage of Vicky and Jacques this coming weekend.

I truly appreciate how the three of us have collaborated in creating a ceremony that really speaks of them as a couple. They are clear on what matters to them, and that will serve them well in their marriage.

I look forward to celebrating with them and with you at their wedding this coming weekend.

Sincerely,

Rev. Lynn Gladstone

Family 2:

Dear Elise and Stephan (parents of the bride),

I want to congratulate you on the upcoming marriage of Jacques and Vicky.

I have very much enjoyed communicating with them and getting to know each of them individually and as a couple. Since they met, they clearly have been building a path together that will grow and flourish.

I look forward to celebrating their wedding ceremony with them and with you this coming weekend.

Sincerely,

Rev. Lynn Gladstone

Chapter Tips

- Family members, especially parents, are deeply invested in the well-being of their children and the wedding process.

18

Day of Wedding (DOW)

There is so much for a couple to remember on their actual wedding day. I have found it very useful for the celebrant to provide a Couple's *Day of Wedding Checklist* a few days before the couple's wedding.

As each ceremony is unique, it is equally helpful for a celebrant to be prepared with her/his own Celebrant's *Day of Wedding Checklist.*

Tools: Couple's Primary DOW Checklist — Important Items to Bring

- Marriage license, two copies and stamped envelope addressed to Clerk's Office
- Vows (or I bring them on cardstock)
- Adult witnesses, if required
- Rings
- Balance of celebrant's fee

Tools: Couple's Secondary DOW Checklist — Suggested Items to Bring

- Programs
- Eyeglasses
- Handkerchiefs
- Wedding canopy
- Ritual altar objects such as:
  - Altar table and ironed cloth
  - Flowers

- ○ Family photos
- ○ Drinking vessel(s)
- ○ Small pitcher
- ○ Ceremonial beverage
- ○ Two cloth napkins
- ○ Box with Love Letters and Wine or simply wine
- ○ Unity candle
- ○ Light bulbs or wine glasses and bag for shards
- ○ Head coverings

Tools: Celebrant's DOW Checklist—Items to Bring

- Directions to the wedding venue
- Ceremony clothing and stole
- Eyeglasses
- Gifts
- Minister's wedding documents and signing pen
- Copies of the ceremony
- Vows and Love and Marriage Readings cards
- Handkerchiefs

Arrive early. Always anticipate traffic delays!

Chapter Tips

- I have found it useful for the celebrant to provide a Couple's *Day of Wedding Checklist* a few days before the couple's wedding.
- Celebrant should also be prepared with her/his own Celebrant's *Day of Wedding Checklist*.

19

Upon Arrival to the Wedding Venue

Tools: Celebrant First Meets with the Couple (10 minutes)

- Address any concerns
- Review rings, veil and train
- Provide vow cards
- Give gifts (optional)
- Sign marriage license (witnesses, if required)
- Secure balance of payment
- Request a testimonial
- Do a brief centering meditation

Tools: Celebrant Familiarizes Self with the Ceremony Site

- Meet with wedding planner for final details

  - If you have not conducted the rehearsal, it will be helpful to know where everyone is entering from, including yourself.
  - Set up altar and ritual objects.

Tools: Celebrant Reviews the Various Wedding Roles

- Remind Ushers to guide guests to seats and/or hand out programs (optional).
- Direct Family Members and Wedding Attendants.
- Meet Photographer/Videographer/Musicians for microphone set up, cues and getting their business cards to ask for photos/video of you and the couple.
- Distribute reading selection cards to Readers and review logistics.

Tools: Celebrant Requests Microphones

1. I highly recommend the use of a microphone, especially in the case of an outdoor wedding or a sizeable group of guests.
2. In order to hold your ceremony notes, you will need a hands-free microphone.
3. For vows to be heard, the couple will need to share your microphone or have their own.

Tools: Celebrant Brings Handkerchiefs

The wedding ceremony is a highly charged and emotional experience. If the couple has not brought their own handkerchiefs, I have found it most helpful to be able to hand them one. Sometimes I need one for myself.

Chapter Tips

- The wedding ceremony is a highly charged and emotional experience. If the couple has not brought their own handkerchiefs, I have found it most helpful to be able to hand them one. Sometimes I need one for myself.

20

Right After the Wedding (RATW)

Tools: Celebrant's Follow-Up RATW

- Take photos with the couple.
- Give a copy of the marriage license to the couple. They may need it as proof of marriage before the original is sent to them.

- Mail in the marriage license to the Clerk's Office by due date.

  - Include any Out-of-State Officiant Certificate.
  - Keep a copy in your files.

- Send a follow-up letter to the newlyweds.

- Contact the photographer and videographer to get wedding photos and video.

  - Follow up a month later.

- Contact the wedding planner as a good will gesture.
- After one week, send a review request to the couple.
- Post congratulations to the couple on social media pages.
- Thank the couple for a positive review.
- Post the couple's review with photo and video (if available) to website and other promotional services.

Tools: Celebrant's RATW Follow-Up Letter to the Couple

A letter to the couple after the wedding serves several purposes. It ties things up and produces some closure to the process we had closely shared. It gives you the chance to express your pleasure in having served them and gratitude for their payment. In the letter you can remind them that you will contact them for photos and request a review.

Below, I share an example of my RATW follow-up letter to the couple.

Dear Tracey and Bernard,

It was truly a pleasure getting to know both of you, and I was very happy to meet your friends and family over the weekend.

I appreciate the opportunity to have been a part of your wedding day and for your trust in me. I thoroughly enjoyed performing the ceremony among people who care for you. It was so sweet and touching to be at the altar closely watching your loving expressions and the connection you shared.

I love the amulet you so kindly gave me as a gift. It echoes the design on your lovely wedding invitation. I have it on as I write to you. Thank you for your generous payment. At the end of the year, you will get notice of a donation made in your honor.

I very much look forward to seeing your wedding photographs and video.

As a reminder, I have a favor to ask: I am a registered vendor with The Knot, the premiere online wedding site. If you were pleased with our creative process and the ceremony, would you be so kind as to respond to a review request that will be sent to you by The Knot? Your review is very important to me and will allow me to serve other loving couples. Thank you for your consideration on my behalf.

I am grateful for your including me to be a part of such a beautiful union. I would love to keep in touch to know how you are doing. And, I would be further honored to participate in any future life celebrations with you.

With warmest wishes for your future together,

Rev. Lynn

Chapter Tips

- A letter to the couple after the wedding serves several purposes.
- Post congratulations to the couple on social media pages.

21

Special Touches by the Celebrant

Tools: Special Touches by the Celebrant

One of the reasons I chose to be a wedding minister was to spread joy in the world. Helping people create and experience their happiness is part of that paradigm. So, I adopted certain rituals of my own to please my couples. Here are ways I achieve that:

- I write congratulatory notes to their parents before the wedding.
- The couple receives a nicely printed copy of their ceremony.
- I give them a small, meaningful wedding gift.
- I create an attractive marriage certificate. The original is rather sterile looking. (See Appendix 5).
- I give vintage hankies to mothers along with a document titled "Vintage Hankie Flirtations" (See Appendix 6). If a mother is not present, then I give one to a father.
- I move out of the frame for "the kiss" photograph.
- I send a note to the newlyweds the day after their wedding.
- I make a donation to a charity of their choice in honor of their marriage.
- I post a wedding announcement of their marriage on my social media (*Facebook* and *Twitter*). (See Appendix 2).
- I send holiday cards.
- I acknowledge their anniversary by sending them a Happy First Anniversary card (See Appendix 2).

I am certain you can each come up with your own gracious gestures.

Tools: Additional Special Touches for the Ceremony

A teacher of mine, Susan Turchin, published some special touches for wedding ceremonies in her book, *The Interfaith Wedding Manual, Creating Meaningful Wedding Ceremonies: A Guide for Clergy and Couples* published in 2009 (147). I find them original and charming and paraphrase them here.

1. The groom (partner) seats his or her mother (parents) before or during the ceremony.
2. The couple may walk down the aisle together.
3. The wedding party and readers may embrace the couple before they take their places at the altar.
4. When a father escorts a bride in the procession, the mother may rise to embrace her (and her partner) before they go to the altar.
5. The couple may kiss before the ceremony begins and even during the ceremony.
6. The front row of seating is for parents. Having parents sit on the opposite side of their children will allow them to see their faces during the ceremony.
7. Have a guest or friend sit with a single parent.
8. Allow people to sit on either side of the aisle in support of the new-to-be melded family.
9. Photos are taken at the altar with and without the officiant.

Tools: Donations

The work of a minister is very rewarding, and so I am moved to donate a portion of my fee to charity at the end of each calendar year. In my *Custom Wedding Questionnaire,* I ask my couples which organization they would like me to donate to in honor of their marriage. I ask the charity to notify them of the donation.

If this idea appeals to you, I suggest you visit *Charitywatch.org* to see the most reputable and highly rated charitable organizations.

Chapter Tips

- As a wedding minister, you spread joy in the world. Helping people create and experience their happiness is part of that paradigm. You can adopt certain rituals of your own to please your couples.

22

Resources for the Couple

During the wedding planning process, couples will find an enormous trove of ceremonial material. To help my clients more easily navigate the abundance of resources available, I share my collections with them, organized into clear and useful categories: *Love and Marriage Readings, Wedding Rituals, Wedding Vows, Ring Exchange Vows* and *Classical Ceremony Music.*

Tools: Celebrant's Resources Letter

> *Dear Maria and Ryan,*
>
> *I hope your wedding plans are coming along well.*
>
> *As per your request, I am attaching several resources. Please let me know if they are helpful.*
>
> - *Love and Marriage Readings*
> - *Wedding Rituals*
> - *Wedding Vows*
> - *Ring Exchange Vows*
> - *Classical Ceremony Music*
>
> *Best wishes,*
>
> *Lynn*

Love and Marriage Readings

Over the years, I have collected a rich sampling of wedding readings. I offer this extensive listing of *Love and Marriage Readings* to my clients to consider for use in their ceremonies. After getting to know my couples, I may be able to extract from this collection a shorter list of selections that I think they may like.

Here are some popular options that couples have chosen as wedding readings for their ceremonies. The entire collection of more than one hundred readings can be found in Appendix 7.

Unless otherwise indicated, the sources for these materials are the Interfaith Seminary program at *onespiritinterfaith.org* and Susan Turchin's book, *The Interfaith Wedding Manual, Creating Meaningful Wedding Ceremonies: A Guide for Clergy and Couples* (22–59).

Tools: Love and Marriage Readings for a Ceremony

This reading was selected by a couple who had been dating since high school.

"Union" by Robert Fulghum

Adapted

You have known each other from the first glance of acquaintance to this point of commitment. At some point, you decided to marry. From that moment of yes, to this moment of yes, indeed, you have been making commitments in an informal way. All of those conversations that were held in a car, or over a meal, or during long walks—all those conversations that began with, "When we're married," and continued with "I will" and "you will" and "we will"—all those late night talks that included "someday" and "somehow" and "maybe"—and all those promises that are unspoken matters of the heart. All these common things, and more, are the real process of a wedding.

The symbolic vows that you are about to make are a way of saying to one another, "You know all those things that we've promised, and hoped and dreamed—well, I meant it all, every word."

Look at one another and remember this moment in time. Before this moment, you have been many things to one another—acquaintance, friend, companion, lover, dancing partner, even teacher, for you have learned much from one another these past few years. Shortly you shall say a few words that will take you across a threshold of life, and things between you will never quite be the same.

For after today you shall say to the world — This is my husband. This is my wife (*English-wedding.com*).

Anne's House of Dreams by L.M. Montgomery

Excerpt

It was a happy and beautiful bride who came down the old, homespun carpeted stairs that September noon — the first bride of Green Gables, slender and shining-eyed, in the mist of her maiden veil, with her arms full of roses. Gilbert, waiting for her in the hall below, looked up at her with adoring eyes. She was his at last, this evasive, long-sought Anne, won after years of patient waiting. It was to him she was coming in the sweet surrender of the bride. Was he worthy of her? Could he make her as happy as he hoped? If he failed her — if he could not measure up to her standard of manhood — then, as she held out her hand, their eyes met and all doubt was swept away in a glad certainty. They belonged to each other; and, no matter what life might hold for them, it could never alter that. Their happiness was in each other's keeping and both were unafraid.

Engaging Family and Dear Friends

A wedding ceremony is an ideal opportunity for the couple to honor those they love. It is a chance to thank those people who have been most significant in their lives.

One such way is to invite them to be a part of the wedding party and the procession. Another way is to have someone read an expressive passage or poem or sing a song during the ceremony. Yet another is to ask that they be a part of a wedding ceremony ritual.

When stepchildren are present, I recommend finding a role for them in the ceremony. Stepfamilies come with complexities that may be assuaged by including the children in a role that is comfortable for them. Some ideas, depending on the child's age, might include being a part of the wedding party, acting as flower bearer or ring bearer, reading a poem, or participating in a ritual.

Traditional wedding rituals are rich with meaning. They are a form of respect for all that has come before and shine a light on the future of the wedding partners. In this section, I will catalogue a variety of wedding rituals. Some are age-old ceremonies while others are more modern. Regardless, I believe rituals are subject to interpretation and based on the wants and needs of the couple marrying. Variations are acceptable and desirable. I consider all of the following rituals to be available and adaptable to all wedding couples, as they prefer.

Tools: Wedding Rituals from World Cultures

For much of this chapter, I have collected the *Rituals* from a variety of wedding- and marriage-related resources found on the Internet. Many materials had no attributed author or source or were defined as public domain material, which may have been further adapted. Material that did have sources I have credited within this book. Finally, additional sources for these materials are the *Interfaith Seminary* program at *onespiritinterfaith.org*, Susan Turchin's book, *The Interfaith Wedding Manual, Creating Meaningful Wedding Ceremonies: A Guide for Clergy and Couples* (78–94), and Maureen Burwell Pollinger's book, *Yes! I Will! I Do! Your Step-by-Step Guide to Creating a Wedding Ceremony as Unique as You Are* (283–318).

Catholic: Unity Candle
Commonly used in Catholic weddings, the Unity Candle also holds a universal significance.* By using three candles, it symbolizes the joining of the couple in marriage, the joining of their two families and the Holy Trinity. Parents may light their individual candles and use them to light the third, thus, showing their support for the couple's creation of a new family. Alternatively, the couple may choose to do the candle lighting.**

* This is a popular ritual for all denominations using a single candle
** Not advised for outdoor ceremonies

Celtic and African: Broom Jumping

In this Celtic and African tradition, a broom is placed on the floor and the couple jumps over it to symbolize the clearing away of negativity with a sweep of the broom and creating a threshold for the couple to cross over into their new life together.

Celtic: Hand Fasting Ceremony

The expression *tying the knot* comes from an old Celtic ritual. In this tradition, the hands of the partners are tied together* with cloth or a wide ribbon. The tying is done in the pattern of the infinity symbol or with simple repeated wrapping to symbolize the bringing together of the two hearts in a marriage of strength and unity forever.

* Best done near the end of the ceremony

Japanese Buddhist: Juzu Beads

The couple carries *Juzu* or prayer beads. They are strings of twenty-one or 108 beads, the number having earthly significance. They are used to offer prayers to Buddha.

Christian: Episcopal

During the ceremony, the celebrant asks the community of guests if they will "uphold these two persons in their marriage?" The community answers, "We will" and a song follows.

Filipino: Coin Ceremony

One partner cups hands under the cupped hands of the other partner. The celebrant sprinkles thirteen silver coins into the upper palms that trickle like a waterfall into the lower palms. Then the coins are placed onto a plate held by an honoree. This represents a sign of fidelity and completes the marriage contract.

Filipino: Veil and Cord

Two of the wedding sponsors are chosen to be *veil sponsors* who pin a large veil on top of one partner's head and the other's shoulder. The veil symbolizes unity and that the newlyweds shall be clothed as one.

Another set of sponsors are *cord sponsors* who place a white cord loosely around the necks of the couple in a figure eight to symbolize their bond.

German: Boughs

Guests lay fir boughs in front of the couple as they leave the ceremony to pave their way with hope, luck and fertility.

Greek: Crown Ceremony, *The Stephana*

Attached wedding crowns are placed on the couple symbolizing the glory and honor that is being bestowed upon them by God. These *Stephana (crowns)* are joined by a ribbon indicating unity and the presence of Christ's blessing, establishing the couple as the king and queen of their home, which they shall rule with wisdom, justice, integrity and self-sacrifice.*

Usually accompanied by the reading about the Wedding of Cana in the Gospel According to John

Hawaiian: Lei

The *lei* is the Hawaiian symbol of love. During the ceremony the celebrant binds the hands* of the partners with leis as a symbol of the couple's commitment to each other.

Best done near the end of the ceremony

Sample I/I/I Ceremony:

In a ceremony I officiated, shortly after same-sex marriages were legalized in the United States, one groom was from Massachusetts and the other groom was from Hawaii. By binding their hands together using a lei, from the Hawaiian culture, the couple pledged their commitment to each other before family and friends.

Hindu: Gath Bandhan

During the ceremony, scarves are placed around the couple symbolizing their eternal bond.

Hindu: Jalastnchana

The parents of the couple marrying bless them by dipping a rose in water and sprinkling it over them.

Hindu: Saptapadi

During the ceremony, the couple walks seven steps together to signify their vows at the beginning of their journey through life together. These steps are traditionally walked around a fire* as the couple recites their seven vows.

First step: To respect and honor each other
Second step: To share each other's joy and sorrow
Third step: To trust and be loyal to each other
Fourth step: To cultivate appreciation for knowledge, values, sacrifice and service
Fifth step: To reconfirm their vow of purity, love, family, duties and spiritual growth
Sixth step: To follow the principles of Dharma (righteousness)
Seventh step: To nurture an eternal bond of friendship and love

* Fire safety to be observed

Indian: Jaimala

The couple exchanges garlands as a gesture of acceptance and respect for one another and for prosperity.

Indian: Salt Ceremony

Indian weddings often include a Salt Ceremony. The bride passes a handful of salt to her groom without spilling any. He then passes it back to her and the exchange is repeated three times. She then performs the salt exchange with all of the members of the groom's family, symbolizing her blending in with her new family.

Indian: The Bhariat

The *Bhariat* is the bridegroom's festive processional.* The bridegroom and his entourage enter the wedding venue dancing. The groom traditionally dresses in the fashion of the Mughal royalty. This ritual is meant to formally establish the bond between the two marrying families.

* *Traditionally, the bridegroom arrives on horseback.*

Sample from an Interfaith Ceremony:

In 2014, I officiated an interfaith wedding between a Muslim man and a Jewish woman. To balance the requests of the groom, the bride and their respective families, the pre-ceremony was the Bhariat with lots of dancing by the groom with his attendees. For the bride's part, traditional Jewish elements were included in the ceremony, including the groom's Breaking of the Glass (see ritual below). In the photograph above, the bridegroom Ahmed arrived dancing with his entourage before the ceremony. I had the pleasure of marrying Ahmed and Alexis that day. Photograph taken by Cole and Kiera Photography.

Japanese: Fans
Bridesmaids carry fans symbolizing happiness because a fan expands suggesting a bigger and better future.*

* Also practiced in Chinese weddings

Japanese: Sake Ceremony
Three different sizes of sake cups are exchanged nine times between the couple before the two families join in to celebrate their union.

Jewish: Breaking of the Glass
A Jewish wedding tradition is the *Breaking of the Glass*. The shattering of glass historically served as a reminder of the destruction of the Temple in ancient Jerusalem. At the end of the marriage ceremony, the rabbi may say, "As we congregate to share the meaning of this most heartfelt moment, let me ask you all to go within and fill yourselves with the best of wishes for this lovely couple." One or both partners stomp on a glass.* Afterward, everyone shouts "*Mazel tov!*" (Good luck!) The recessional follows.

* A glass or light bulb is wrapped in a cloth napkin or bag

Commentary:
This symbolism today can be a reminder of the fragility of human relationships. Even the strongest love can be subject to frailty, thus requiring the utmost care.

Jewish: Chuppah

The wedding canopy in a Jewish wedding is called a *chuppah*. In one traditional explanation, the chuppah represents the home the couple will share. The opening on the top can be thought of as a roof window that will allow sunshine to glow upon them. The uncovered sides suggest that their home shall always be open, as may their hearts be, to welcome all who are a part of their lives.

Commentary:
One might ask, "But what if it rains?" It's true that there may be times when rain comes flowing in, but it is then that you can find shelter in your love, and the sun will surely follow. The chuppah is a place of joy. Did you know that in biblical times it was customary for couples to spend their first wedded night sleeping under the chuppah?

In the photo above, I had the pleasure of marrying Roberta and Zack under their chuppah. Photograph taken by *FarnazKStudio.com*.

Jewish: Ketubah

The *ketubah* is the Jewish marriage contract as commanded by the Torah. The ketubah ceremony is usually held right before the larger wedding ceremony. Selected guests are invited and of them two adults are honored to be witnesses* to the signing of the Jewish marriage contract. It is a ceremony within a ceremony, so to speak, and may be mentioned or read during the general gathering of all the guests.

Ask the couple and witnesses to bring their Hebrew names in writing to this ceremony.

In the photo above, I had the pleasure of conducting the Ketubah Ceremony for Frances and Gene. Photograph taken by *GregKesslerWeddings.com*.

Jewish: Seven Circles Ceremony
The following ceremony is read out loud by the celebrant as the couple takes turns circling one another:

Seven times encircling my beloved beneath this fragrant canopy, our home
The seven circles of my love for you
The seven blessings of our wedding day
Seven are our vows today, my love
Seven the days of the week
And the Sabbath is the seventh day
The Holy Bride, the Sabbath Queen.
The first circle is *chesed* — I circle you with loving kindness
The second circle is *gevurah* — I bless you with strength
The third circle is *tiferet* — May harmony rule in our home
The fourth circle is *netzach* — The circle of victory
May goodness triumph always
The fifth circle is *hod* — The shining radiance of God's glory
Reflected on our faces today
On our wedding day
The sixth circle is *yesod* — The firm foundation
May the bedrock of our love and faith
Sustain us come what may
The seventh circle is *malchut* – The sphere of Kingship
Today I am your Sabbath Queen
Yasis Alayich Elohayich
Kimsos Chatan Al Kallah
Your God shall rejoice in you
As a Bridegroom rejoices
In his Bride
Ve'erastich li

> I shall bind you to me *Be'emunah*—in faith *Be'chesed*—in loving kindness
> *Uv'rachamim*—and in compassion

With this dance, I thee wed.

The following connects to the "Wedding Film" video link for a wedding I conducted that included the seven circles ceremony ritual: *Mediazilla.com/pny4w7xm3*. Video created by *Timeless-Cinema.com*.

Korean: Ducks

Ducks are included in the wedding procession, because they are considered lucky, as they mate for life.*

* Best suited for outdoor ceremonies

Mexican: Rosary

A lasso of a very large rosary is wound around the couple's shoulders and hands during the ceremony to symbolize their union and the protection of their marriage.

* Best done near the end of the ceremony

Muslim: *Nikkah*

During a Muslim ceremony, each partner says *"qubool"* (yes) three times for the marriage to be valid. This is done during the *nikkah* portion of the ceremony. The *nikkah* is a very intimate and short wedding ceremony.

Muslim, Sikh: Pink Sash

In a Muslim ceremony, a parent places a pink sash on one partner who ties it to the other partner to symbolize their unity.

Native American: Butterfly Release

A Native Indian legend says that if you catch a butterfly and make a wish, when you release it your wish will come true. Many people choose to have this charming ritual performed at the end of their wedding ceremony.*

* This ritual is time sensitive for the well-being of the butterflies.

Quaker: Meditation and Speak Out

A quiet meditation is often held in this tradition. Guests are welcome to speak out.

Quaker: Signing the Wedding License

After the ceremony, the whole community is invited to sign the Quaker Wedding License. In the photo above, the Quaker Wedding License for Jennifer and Colin awaits to be signed by their wedding guests. The Quaker Wedding License and photograph above were created by Miss Design Berry Inc. at *Etsy.com/shop/ MissDesignBerryInc.*

Rose Ceremony

Here, the couple may choose during the ceremony to present roses to the mothers and grandmothers as a way of showing appreciation for their support. Or, the roses can be exchanged as the first gifts that the pair gives to each other as a married couple.

Salt Covenant Ceremony

In this ritual from biblical times, the couple will combine two similar containers of salt into a single vessel. The separate containers represent each partner's life and experiences up to their wedding day. This act has its origin in the Old Testament. Humankind has long considered salt to be an agent of exchange and a pure substance that adds flavoring to life. It is a symbol of prosperity, luck and an agent of long-lasting preservation—all good things in a marriage.

By pouring* the separate containers of salt into one, the covenant of marriage and joining of the two families is symbolized. Just as they are not able to separate grains of salt, they will not be able to break their commitment to each other. Their families will enduringly maintain their support of this union. This single container of salt is sealed and shall be placed prominently in the newlyweds' home** as a remembrance of their wedding day.

Use of a funnel is recommended
**Rock salt withstands moisture better*

Sand or Rice Rituals
Though not biblically based, this ritual is conducted just like the Salt Covenant Ceremony above. Couples may choose to use different colored elements in place of the salt.*

This ritual is particularly appropriate for including children

Scandinavian: Care Cloths
After the closing blessings, wedding attendants hold "care cloths" over the couple to protect them from evil.

Scottish: Bagpipes
A piper plays the bagpipes heralding the couple's exit from the ceremony.

Scottish: Tartan
After vows are exchanged, partners drape a shawl or sash in their clans' tartans over each other's shoulders to symbolize unity. At the wedding ceremony I performed for Ellen and Steven, the groom and groomsmen wore tartans celebrating their Scottish heritage.

Spanish (Spain)

Parents act as the best man and matron of honor.

Stone or Shell Collection

Have every guest hold a small stone or shell during the ceremony that they will silently bless the couple with. Have the stones collected in a pretty, clear container the couple will keep as a reminder of their guests' support for the marriage.

Tree Planting*

During the ceremony, the couple may plant a small evergreen tree in a pretty container symbolizing the establishment of roots that will be the foundation of their marriage and the growth that will continue in their future together.

* Best suited for outdoor ceremonies

Various Cultures: Wine

Many cultures incorporate a wine ritual in their weddings. In this ritual, the couple will drink from a special vessel of wine.* It is a traditional way of sharing their love and the joy that comes from the fruit of the vine. The wine (or other beverage) is blessed.** In this sharing, they are displaying to their loved ones their commitment to the sanctity of their marriage. The celebrant hands the pre-filled cup to one partner who sips and passes it to the other partner who sips. Sometimes the couple will entwine their elbows while drinking. The cup is handed back to the celebrant.***

*White wine is recommended near a wedding dress.
**For Jewish ceremonies, the following prayer is recited:

וְפגה ירפ ארוֹב םלוֹעה דְלמ וּניהלֹא חוחי התּאַ דְוּרבּ.

Baruch ata Adonai Eloheinu melech ha'olum, borei p'ri hagafen.
Blessed art Thou, our God, Ruler of the universe, creator of the fruit of the vine.
***A toast by the community works especially well here.

Commentary:

One of my grooms manufactured beer in his basement, so that was the beverage of choice to be shared. Another couple chose *maracuyá* from South America where they had traveled together. Other couples have chosen to drink from a bottle of wine dated the year they met.

Various Cultures: Wine Box/Love Letters

In this ritual, the couple has written love letters to each other before the wedding day. At this ceremony they will place a favorite bottle of wine and the love letters into a special wine box. The couple will seal the box and vow not to open it until their anniversary of choice. At that time, they will share the wine as they read their love letters.

Couples may also reference/adapt any of the above rituals to help them create a new ritual for their ceremony. For further illumination of a myriad of other wedding rituals, I refer you to *Yes! I Will! I Do! Your Step-by-Step Guide to Creating a Wedding Ceremony as Unique as You Are* by Maureen Burwell Pollinger, and *Wedding Planning for Dummies*, 3rd edition, by Marcy Blum (164–181).

Vows for Weddings

While some couples choose to put their own stamp on the ceremony, others prefer to stick to traditional vows that have been spoken for centuries. There is no right or wrong approach here—it is simply a case of what works best for the partners. Please note that the couple's spoken vows may or may not be the same and couples may opt to alter the vows below to their liking.

For much of this chapter, I have collected the *vows* from a variety of wedding- and marriage-related resources found on the Internet. Many vows had no attributed author or source or were defined as public domain material, which may have been further adapted. Vows and materials that did have sources I have credited within this book. Finally, some of the vows are from writings by my eloquent colleagues in *Interfaith Seminary* program at *onespiritinterfaith.org*, *myweddingvows.com*, *TheKnot.com* and *weddings.about.com*.

Tools: Examples of Traditional Vows

Vow 1:

I, (name), take you (name), to be my (wife/husband), to have and to hold, for better or for worse, for richer, for poorer, in sickness and in health, to love and to cherish; from this day forward until death do us part.

Vow 2:

I, (name), take you, (name), to be my [optional: lawfully wedded] (husband/wife), my constant friend, my faithful partner and my love from this day forward. In the presence of God, our family and friends, I offer you my solemn vow to be your faithful partner in sickness and in health, in good times and in bad, and in joy as well as in sorrow. I promise to love you unconditionally, to support you in your goals, to honor and respect you, to laugh with you and cry with you, and to cherish you for as long as we both shall live.

Vow 3:

(Name), I take you to be my lawfully wedded (husband/wife). Before these witnesses, I vow to love you and care for you as long as we both shall live. I take you with all your faults and your strengths as I offer myself to you with my faults and strengths. I will help you when you need help, and I will turn to you when I need help. I choose you as the person with whom I will spend my life.

For more examples of traditional vows see Appendix 8.

Tools: Vows from World Cultures

The following time-honored vows, prayers and poems come from cultures all over the world. They can be used to inspire a couple's own vows, or included as a part of their ceremony.

BAHA'I

I (groom), take you (bride) to be my wife,
Knowing in my heart that you will be my constant friend,
My faithful partner in life and my one true love.
I add my breath to your breath,
That our days may be long on the earth,
That the days of our people may be long,
That we may be one person,
That we may finish our roads together.

Celtic Handfasting

Handfasting for a year and a day
Bound together for a lifetime.
I will always hold your hand fast,
And we shall have the time of our lives.

We are the air it surrounds us.
We are the fire it burns within us.
We are the water it flows through us.
We are the earth it sustains us.

Chinese

From sixth-century China:
And we will make our bed beneath the bright and ragged quilt
Of all the yesterdays that makes us who we are.
The strengths and frailties we bring to this marriage,
And we will be rich indeed.

Humanist

I promise to love, cherish and protect, in good fortune and adversity.

Irish

As light to the eye, as bread to the hungry,
As joy to the heart, may thy presence be with me.

Here is my hand to hold with you,
To bind us for life and grow old with you.

I take you in all love and honor,
In all duty and service,
In all faith and tenderness.

Jewish
We come together to record in the minds and hearts of all present the ripe event of a love that's bloomed.

Lutheran
I give you my hand and my heart as a sanctuary of warmth and peace.

Marriage a Poem by Susan Schuette
When I look into your eyes I see the love I have for you reflected back at me;
As I walk this joyous path with your hand in mine,
I think of all the special things both mundane and sublime;
The passion and the joy our love has grown to be;
The wonderful safe harbor it has become for "We."

Medieval Christian
You cannot possess me, for I belong to myself.
But while we both wish it, I give you what is mine to give.

Methodist
The peace and serenity of the heavens be with you always.

Presbyterian
I enter this marriage with you knowing that the true magic of love is not to avoid changes but to navigate them successfully.

Pueblo Indian

Together we will remain faithful and lifelong partners . . . .

Together we will cherish each other and our families in sorrow and happiness.

Wiccan Handfasting

You are the star of each night.

You are the brightness of each morning.

You are the story of each quest.

You are the report of every land.

Tools: Personal Vows

The following are a sampling of original vows written by couples I married. To protect their privacy I am using pseudonyms.

Groom:

"I have to admit that writing this wedding vow was a bit daunting. My first step was to read through a list of thought provoking poems, sayings and blessings provided by Reverend Lynn (all 105 of them). This would be a good starting point. There (of course) would also be a need to scour the Internet for example after example, to make sure that I did not miss an important emotion to express.

But I was wrong (it won't be the last time.) On the very first day of writing, I spotted this poem by Rainer Maria Rilke:

Understand, I'll slip quietly away from the noisy crowd
When I see the pale stars rising, blooming over the oaks.
I'll pursue solitary pathways through the pale twilit meadows,
With only this one dream: You come too.

We have known of each other for some time now, but we didn't truly meet until five years ago. From that moment, I knew that we would be standing here one day. As we traveled the path to this day, I admired the academic and professional accomplishments that you achieved in a short period of time. I learned that you are Strong, Smart, Supportive, Skilled and Successful at everything you do, and it doesn't hurt that you are Strikingly beautiful. Those are a lot of words that start with "S." You should have a cape with an "S" on it; you are a superhero. I also learned to always have extra napkins, because no filled glass of liquid is safe near you.

My hopes and aspirations for the future are now much less complicated than I had ever thought possible. Now, when two roads diverge in a yellow wood, it will not matter which one I take, as long as you come too.

Kimberly, amidst all of the complexity that is surrounding us today, among all of life's day-to-day challenges, and within all of the calamities that may occur in the future, I have no worries. My every day, every hour, every minute will be a dream come true, as long as you come too."

Bride:

"André, when we took our first vacation to Ocean City together, I didn't realize that it would forever change my life. This is when I realized that I loved you and that I couldn't imagine my life without you. (Even if you were a sore loser in Pictionary.) We encourage each other to be the best versions of ourselves. We balance each other flawlessly. As most of you know, I can be a little type A. You are my perfect balance, and as Mike calls you, the 'Kim Whisperer.' As you told me the only thing that will be completely perfect on our wedding day is us, because we are perfect together and for each other. Today and every day I promise to love and support you unconditionally for the rest of our lives. I vow to walk with you, be your partner, best friend and rock. I love you with all of my heart and soul and I am so blessed to have found you, my perfect match."

For more examples of personal vows see Appendix 9.

Tools: Tips for Couples Writing Their Own Vows

Blog: Vows? Wow! Where Do I Begin?

The following tips were adapted from one of my blogs, "Vows? Wow! Where Do I Begin?" at *LynnGladstone.com*, to aid couples interested in writing their own original vows.

Vows are a very important part of a marriage ceremony. It is with the vows that the couple pledges their most heartfelt intentions to one another, witnessed by the most important people in their lives.

Writing and delivering your own vows can be intimidating. They center on your intimate feelings and sometimes feelings are difficult to put into words. However, they can be the greatest wedding gifts you can give to each other, because, it is a generous, loving surprise.

Try to relax. Remember that you simply want to do something to make your fiancé happy. It does not have to be the greatest speech in the history of the world. When you sit down to compose your vows, imagine you're sitting across from one of your close friends (or have that friend sit there in person) as you casually tell your friend the story of your fiancé, as if they never met. Add something about how you imagine your lives together in the future. Jot down notes or have your friend do it for you. Refer back to these notes when writing your actual vows.

Here are some tools to help you write your marriage vows:

- List three to five words describing your fiancé.
- List three to five words describing your feelings for your fiancé.
- List three to five words about how your fiancé makes you feel.

  ○ How did you meet? What did you think and feel when you first met?
  ○ What incident(s) let you know this is a solid human being?
  ○ Describe when you first fell in love with your fiancé. And what followed?
  ○ Talk about dreams you share for your future together.
  ○ What do you want to pledge to your fiancé?
  ○ List three to five promises that you can keep.

Use the information gathered above when considering the following:

Opening section of your vows:

- Imagine you are writing a public love letter to your beloved, because you are!

General Tips:

- The most important aspects of wedding vows are the promises you make.
- Stay with positive language.
- Humor is always appreciated. Include some if you are comfortable with it.

- Vows may be as short as a well-formed sentence or much longer.
- Vows may even be in the form of a poem or song.
- Feel free to be imaginative.
- Google: "Love Poems" and "Quotes About Love" and see what speaks to you.

Closing section of your vows:

- Use your deepest words of appreciation and intention.
- Offer your greatest promise.

Photography above is from iStockphoto ©nikolasvn.

Tools: Suggested Vow Vocabulary List for Couples

- Accept, admire, adore, always, appreciation, authentic
- Beautiful, beloved, best friend, blossom
- Care, challenge, charm, cherish, comfort, commit, complete, create, cry
- Dear, delight, desire, devotion, divine
- Elation, endearing, embrace, encourage, enduring, enjoy, eternal, everlasting
- Faith, flow, forever, free, friend, fun, funny
- Gentle, give, glow, grow, generous
- Happy, holy, honest, honor, hope
- Important, inspire, integrity, intimate
- Join, joy
- Kind, kindred-spirit
- Laugh, learn, long, love, lovely, loyal
- New, nurture
- Offer, only
- Partner, passion, peace, positive, precious, priceless, promise, protect
- Real, reliable, respect, revere, romantic
- Sacred, secure, sensitive, share, sincere, singular, soul mate, special, spirit, strive, support
- Teach, thoughtful, thrill, total, treasure, true, trust, try
- Understand, unity

- Values, virtue
- Warmth, wonderful, worthy

Or use your own words.

Tools: Examples of Traditional Ring Exchange Vows

Ring Vow 1:

I, (name), give you, (name), this ring as a token of my love. I marry you with this ring, with all that I have and all that I am.

Response: (Name), I, (name), will forever wear this ring as a sign of my commitment and the desire of my heart for you.

Ring Vow 2:

I give you this ring in God's name, as a symbol of all that we have promised and all that we shall share.

Ring Vow 3:

Let this ring be a symbol of my promises to you and a reminder of my devotion to you. I am honored to call you my (wife/husband).

For more examples of ring exchange vows see Appendix 10.

Tools: Traditional Jewish and Muslim Ring Exchange Vows

Jewish Ring Vow

For the groom placing the ring on the bride's finger:

לארשיו השמ תדכ ,וז תעבטב ,יל תשדקמ תא ירה.

Harei at m'kudeshet li b'taba'at zo k'dat Moshe v'Yisrael.

And for the bride, placing the ring on the groom's finger:

לארשיו השמ תדכ ,וז תעבטב ,יל שדוקמ התא ירה.

Harei atah m'kudash li b'taba'at Zoe k'dat Moshe v'Yisrael.

Behold, thou art consecrated unto me with this ring according to the Law of Moses and of Israel.

Muslim Ring Vow

Rings are traditionally exchanged during the *mangni*, a betrothal ceremony or at the reception, but not during the wedding ceremony *(nikkah)* itself.

Tools: Classical Ceremony Music

Couples occasionally ask for my suggestions for classical ceremony music. I have a collection of classical music selections appropriate for the processional entrance and recessional exit parts of a ceremony. I have collected the *Ceremony Music* from a variety of wedding- and marriage-related resources found on the Internet. Some of the sources for these materials are *classicalarchives.com*, *imslp. org*, and *britannica.com*. An additional source is Diane Berke's book, *Interfaith Minister's Training and Reference Manual, Second Year Training Program* (343–345).

Air on a G String by Johann Sebastian Bach
"Ave Maria" by Johann Sebastian Bach and Charles-François Gounod
Cantata No. 29 by Johann Sebastian Bach
Cello Suite No. 1, Prelude by Johann Sebastian Bach
Gigue from Orchestral Suite No. 3 in D Major by Johann Sebastian Bach
"Jesu, Joy of Man's Desiring" by Johann Sebastian Bach
Concerto for Two Violins in D minor, Largo by Johann Sebastian Bach
"Notebook for Anna Magdalene Bach" March in D Major by Johann Sebastian Bach
"My Heart Ever Faithful" by Johann Sebastian Bach
Prelude and Fugue in C Major by Johann Sebastian Bach
Cantata No. 208, "Sheep May Safely Graze" by Johann Sebastian Bach
Cantata No. 156, Sinfonia by Johann Sebastian Bach
Cantata No. 140: "Wachet auf, ruft uns die Stimme," (Sleepers, Awake) by Johann Sebastian Bach
Symphony No. 9, "Ode to Joy" by Ludwig van Beethoven
"Marche Troyenne," *Les Troyens* by Hector Berlioz
"Rigaudon" by André Campra

"Te Deum" by Marc-Antoine Charpentier

"The Prince of Denmark's March" by Jeremiah Clarke

"Trumpet Voluntary" by Jeremiah Clarke

"The Flower Duet," *Lakmé,* by Léo Delibes

"Messe Solennelle," Op. 12, No. 5, by César Franck

"Panis Angelicus" by César Franck

Canzon V by Giovanni Gabrieli

"Wedding Day at Troldhaugen" by Edvard Grieg

Water Music, Suite No. 1 in F Major, Air by George Frideric Handel

Water Music, Suite No. 2 in D Major, "Alla Hornpipe" by George Frideric Handel

"Music for the Royal Fireworks," *La Réjouissance* by George Frideric Handel

Largo, *Xerxes* by George Frideric Handel

Ouverture, *Music for the Royal Fireworks* by George Frideric Handel

"Processional of Joy" by Hal H. Hopson

Trumpet Tune in A Major by David N. Johnson

Cavalleria Rusticana, Intermezzo by Pietro Mascagni

Organ Sonata No. 3 in A major, Op. 65,

Con Moto Maestoso, by Felix Mendelssohn

"Wedding March" from *A Midsummer Night's Dream* by Felix Mendelssohn

Toccata, *L'Orfeo* by Claudio Monteverdi

Andante, Divertimento No. 1, *Salzburg Symphony* by Wolfgang Amadeus Mozart

Ave Verum Corpus by Wolfgang Amadeus Mozart

"March of the Priests" from *The Magic Flute* by Wolfgang Amadeus Mozart

Piano Concerto No. 21 in C Major by Wolfgang Amadeus Mozart

"Romance" from String Quartet by Wolfgang Amadeus Mozart

"Wedding March," from *The Marriage of Figaro* by Wolfgang Amadeus Mozart

Promenade, *Pictures at an Exhibition* by Modest Mussorgsky

Canon in D by Johann Pachelbel

Trumpet Tune by Henry Purcell

"Procession of Nobles" by Nikolai Rimsky-Korsakov

Trumpet Voluntary by John Stanley

"Coronation March" for *Tsar Alexander III* by Peter I. Tchaikovsky

"Love Theme," Overture, *Romeo and Juliet* by Peter I. Tchaikovsky

March, *Aida* by Giuseppe Verdi

"Spring," *The Four Seasons* by Antonio Vivaldi
"Winter Largo," *The Four Seasons* by Antonio Vivaldi
"Bridal Chorus," *Lohengrin* by Richard Wagner

Think Outside the Box

What is most important is that the couple has the ceremony they have dreamed of, and that means officiants need to be open-minded. The only rule I have for couples is that nothing be planned that would knowingly hurt someone. That still leaves a lot of room for imagination.

Two of the sweetest touches that have happened in my ceremonies involved dogs. In one instance, a beloved canine was the flower bearer and in another, a best man!

Chapter Tips

- A wedding ceremony is an ideal opportunity for the couple to honor those they love.
- Couples may reference or adapt any of the rituals to help them create a new ritual for their ceremony.
- While some couples choose to put their own stamp on the ceremony, others prefer to stick to traditional vows that have been spoken for centuries. There is no right or wrong approach here—it's simply a case of what works best for the partners.
- What is most important is that the couple has the ceremony they have dreamed of, and that means officiants need to be open-minded.

23

Ceremony Outline and Flow

There are many ways to conduct a ceremony. After ongoing discussion, I always defer to the couple's wishes. Below is an example of a typical wedding *Ceremony Outline and Flow*. Use it as a general guide, but not as gospel.

A Word about Involving the Gathered Community of Guests

I am of the belief that guests will be more invested in the ceremony, less restless, and will remember it better if they actually participate. With the couple's input, I try to find an appropriate way to include them. This is a perfect chance to be creative. Some of the ideas I have used are:

- A virtual glass-raising toast by the guests
- A blessing for the couple by the gathered community
- A sing-a-long

Tools: Ceremony Outline and Flow

Being an I/I/I minister, I am open to both traditional and creative ceremonies. When I talk about the flow of a ceremony, I'm interested in the order in which events will occur. If a couple wishes to veer from 'the way it's always done,' I am fully comfortable with that and work with them to find the right structure for them. Most of my ceremonies will last twenty to thirty-five minutes.

While there are no hard and fast rules to my ceremonies, there are two legal requirements:

- Establish that both partners are marrying of free will.
- The officiant pronounces the couple as legally married.

Below is one example of a general ceremony outline presented in *gender-neutral* terms. As the ceremony creation process is a collaboration between the couple and the celebrant, I give them a ceremony outline to help them think about what they want in their ceremony. The outline is also useful to them in designing their *Wedding Program.*

Ceremony Outline and Flow:

1. **Wedding Title**
   Couple's names, wedding date and venue

2. **Entrance and Seating Guests to Music**
   Ushers conduct seating and distribute wedding programs

3. **Entrance of Celebrant**
   Celebrant walks to the altar and quiets guests

4. **Announcements**
   Celebrant addresses the community of guests with greetings and any requests from the marrying couple (e.g., no cell phones or photographs during the ceremony)

5. **Processional to Music**

   - Partner 1 enters to music, alone or accompanied
   - Partner 1's attendants follow and line up in a row at the altar facing the guests
   - Partner 2's attendants enter and line up on the opposite side of the altar
   - Flower bearer enters tossing flower petals
   - Ring bearer enters and delivers the ring to main attendant 1
   - Celebrant indicates that guests should rise
   - Partner 2 enters to music, alone or accompanied
   - Couple meets in the aisle and greets their parents
   - Couple walks together to the altar
   - Main attendant 2 takes bouquet and straightens train

6. **Celebrant's Introductory Remark**
Celebrant presents a short poem or prose reading to set the tone of the ceremony

7. **Celebrant Welcomes and Introduces**

   - The couple
   - Self
   - The parents and family
   - The wedding party
   - The community of guests

   Then, blesses the community

8. **Celebrant Remembers**
Honored ancestors

9. **Celebrant's Invocation**
Celebrant requests a blessing for the couple from God or a Universal Spirit

10. **Love and Marriage Reading**
An honored guest presents a pre-selected reading

11. **Words About Love and Marriage**
Celebrant speaks about love and marriage

12. **Words About the Couple**
Celebrant speaks about the couple

13. **Ritual**
A ritual is performed that may or may not include family participation

14. **Virtual Toast by the Community or Blessing by the Celebrant**

15. **Intentions and I Do's**
   - Free will: The couple establishes they are marrying of free will
   - Vows: The couple exchanges traditional or original vows
   - Rings: The couple express promises to one another as they exchange rings

16. Celebrant's Charge

Celebrant offers words of wisdom to the couple

17. Community Blessing

Blessing of the couple by the gathered community

18. Closing Blessing by the Celebrant

19. Pronouncement of the Couple

Celebrant announces the couple as legally married

20. Optional Closing Ritual

21. The Kiss

A veil may be raised

22. Recessional to Music
- Bouquet and train are tended to
- The couple exits
- Attendants pair off to exit
- Celebrant exits
- Parents exit
- Close family exits
- Guests exit

Tools: Detailed Ceremony Outline and Flow

Now that we have reviewed a general ceremony outline and flow above, the following is an example of one of my ceremonies.

Detailed Ceremony Outline and Flow:

The Wedding of Cara Anne and Peter

This ceremony is the wedding of Cara Anne Mathison and Peter James Lee on August 14, 2015, at Gedney Farm, Massachusetts.

Entrance and Seating of Guests to Music

Ushers seat guests and distribute wedding programs.

Music: Musical Prelude by Intermezzo Chamber Players.

Entrance of Celebrant

Celebrant goes to altar and quiets guests.

Announcements

Celebrant says:

"Welcome everyone! May I please ask for your silence? We are about to begin the marriage ceremony.

"I imagine many of you have come here expecting a traditional wedding. You are right—there will be that. However, there will be a lot more. This is going to be a soulful ceremony, filled with your participation and fabulous music. Please get ready to let your hair down, do some singing, and laughing and what have you! You will best honor Cara and Peter by actively taking part in their marriage ceremony.

"To get us started, please turn to someone you do not know and shake their hand and say hello. Okay, please clap or holler to show me that you are ready to have some serious fun! Thank you. Let the procession begin."

Processional to Music

Music: "Marry Me" by Train

Entrance:

- Partner 1 (traditionally the groom), enters from a side aisle and stands at the altar
- Attendants 1 enter from a side aisle and line up at the altar next to Partner 1
- Attendants 2 enter center aisle and line up at the opposite side of the altar

Music: "Love Theme" from *Romeo and Juliet* by Peter I. Tchaikovsky

Entrance:

- Flower bearer enters tossing flower petals in the aisle, then sits
- Ring bearer enters with the rings, delivers the rings, and then sits

Music: "The Prince of Denmark's March" by Jeremiah Clarke
Entrance:

- Guests are directed to rise
- Partner 2, traditionally the bride, enters to music accompanied by parent(s)
- The couple meets in the aisle and embrace the parent(s), and parents then sit
- Couple walks to the altar
- Bouquet is taken and train straightened
- Guests are directed to sit

Celebrant's Introductory Remark

Celebrant says:

"To set the tone of this nuptial ceremony I share these words written in the 13th century by the Persian poet, Rumi:

> The real beloved is that one who is unique,
> who is your beginning and your end.
> When you find that one,
> You'll no longer expect anything else . . . .

The source is *goodreads.com/quotes*.

Celebrant Welcomes

Celebrant says to each:

First the Couple:

"Cara Anne and Peter James, it seems we met so long ago that this feels especially heartwarming to at last welcome you to this altar tonight. Here you are celebrating your marriage. Now is when you have chosen to sanctify your commitment to one another. In some magical way, this could be the moment you have always sensed would someday arrive. After nearly five years of knowing one another, something is about to become eternally deeper between you. Thank you both for the ways you helped me to make this day so meaningful."

Then Introduces Self:
"I am Reverend Lynn Gladstone and am honored to be here to conduct this service for this lovely bride and groom. Regardless of how many times I have stood at the altar with couples that are getting married, I always celebrate with joy the opportunity to take part in a wedding ceremony. I invite you to do the same."

Next the Parents:
"I would like to bring marked attention to those who gave life to this young woman and young man and raised and loved them. In indefinable ways, Karen, David, Su-ye and Han have pointed Cara and Peter towards this singular and joyous occasion. Congratulations dear parents and the families by your sides. Please bask in how much your children appreciate you, and all you have done for them, always.

"While a wedding indicates the joining of the past, present and futures of two individuals, experience reminds us that marriage is also the wedding of two families and their histories. Each family offers different and rich gifts for this couple."

Then the Wedding Attendants:
"I thank this gracious wedding party for your supportive roles as attendants. May your abundance in numbers reflect the great care and loyalty you feel for this precious wedding couple going forward in life by their side."

Next the Guests:
"Beloved guests, because you signify something very real to them, Cara and Peter have invited you to witness them as they heighten their dedication to one another. By being here tonight to participate in this ritual of marriage, it is clear that you hold them sincerely in your hearts. On their behalf, I thank you all for being here.

They are deeply moved and appreciative of those who have traveled great distances to make this memory a cherished one. As a whole, everyone here makes up the circle of love and care that will help them embark on a life of even more meaning together."

And, Finally Blesses the Community:
"Cara and Peter know that their own love is very special, and they would like to extend it to all of you. So, they have asked me to bestow a blessing upon you, from them. We ask you, the Universal Spirit of life, love and of all beliefs, to regard with affection these dear family and friends who have been invited because of their importance in our lives. Please bestow your caring consideration, your generosity and wise guidance upon them. Provide them with good health or healing should they need it. We are so grateful to you, our dear guests, and for the Spirit listening to our hearts."

Celebrant Remembers
Celebrant says:

"In this moment we choose to recall those beloved people who cannot be here in body, but are certainly remembered. We invite them to join us, and we recognize that in some inexplicable manner, they too are here smiling and rejoicing in what is best about the human heart."

Celebrant's Invocation
Celebrant says:

"Dear God, we are here tonight for the marriage of Cara and Peter. Confident in your abiding presence alongside us, I ask you to please bless this couple generously by inspiring and sustaining them in their love for all of their days together unto eternity."

Celebrant's Commentary:

"Here we are at an auspicious moment, because today is the winter solstice. It is the shortest day of the year, but from this day forward sunlight increases. We are also nearly at the eve of Christmas, Cara's favorite holiday and time of year.

Both of these concurrent happenings have happy and hopeful overtones. What a perfect time to be married!

"In this pair, Cara and Peter, we have the representation of different religions and five ethnicities. As we watch more and more people marrying outside of their birth faith or cultural background, the world actually is brought closer together by the blending of the beautiful in each tradition. I have yet to find a religion in which the deepest original elements are not kindness and decency. This recognition of the common values of goodness and the increasing trend toward interfaith marriages provide an immeasurable chance to foster greater understanding, appreciation and peace in the world."

Love and Marriage Reading

Celebrant says:

"We know that so very much goes into building and maintaining a successful marriage. Now we will hear from Peter's brother, Stephen, with a reading about how love and marriage can be encouraged to evolve."

Honored Guest reads:

"To His Wife Mary" by William Wordsworth

> *Every day every hour every moment makes me feel more deeply how blessed we are in each other, how purely how faithfully how ardently, and how tenderly we love each other; I put this last word last because, though I am persuaded that a deep affection is not uncommon in married life, yet I am confident that a lively, gushing, thought-employing, spirit-stirring, passion of love is very rare even among good people . . . O, I love you with a passion of love which grows 'til I tremble to think of its strength.*

Words about Love and Marriage

Celebrant says:

"Is there anything more wonderful than love? Can anyone here disagree with the statement that love is the bottom line – the love of family, friends, and the love of couples? The desire to love and be loved is both irresistible and universal. When we are fortunate enough to find our true partner, it's as if a divine voice is telling us, 'Take this hand and heart, become bigger than you were on your own and go forth into goodness together.'

"In addition to the good will of a Divine Spirit, where does a good marriage begin? It takes two people who can laugh and cry, sing and dance, be quiet together, respect and be respected, communicate, make plans together, dream of their future, be vulnerable and sometimes disagree, but have a committed strategy for resolution. And perhaps, most important, amid their unquestioning love and devotion, they recognize that each individual must forge their own path while the other plays their cheerleader.

Love is something that has been around for eons. Something that is always being delightfully sought after and discovered, eternally felt, and forever written about. It crosses all boundaries of faith and belief systems as if made of one, single language."

Words about the Couple

Celebrant says:

"Let's talk about these two cheerleaders. When I met them, I found Cara to be the talker, and Peter to be more of the listener. Though their personal styles are different, it became evident to me that this is an equal partnership. They are clearly in sync about what they want. While Cara is the first to speak, she is respectful to check for Peter's input in the decisions we needed to make for this ceremony. When Peter added his opinions, he was gentle while being clearly definitive.

Cara, a human resources manager, and Peter, a senior technical consultant, met at work in 2009 and immediately hit it off. Cara told me that her initial attraction to Peter was his sincerity, his gentlemanly manner and, in parentheses, his good looks. Peter's early attraction to Cara was her outgoing personality, good looks and beautiful blue eyes—no parentheses. Casual weekday lunches slowly evolved into weekend dates that, at first, they kept secret from their colleagues.

That secret didn't last, and they became *the office couple*. With their love continuing to blossom, years later they found themselves living in a condo in Somerville with a beloved roommate, their cat, Bruiser.

Having been invited to a destination wedding in Montego Bay, Jamaica, a light bulb went off in Peter's mind. What a perfect opportunity to propose marriage to Cara. Before the trip, Peter called Cara's father to ask for his blessing. In Jamaica, he cleverly and thoughtfully managed to pull off a no-holds-barred proposal scenario.

He had arranged for a private setting at a floating table on the pool, replete with candles and a private chef. Before the meal was served, Peter got down on one knee, pulled out a ring and popped the question! Cara was overcome with surprise and immediately lost her appetite. It was the stuff that reality shows are made of. By the virtue of us being here tonight, we know how she responded.

As their relationship grew, Cara came to admire Peter as one of the most humble people she knows. She appreciates his attention to detail. Peter makes her feel special by his words and deeds. He demonstrates respect for her one hundred percent. When summed up, Cara describes Peter as her ultimate best friend.

As for Peter, he sees Cara possessing a remarkable ability to get along with everyone. He loves that she has great family values. Cara is socially outgoing and someone who also loves a home-cooked meal. They really enjoy cooking as a team, with Cara being the sous chef to Peter's role as chef.

In the nearly six years since they met, Peter and Cara have grown very close. While Cara likes to work out and go to the beach in her free time, Peter enjoys the chillier sport of snowboarding. Together they have a joint sense of curiosity, pursuing new experiences, and traveling to new places. They share a love of music, the outdoors and simply spending time in each other's company.

They know how to communicate honestly, with the willingness to face head on both the good and the difficult subjects. Most significant is their utmost trust and respect for one another.

Both of them say that they see marriage as a lifelong commitment through joyful and challenging circumstances. They look forward to building a loving family. The elements by which Cara and Peter measure love are: open communication, encouragement of one another, trust, respect, laughter, happiness, and the elusive feeling of butterflies. That's a high bar that they have set, and I believe they will honor it."

Ritual
Wine Ritual:
Parents walk to the altar with two goblets and stand for the duration of the ritual.

Celebrant says:
"Many rituals accompany weddings throughout history and across all faith practices. Cara and Peter will now partake in the sharing of wine from family goblets. The couple's use of a libation in many traditions is a symbol that serves to seal their love and unite their families. In drinking of the fruit of the vine from the same cups, they are also displaying their commitment to the miracles of life, the wonders of nature, and to the sweetness of their marriage."

Celebrant pours wine into both goblets. *White wine is recommended in case of spillage.*

"We bless the wine. Cara and Peter and anyone who wishes to join in, please recite after me this prayer over the wine that says:

Blessed art thou, Creator of the Universe, Creator of the fruit of the vine. Amen."

The two goblets of wine are shared and handed back to the celebrant.

Blessing by Celebrant or Community Toast
Celebrant says:
"A blessing from Hawaiian culture, where they will honeymoon:

Ka mau ki aha.
"May you never thirst again."

Intentions

Celebrant says:

"The time has come. Please face each other as I ask this important legal question of each of you. Do you Cara come here tonight to be wed to Peter of your own free will? *(Yes.)* Do you Peter come here tonight to be wed to Cara of your own free will? *(Yes.)*

"The interesting part of that question is that if either of you had answered, 'No,' I would not have been legally authorized to marry you. So, thank you for making it easy for me to confirm that free will is duly established."

Vows and I Do's

Celebrant says:

"Wedding vows are the sincerest promises you make to one another and will stand as the underpinnings of your entire relationship. Please turn to each other, and before all those you hold dear, speak your vows now."

Partner 1 says:

"I, Peter, take you Cara, to be my beloved wife, my constant friend, my faithful partner and my love from this day forward. I promise to be true to you in good times and in bad, in plenty and in want, in joy and in sorrow, in sickness and in health. I promise you this from my heart, and I will love you and honor you all the days of my life."

Partner 2 says:

"I, Cara, take you Peter, to be my beloved husband; together we will remain faithful and lifelong partners, and we will cherish each other and our families in sorrow and happiness."

Celebrant says:

"Peter, do you stand by these vows?"

Partner 1 says:

"I do."

Celebrant says:
"Cara, do you stand by these vows?"

Partner 2 says:
"I do."

Rings
Celebrant says:
"Peter and Cara, it is now time for the exchanging of your rings."

Rings are presented to the couple by the Best Man.

Partner 1 says:
"This ring is a token of my love. I marry you with this ring, with all that I have, and all that I am."

Partner 2 says:
"I will forever wear this ring as a sign of my commitment and the desire of my heart."

Celebrant says:
"Cara and Peter, to seal your marital union, please recite these biblical words after me: 'I am my beloved's and my beloved is mine.' "

(They repeat the words.)

Celebrant's Charge to the Couple
Celebrant says:
"Cara and Peter, the time you have been together has been so well spent and shows that you know a lot about what will make a marriage work. That said, here are some of my words of advice.

"Find ways and make time to cherish one another.
Practice respect and kindness.
Be honest with yourself and each other.
Use words wisely and gently.
Be willing to apologize and to forgive.
When you don't understand, try your best to step into the other's shoes.

It does not matter much if you say "tomato" or "tomahto." Sometimes you are essentially saying the same thing, just in different ways.

Keep the candle of romance lit.

Always try to act from the depth of love that you feel today.

I know that your shared sense of humor will serve you well, so continue to laugh a lot."

Celebrant says:

You will now hear from your community of guests and family.

Community Blessing

Community of guests read from the back of the Wedding Program:

"Dearest Cara and Peter, we are gathered here this evening to celebrate wholeheartedly as you become husband and wife. We want to demonstrate our loving support by wishing you the sincerest blessings of home, health, and love from this day forward. Should you ever need us for support or celebration, we will be here for you. Amen."

Closing Blessing by Celebrant

Celebrant says:

"May the Universal Spirit of life at its best bless you both and be gracious to you in your marriage.

May your faith in one another and in yourselves forever bring you the stability and discernment that will guide you through all your days together.

"May joy, peace, wisdom and good humor abound in your marriage and in the world.

"May God travel alongside you and inspire you in your wedded years together.

"May you build a life that increases in richness with even more wonderment of one another than you possess at this moment.

"May you remember that when you look into each other's eyes, you are looking into the eyes of all of humanity."

Pronouncement of the Couple

Celebrant says:

"With the power vested in me by the Commonwealth of Massachusetts and the strength of your love, it is my great pleasure to pronounce you wife and husband for the first time: Mr. and Mrs. Cara and Peter Lee.

It is time for a kiss!"

The Kiss

Cara and Peter kiss, their guests clap and cheer, and the music plays.

Recessional to Music

Music: "Higher and Higher" ("Your Love Keeps Lifting Me") by Jackie Wilson
Other: Bouquet and train are tended to
Exiting the Ceremony:

- The couple exits
- Attendants pair off to exit
- Celebrant exits
- Parents exit
- Close family exits
- Guests exit

Chapter Tips

- There are many ways to conduct a ceremony.
- Guests will be more invested in the ceremony, less restless, and will remember it better if they actually participate.
- While there need be no hard and fast rules to ceremonies, there are two legal requirements:
  1. Establishing that both partners are marrying of free will.
  2. The officiant pronouncing the couple as legally married.

24

Who is at the Altar?

The subject of stepparents can be a delicate issue, and may or may not be a complex concern. Families can be complicated and stepfamilies even more so. Rarely have I served couples where both sets of parents were still married. Many couples' parents are either divorced, deceased or voluntarily chose single parenthood.

I spend a fair amount of time discussing ceremony decisions with regard to parents and family members. The rule of thumb that I share with my couples is that they do not knowingly hurt anyone's feelings or make decisions they may later regret.

For example, if they choose to have one stepparent at the altar it makes sense to have the other one there too. My belief is that weddings are happy occasions and are not the time to act upon any negative, residual feelings. By the same token, I think it is perfectly appropriate to choose to have only their birth parents at the altar.

Each family can be fairly honored by keeping decisions balanced and aiming for parity. That has to be carefully considered in order to maintain the atmosphere of happiness and good will for the wedding day.

Chapter Tips

- The subject of stepparents can be a delicate issue, and may or may not be a complex concern.
- Each family can be fairly honored by keeping decisions balanced and aiming for parity.

25

Rehearsal

A wedding rehearsal may be conducted by a wedding planner, a venue manager or an officiant. If the rehearsal is included with the contracted price for the wedding planner or venue, I encourage couples to use their services. If they prefer to have me handle the rehearsal and I am available, I will do it for a small additional fee.

A word of advice to officiants: Make it clear to the couple that if we are conducting the rehearsal, we should be in charge and the wedding planner or manager should be notified. This avoids last-minute confusion.

I will generally accept a gracious invitation to the rehearsal dinner in order to meet the close family members and wedding party. Most couples really appreciate this, and I enjoy doing it.

As every ceremony is unique, so will be each rehearsal. I have outlined below the general elements of a rehearsal.

Tools: Celebrant's Rehearsal Checklist

The Celebrant

- Confirms time and location of rehearsal
- Prints a copy of the ceremony highlighting salient information
- Meets with the wedding planner or venue manager to discuss logistics
- Checks microphones and reviews placement
- Meets family members and wedding attendants by name
- Reviews items required for altar table and who is bringing them

Role of Ushers/Programs/Seating

- Determine where disabled guests will sit
- Decide how and where primary family members will sit
- Review celebrant's announcements
- Establish order of processional

Processional

- Review music selections and cues
- Confirm where entrances will be
- Give special attention to flower and ring bearers
- Establish pacing and placement of wedding attendants at altar
- Discuss when guests will rise
- Decide where the couple will meet — in the aisle or at the altar
- Confirm placement of partners at the altar
- Review how and when bouquet is taken and train straightened
- Discuss when guests will be seated

Additional Ceremony Elements

Note, the rehearsal is a review of important sections, not a full enactment of the wedding ceremony.

We will want to leave room for an element of surprise on the wedding day. Address the order of the following with special attention to how the ritual will be done:

- Family roles during the ceremony
- Welcome, remembrance and invocation
- Minister introduction
- Wedding readings
- Words by celebrant
- Words about the couple

- Ritual steps
- Words about marriage
- Blessing
- Intentions and I do's
- Marriage vows

Rings

- Confirm who delivers them to the couple
- Practice their presentation
- Have rings presented to the couple while facing guests

Closing Elements

- Community blessing
- Minister's blessing
- Pronouncement
- Veil raising
- Kiss

Recessional

- Bouquet returned and train straightened
- Music selection begins
- Review order and pace of recessional

Reminders to the Couple

1. Short meeting with celebrant before the ceremony
2. Bring the license, two copies and stamped envelope, addressed to the Clerk's Office
3. Pay the balance of officiant's fee before the ceremony

Chapter Tips

- A word of advice to officiants: Make it clear to the couple that if you are conducting the rehearsal, you should be in charge and the wedding planner or manager should be notified. This avoids last-minute confusion.

26

Pre-Ceremony Meeting

Calming the Couple

I have discovered that even the most self-assured couples tend to become nervous when anticipating being at the altar. Sometimes it is about the idea of getting married for real, other times it is about speaking in front of so many significant people in their lives, and finally some do not want to be seen becoming emotional.

All of these fears are perfectly natural. In my pre-ceremony meeting, I address these possibilities and try to help them find effective methods to calm themselves should they become unsettled during the ceremony. Often, they are able to think of ways to calm themselves during the service. If they cannot, I suggest the following:

Tools: Tips for the Couple on Staying Calm During the Ceremony

- Hold hands and look into each other's eyes
- Conjure up "their song" in their minds
- Imagine walking on a beautiful beach, hand in hand
- I will offer them a centering thought such as:
  "The present moment, like the spotted owl or the sea turtle, has become an endangered species. Yet more and more I find that dwelling in the present moment, in the face of everything that would call us out of it, is our highest spiritual discipline ("October 9 — Philip Simmons" *Onespiritinterfaith.org*.)."

Tools: Celebrant's Pre-Ceremony Meeting Note/Gifts to the Couple

During our pre-ceremony meeting, I give the couple:

- A gift and note
- A copy of their ceremony
- A pretty marriage document (Appendix 5)

Chapter Tips

- Even the most self-assured couples tend to become nervous when anticipating being at the altar.
- In the pre-ceremony meeting, address these possibilities and try to help the couple find effective methods to calm themselves should they become unsettled during the ceremony.

27

Wedding Program

Sometimes couples ask me to provide a layout for their *Wedding Program,* and I am happy to oblige. Below is one I created for Susan and Andrew based on the ceremony outline and flow that was selected.

Tools: Wedding Program Example

Susan Lynn Arch & Andrew Scott Burnham
Oct. 17, 2015
The Langham • Boston, Massachusetts

Prelude
Musical selection

Entrance
Rev. Lynn Gladstone

Processional
Music title(s) and composers
Names in order of entrance
Bride escorted by father

Welcome and Remembrance

Invocation

The Chuppah

Love and Marriage Reading
Title, author and reading by

Reflection — Words by Reverend

Exchange of Vows and Giving of Rings

Sharing Ritual

Reverend's Blessing

Presentation of the Newlyweds

Breaking of the Glass

Recessional
Music title and composer

The actual wedding program was printed on three narrow pages. Susan and Andrew added a note of appreciation to their guests.

The wedding program is also the perfect place to include any words or blessings the guests may speak during the ceremony.

28

Announcements

Announcements are made before the Processional begins. The content varies as these are directives from the couple about things they want their guests to know before the ceremony begins.

Tools: Celebrant's Announcements

Example 1:

Celebrant's says:

"Welcome everyone! May I ask all of you, after the ceremony, to convene to the patio and please partake in the family and Quaker tradition of signing Rob and Sarah's wedding certificate? By signing this document, you demonstrate your support of their marriage. Thank you. Let the Processional begin."

Example 2:

Celebrant's says:

"Welcome everyone! May I ask for your silence, as we are about to begin the ceremony? The wedding couple has two special requests of everyone gathered here. They have asked that you kindly put away your cameras and turn off your cell phones. Please sit back and enjoy the ceremony. Arrangements have been made for these lovely photographers over here to document the ceremony. So do not worry, there will be plenty of photographs to go around. Thank you and now let us begin."

Example 3:

Celebrant's says:

"The bride and groom have requested that after the ceremony please go directly and swiftly down the hill to the reception area for cocktails and hors d'oeuvres. Lisa and James will happily join you there after their photographs are taken. Thank you. Let the Processional begin."

For more examples of announcements see Appendix 11.

29

Minister's Introductory Remark

After the Processional, in a quiet moment of reverence, I begin with a short *Introductory Remark* to set a contemplative tone before the service. A carefully selected introductory remark can help family and guests relax around religious issues at an interfaith event. I have included some of my favorite examples below.

Tools: Celebrant's Introductory Remarks

Unless otherwise indicated, the sources for these materials are the *Interfaith Seminary* program at *onespiritinterfaith.org* and Susan Turchin's book, *The Interfaith Wedding Manual, Creating Meaningful Wedding Ceremonies: A Guide for Clergy and Couples (11–15)*.

"All About Love" excerpt by Robert Frost
Love is the irresistible desire to be desired irresistibly.
To love is to place our happiness in the happiness of another.
There is no remedy for love but to love more.
Love is the triumph of imagination over intelligence.

Words by Jalaluddin Rumi
The real beloved is that one who is unique,
Who is your beginning and your end.
When you find that one,
You'll no longer expect anything else.

The Song of Solomon
These passages beckon us:
My beloved speaks and says to me:

"Arise, my love, my fair one,
and come away . . . ."

~

Many waters cannot quench love,
Rivers cannot wash it away . . . ."

For more examples of introductory remarks see Appendix 12.

Chapter Tips

- Begin with a short *Introductory Remark* to set a contemplative tone before the service.

30

Invocations

Two people discover each other, fall in love and decide to marry. They invite their closest family and friends to witness this intimate act. Something sacred is surely taking place. Everyone in the room is experiencing at least a bit of awe and respect for the ceremonial event. While we share in the height of the moment, it seems natural and appropriate to address a force bigger than we are, and ask for a blessing. That is why I like to present an invocation in my I/I/I ceremonies. Here are some ways I call upon that bigger force.

Tools: Celebrant's Invocations for I/I/I Ceremonies

The following are my original invocations:

Interfaith:
Celebrant says:
"Let us take this moment to thank the gods of both of these families' traditions for being present here with us and to ask for the protection of this couple in their life together."

Religious:
Celebrant says:
"We are joined here by the unfailing and loving presence of The Father, The Son and The Holy Spirit. At this time, we faithfully invoke God's love and support.

Deborah and Seth, may every form of blessing be given to you. Dear God, please be generous with this couple offering your wise guidance to them.

Inspire and sustain them in their love for all the days of their lives. We ask you, O Universal Spirit, to also regard their family and friends. Please bestow upon them your caring consideration, providing them all with good health and healing, if needed. Let us be grateful for God's listening heart."

Spiritual:

Celebrant says:

"We are joined here by a Universal Spirit of love that belongs to all people of all faiths. Dear God, we are here tonight for the marriage of Alexandra and Martin, and I ask of your presence to witness this ceremony alongside all of us. Please be generous with this dear couple by inspiring and sustaining them in their love for all the days of their lives."

For more examples of the invocations for I/I/I ceremonies see Appendix 13.

Chapter Tips

- Two people discover each other, fall in love and decide to marry. They invite their closest family and friends to witness this intimate act. Something sacred is surely taking place.

31

Blessings by Celebrant

Blessings are opportunities for the celebrant to offer a very personal statement of overall good will and care to the couple. Blessings may be placed throughout the ceremony, or simply used as a vehicle for opening or bringing the ceremony to a close.

Tools: Blessings by the Celebrant

The following are examples of my original blessings.

Example 1:

This is from the wedding of Sofia and Jason, Boston, Massachusetts, 2013.

Celebrant says:
"May the Universal Spirit of life at its best
Bless you both and be gracious to you in your marriage.
May your faith in one another and in yourselves
Forever bring you the stability and discernment
That will guide you through all your days together.
May joy, peace, wisdom and good humor abound in your marriage
And in the world.
Please remember that when you look into each other's eyes,
You are looking into the eyes of all of humanity."

Example 2:

This is from the wedding of Antonia and Miguel, New York, New York, 2014.

Celebrant says:
"May the Spirits of God and of love bless you and be gracious to you.

May your faith, as it is told,
Be like that of Jesus when he turned water into wedding wine,
Forever bring you abundance.
May joy, peace and good humor abound in your marriage and in the world."

Example 3:
This is from the wedding of Brandon and Jeff, Malibu, California, 2015.

Celebrant says:
"Brandon and Jeff, may the Spirit of God travel by your sides and inspire you as you walk into the future and your maturity together. May you build a life that increases in even more love and wonderment of one another at each passing day than you possess at this moment. So be it."

For more examples of blessings by the celebrant see Appendix 14.

Tools: Blessings from World Cultures

For much of this chapter, I have collected the *world culture blessings* from a variety of wedding- and marriage-related resources found on the Internet. Many materials had no attributed author or source or were defined as public domain material, which may have been further adapted. Material that did have sources I have credited within this book. Finally, an additional source for these materials is *weddingdells.com.au*.

African
O God, give the joy and God the love
To those who are lovers true
Shed down benedictions from above
As in one are joined the two
You are the star of each night.

Native American
Like a star should your love be constant
Like a stone should your love be firm

The good spirits will be their cushions
so that not a hair of their heads shall be harmed.

Native American
May your life be like a wildflower,
growing freely in the beauty and joy of each day.

Sufi
May these vows and this marriage be blessed.
May it be sweet milk, this marriage, like wine and halvah.
May this marriage offer fruit and shade like the date palm.
May this marriage be full of laughter, our every day, a day in paradise.
May this marriage be a sign of compassion, a seal of happiness here and hereafter.
May this marriage have a fair face and a good name, an omen as welcome as the moon in a clear blue sky.
I am out of words to describe how spirit mingles in this marriage.

For more examples of blessings from world cultures see Appendix 15.

Chapter Tips

- Blessings are opportunities for the celebrant to offer a very personal statement of overall good will and care to the couple.

32

Community Blessings and Meal Blessings

Community Blessings are twofold. They are wonderful ways for the couple to express gratitude and appreciation for their guests and the guests to express gratitude and appreciation for the wedding couple. Blessings for the guests are well accomplished during the *Welcome Section* of the ceremony. Blessings for the couple can be easily inserted into the wedding program to be recited during or toward the end of the ceremony. This is one way for guests to be invested in the couple's ceremony and future happiness.

On occasion, I am asked to present a *Meal Blessing* at the start of the wedding reception. I am pleased to provide this service and have included some examples of meal blessings in this section.

Tools: Couple's Blessing for the Community

If a couple wishes to bless their community, they can recite something like the following or have the celebrant do so after the welcoming of the guests. This is my original blessing for the guests:

Celebrant says:
"We ask the Universal Spirit of love and life, of every belief, to thank you all for your presence at this wedding. You stand as witnesses to the sacred marriage of Theresa and Franklin. And, you are demonstrating your care and support of this dear couple as they move from their pasts and forward into the welcoming light of their present and future. Having each and every one of you present adds

meaning and enriches their union. They pray to keep you in their hearts and they in yours forever."

Tools: Community Blessings for the Couple

The following are examples of my original community blessings, unless otherwise noted:

Example 1:
Gathered Guests say:
"Dear Henia and Adam,
We offer this to you:
We are here with you tonight to share in your happiness.
We have come to honor your love for one another.
And, we recognize the warmth of your love for family and friends.
We wish to demonstrate our love for you as you become a newly married couple,
     and as you go forward to build and spend your whole life together.
Should you ever need us for support or celebration, we will be here for you.
Amen!"

Example 2:
Gathered Guests say:
"Dearests Jasmine and Jamahl,

We have watched your love begin, and we were with you as it grew. Today we are here, as family and friends to witness the great spirit of your love. You have shared the beauty of your happiness with us in good times and tough ones. It has marked us and taught us to be ever more generous with our hearts and to believe in the power of meaningful relationships. Should you ever need us, we are available to protect you in challenging moments as is the Divine Spirit."

Example 3:
Gathered Guests say:
"We are here with you tonight to share in your happiness.

We have come to:

- Honor your love for one another
- Joyfully recognize your love for your family and friends
- Demonstrate our love for you as a newly married couple going forward to spend and build your whole life together

Should you ever need us for support or celebration, we will be here for you.

And so it is!"

Quaker Blessing
"So, while ye tarry here with us we would have thee enjoy the blessing of a *home, health, love and freedom, and we pray that thou mayst find the final blessing of life. Peace.*"

Tools: Celebrant's Meal Blessings

Celebrants are sometimes asked to bless the wedding meal. There are so many beautiful prayers for meal blessings: traditional, religious and cultural. Feel free to adapt them appropriately for each couple's wedding in keeping with the tone of their ceremony. Below are a variety of meal blessings, some of which are original while others are scriptural or traditional prayers.

For much of this chapter, I have collected the *Meal Blessings* from a variety of wedding- and marriage-related resources found on the Internet. Many materials had no attributed author or source or were defined as public domain material, which may have been further adapted. Material that did have sources I have credited within this book. Finally, an additional source for these materials is *indifferentlanguages.com.*

Irish
Bless, O Lord, this food we are about to eat; and we pray to You, O God, that it may be good for our body and soul; and if there be any poor creature hungry or thirsty walking along the road, send them into us that we can share the food with them, just as You share your gifts with all of us.

By Rabbi Rami M. Shapiro
We give thanks to Life.
may we never lose touch with the simple joy and wonder
of sharing a meal.

By Rev. Lynn Gladstone
I feel so much joy in this room. Who agrees with me?
As we gather at this pre-nuptial table,
surrounded by the plentitude of love among us,
and the abundance of nourishment that we are about to savor,
let us be grateful to you, O God, and allow ourselves
awareness of those less fortunate.
May they soon share in all we have.

For more examples of meal blessings see Appendix 16.

Tools: "Bless this Food" in Seventeen Different Languages

The source for the following material is *indifferentlanguages.com.*

Bless this food
English
Benedicte hunc cibum
Latin
Bendita sea esta comida
Spanish
Benis ce repas
French
Benedetto questo cibo
Italian
Segne diese speisen
German
Eulogayte wkaynon aptov
(Cl.) Greek
Barek natra aet'taam

Arabic

Blagaslavee aetoo yedoo

Russian

Hamotzi lechem min ha'aretz

Hebrew

Ae kanae koo asheez doo

Hindi

Valsigna maten

Swedish

Kyoo no shoku ji ni kan sha I ta ma su

Japanese

Choo foo sheh oo

Chinese

Abencoe esta comida

Portuguese

Zaegeb de maaltid

Danish

Signe maden

Norwegian and Danish

Chapter Tips

- *Community Blessings* are wonderful ways for the couple to express gratitude and appreciation for their guests and the guests to express gratitude and appreciation for the wedding couple.

33

Ceremony Toasts

As a celebrant, I like to use a short toast in my ceremonies. It engages the guests while bringing a bit of zest to the event. I ask the guests to raise their "virtual glasses" for the toast.

One way to customize the toast is to find traditional toasts related to the cultural background of the couple. The couple's families are good resources, and can provide you with toasts that are expressive of them.

Tools: Ceremony Toasts from World Cultures

For much of this chapter, I have collected the *ceremony toasts* from a variety of wedding- and marriage-related resources found on the Internet. Many materials had no attributed author or source or were defined as public domain material, which may have been further adapted. Material that did have sources, I have credited within this book. Finally, an additional source for these materials is *theknot.com*. © Copyright 2016, *TheKnot.com*. Reproduced by Permission. All Rights Reserved. Credit to: *TheKnot.com*.

Greek
In 2015, at Cary and Nikos's interfaith wedding, I included the beautiful *Stephana* (Greek crowns) ritual. At the end of the ceremony, the guests shouted this traditional Greek toast:

Εἰς υγείαν! Transliteration: Ees-ee-YEE-an!
To your health and happiness!

Italian
Per cent'anni!
For a hundred years!

Jewish
Mazel tov!
Congratulations!

Traditional American
May your love be as endless as your wedding rings.

For more examples of ceremony toasts from world cultures see Appendix 17.

Tools: Historical Quotes as Toasts

For much of this chapter, I have collected the *historical toasts* from a variety of wedding- and marriage-related resources found on the Internet. Many materials had no attributed author or source or were defined as public domain material, which may have been further adapted. Material that did have sources I have credited within this book. Finally, an additional source for these materials is *TheKnot.com*. © Copyright 2016, TheKnot.com. Reproduced by Permission. All Rights Reserved. Credit to TheKnot.com.

Numbers 6
The Lord bless you and keep you!
The Lord let His face shine upon you, and be gracious to you!
The Lord look upon you kindly and give you peace!

The Tempest by Shakespeare
Look down you gods,
And on this couple drop a blessed crown.

The Merchant of Venice by Shakespeare
I wish you all the joy you can wish.

For more examples of historical quotes as toasts see Appendix 18. Additional toasts published online by The Knot see Appendix 19.

Chapter Tips

- Use a short toast in ceremonies. It engages the guests while bringing a bit of zest to the event.

34

The Demanding Family

Generally, families, mostly parents, are invested both emotionally and financially in their children's wedding. It is understandable that the parents have long dreamed of this wedding day and want to be involved in the decision-making. The framework I use in dealing with overly demanding family members is that the wedding belongs to the couple. This is easier said than done. I feel it is my role to advocate and be supportive on behalf of my couples. If conflict arises, I offer respectful strategies to negotiate within the families. If my advice fails my couples, I then offer to speak directly to the family members involved to see if a compromise can be reached.

Tools: Hey! Whose Wedding Is This Anyway?

The following blog was written to help guide couples in dealing with demanding families while planning their wedding. "Hey! Whose Wedding Is This Anyway?" is adapted below having originally been written in 2013 and published on my website, *LynnGladstone.com*. Photography above is from iStockphoto ©Voyagerix.

Blog: Hey! Whose Wedding Is This Anyway?

The proposal takes place and is accepted. The prospective marital couple starts to imagine what their wedding will be like. What is not immediately thought of is there will likely be two families imagining the same scenario.

Thus begins the conversation—the one where each significant player expresses their dreams, their hopes and yes, their demands for this long-awaited day.

Inevitably, there will be differences of opinions, people invested in certain details and rituals and perhaps divided loyalties. *This is typical.*

It may seem to the partners that everyone is claiming their piece of the action—especially when their parents are contributing financially to the special event.

What is a couple to do? With the abundance of love they feel deep in their hearts at this time, they surely do not want to offend or hurt anyone. Is it possible to please everyone and every insistence? Probably not! Is it possible for a couple to create a wedding of *their* dreams without causing undo strife? Yes.

The key to any challenging life situation is communication.

- Communication must first be initiated between the couple to be married. Once there is a clear picture of what *you two* envision, you will be able to present a united front to your families and minimize the prospect of conflict. As a pre-emptive measure, don't wait too long after the proposal to sit down with your parents and talk honestly, gently, respectfully and openly.

- Listen to your parents and then ask them to listen to you. As the leading roles you are entitled to take command!

- You, as the couple, can present your expectation that this is to be *your* wedding, your day of a lifetime, while explaining your appreciation for their generosity and support and inviting them to submit *five* requests that they would like to see happen.

- You might tell them that you will take their five under consideration and come back to them with at least *three* that you will implement. This is excellent practice for negotiating within marriage and with your families going forward.

With love in your heart, remember to be clear about your desires — what you can be flexible about and what is non-negotiable and stand, as a twosome, firm.

I wish you a celebration with a roomful of smiles.

Rev. Lynn

Chapter Tips

- The framework you can use in dealing with overly demanding family members is that the wedding belongs to the couple. It is your role as celebrant to advocate and be supportive on behalf of your couples.

35

Trouble in Paradise

Alas, among all this talk of love and good will, there are bound to be some snags. No matter how much preparation we do or anticipation of what could possibly go wrong, something could still go wrong. Life happens.

Remember, it's not the end of the world. We must keep our good graces and quick wits about us, breathe and handle each mishap thoughtfully.

One prospective client asked me, "What has been your greatest challenge?" It was a good question, and I had to think. In fact, there have been numerous challenges, and I'd like to share some of them.

Tools: Trouble in Paradise

Situations and Lessons Learned

Situation 1:
A bride had worked long and hard on her personal vows. When she arrived at her wedding venue, she realized she had left them at home, a good distance away. She started to panic until I said I had brought a copy.

Lesson Learned:
I explain to couples that I like to see a copy of their vows before the wedding day, partly to avoid such a calamity. I make sure to bring them along to the ceremony. When I do have them, I put them on cardstock for a prettier presentation.

Situation 2:

A father said, with a slightly heavy heart, that my "About the Couple" portion of the ceremony had stolen his thunder from his own upcoming speech.

Lesson Learned:

The only solution I have come up with is to have the couple share my "About the Couple" section of the ceremony with the people who will be speaking at the reception.

Situation 3:

A bride and groom decided they wanted to be married during the Christmas season. When we discussed whether or not they wanted me to include God or Jesus in the ceremony, they emphatically said, "No," sharing with me their reasons.

After the ceremony, the mother of the bride was irate, asking how I could not mention Jesus, especially with all the guests being Christian and it being so close to Christmas? I was abashed, as I always ask in advance if there are any family issues I should know about. I replied that this was the ceremony her daughter and son-in-law had chosen. She retorted that her daughter had just told her that I had made a mistake and had forgotten to include the religious references.

Lesson Learned:

In order to not involve her daughter at that celebratory moment, I thought it best to let it pass, but I do feel I was set up. It took me several conversations with the mother and a week to get paid.

I received an outstanding review from the newlyweds, who apparently had not known how to handle the awkward situation. Eventually, I did receive an appreciative note from the mother-of-the-bride.

Situation 4:

At one wedding when the bride entered, I motioned for the guests to rise. After she was situated at the altar, I forgot to indicate that they could sit. The guests remained standing for quite a while before the groom discreetly leaned over and pointed out my error.

Lesson Learned:

I need to be more mindful, and it's okay to apologize to the guests during the ceremony and simply move on.

Situation 5:

I keep a list of colleagues to whom I make referrals, if I am unavailable on a couple's wedding date. On one such occasion, the person to whom I referred a couple made an error on their marriage license, making it invalid. The couple notified the celebrant who was out of town for an extended period, and his presence was required to correct the document. The couple needed the marriage license pronto for medical insurance. The celebrant refused to come back into town. After much ado, the matter got settled after a lot of aggravation, at much expense to the couple, and with the aid of affidavits and overnight FedEx.

Lesson Learned:

I was mortified and disappointed trying to come up with a way to help the couple to no avail. What I have garnered from this is to be extremely careful in making referrals, unless I am fully familiar with a particular colleague's demonstration of a high level of professionalism.

Situation 6:

I was hired to perform a wedding ceremony at a lovely botanical garden. Fifteen minutes before the ceremony was to start, with all of the guests seated outdoors, it began to rain. The string quartet understandably refused to jeopardize their instruments. There was no indoor backup plan.

I was able to convince the musicians to set up under a large band shell in the garden so that there would at least be distant music while we waited out the rain. It was very uncomfortable for the guests.

Lesson Learned:

I added a question to my questionnaires asking couples what their backup plan is should it rain on their wedding day.

Situation 7:

For a medium-sized, outdoor wedding, a couple asked that we not use microphones. I reluctantly agreed. In their review, which was mostly very positive, they did mention that people in the back rows could not hear the ceremony.

Lesson Learned:

I learned to insist upon a microphone, especially for outdoor or a sizeable number of guests at a wedding. Microphone usage is referred to in my questionnaires and several of my letters and emails with the couple before the wedding day.

Situation 8:

I conducted the marriage for a couple from Washington, D.C., in New York City. After the ceremony, I mailed in their signed marriage license to the County Clerk's Office, as I always do. This is the only option available: to mail the marriage license by regular mail with no receipt.

The newlyweds were moving immediately to Italy for two years to work. The bride was experiencing some medical problems and needed her husband's health insurance to get proper care.

Their marriage license never arrived, having been lost in the mail. The logistics were demanding. It required that they come back to New York to be sworn in and be supported by a verifying letter from me, their celebrant.

Lesson Learned:

This particular bureaucratic glitch happens from time to time and can be resolved, even in urgent circumstances. This situation is a perfect illustration of why we must keep a copy of the original marriage license so that a paper trail is established. Below is the letter that the County Clerk's Office required from me.

New York City Clerk's Office Marriage Bureau
141 Worth Street
New York, NY 10013

To Whom It May Concern,

This letter is to verify that I was the ordained minister (ID number) who performed the wedding ceremony for Karen Ann Smith and Graham Peter Louis on December 21, 2013 who reside at 1003 K St. SE Apt 1, Washington, D.C. 20003.

The ceremony took place at NoMad Hotel Rooftop, 1170 Broadway, New York, N.Y. at 4:30 p.m.

The witnesses for the marriage license were Becky Louise Smith (witness 1) and George Thomas Louis (witness 2).

I mailed the signed marriage license form in a self-addressed envelope on December 23, 2013. I have been informed that the original license has not arrived to Mr. and Mrs. Louis, and that they need to reapply with my written avowal.

This matter has time urgency as Mr. and Mrs. Louis are scheduled to move abroad for work in the near future. They need their official license in order to secure the proper visa and travel documents among other legal matters.

Thank you very much for your speedy assistance in this matter.

Yours truly,

Rev. Lynn Gladstone

Chapter Tips

- Alas, among all this talk of love and good will, there are bound to be some snags.

36

Working with Vendors

The value of networking is inestimable for growing a professional wedding practice. At each wedding we are likely to be working with wedding planners, venue managers, photographers, videographers and musicians, and others. It is important to make sure to meet them and exchange business cards. It is a good idea to keep a file of the vendors that stand out. I will only recommend vendors with whom I've worked, and whose professional style I find impressive. As I've mentioned before, recommendations that we make are a reflection on us.

When we perform the ceremony and have done an admirable job, vendors will take note. And, we will observe the quality of their work, too. We must strive to be the professional that is remembered, and it may very well bear fruit in the form of mutual referrals.

Wedding day photographs and videos enhance our websites, allowing potential clients to experience us performing a ceremony. Therefore, I purposefully ask photographers and videographers to please include me in some of the photographs and video footage taken of the ceremony, and me with the couple. I have found that vendors are most willing to do so.

If the couple has given written permission for use of their photographs and videos, I contact the vendors. Each vendor receives a note of gratitude, a link on my website, and is placed on my recommended *Vendors List* once I receive the wedding couple's visual materials.

Tools: Recommending Vendors Letter

This letter was sent to the mother of a bride who was residing in Tokyo. Being so far away from home, she was unable to do wedding vendor shopping and asked for her mother's help. Her mother, in turn, asked for my help.

> *Dear Paula (mother of the bride),*
>
> *I want to let you know that I have been compiling a selection of wedding venues and photographers for Abigail and Akio's wedding for you to review. I will send them off to you tomorrow. If any appeal to you, please let me know. If not, we can continue to search further.*
>
> *Sincerely,*
>
> *Rev. Lynn Gladstone*

Tools: Vendor Email Request

> *Subject: Wedding Photo request from Rev. Lynn Gladstone for Mercado-Bickerman married*
>
> *August 1, 2015*
>
> *Dear Amanda Shaw (photographer),*
>
> *I am the interfaith minister who married Mercado-Bickerman (Wedding August 1, 2015, The Langham Boston). The couple gave me written permission (attached) to get a link from you to their wedding photographs to show on my website and storefronts on The Knot.*
>
> *I will be happy to give you photography credit and add your website link to my recommended Vendors List. Here is a link to my website: http://lynngladstone.com/.*
>
> *Thank you,*
>
> *Rev. Lynn*

Note: I send similar letters to videographers.

Tools: Follow-Up Emails to Other Vendors

I contact selected wedding professionals with whom I have worked. I send them follow-up emails expressing my pleasure in having made their acquaintance, and my hope that we will work together again.

Chapter Tips

- The value of networking is inestimable for growing a professional wedding practice.

37

Reviews

The best way a wedding minister can grow their practice is by receiving rave reviews. Some couples will provide this on their own. But, I have learned that reminding couples by email is most effective in getting a review. In general, a couple pleased by their ceremony and the process of working with me are enthusiastic about providing a review. Some newlyweds will need a couple of email reminders. Don't be shy in asking for a review; you have worked hard for it. Never be demanding in tone. Instead, explain why their written review is an important aspect of your professional life and will enable you to connect to other couples planning their weddings.

Close to the wedding date, I will ask them to keep a review in mind. After the wedding, I ask them again. They have a lot on their minds and my reminder is helpful. It may feel a little awkward to make this request, but a well-delivered ceremony deserves recognition, and it helps the wedding minister enormously to reach other loving couples.

The Knot, the most popular online wedding site today, allows wedding vendors (such as officiants) to create professional storefronts to advertise their services. Once an account is established, you can use their online partner tools to request a review from a couple. Not only will *The Knot* post the review with three rating categories, but, they will also verify the source who provided the review.

Tools: Email Review Request Sent to Couples

Subject: Review Rev. Lynn Gladstone on TheKnot.com!

From: Rev. Lynn Gladstone, NY, LA & Beyond

Dear Antonia and Dean,

I was so pleased to officiate at your beautiful wedding ceremony. Congratulations once again.

I am writing to ask for your assistance. Your written review is a very important aspect of my professional life. As in many careers, the recommendations I receive online provide me with visibility on the web and on The Knot. This helps me connect to other loving couples.

I would be very grateful to you if you would submit a review for me on The Knot. Simply click the link (Theknot.com) in this email, login for free and post your review. To see my other reviews, go to http://lynngladstone.com/reviews/.

Thank you for allowing me to be a part of such a lovely union. I am always here for you.

With warmest wishes for your future together,

Rev. Lynn Gladstone

Tools: Thank You Email for a Couple's Review

Dear Antonia and Dean,

I have received your glowing review and thank you deeply. I am delighted that you were so pleased with your ceremony. It means a great deal to me.

Wishing you the very best,

Lynn

Chapter Tips

- The best way to grow your practice is by receiving rave reviews.

38

Ministry Legal Documentation

When dealing with legal matters related to our ministry, it is essential that we dot all of our i's and cross our t's. Without this diligence, a marriage we performed could be deemed invalid.

Tools: Ministry Legal Documentation

There are several components to our work that require legal documentation.

Officiant's Legal Requirements:

- You must have *Proof of Ordination and Good Standing* for legal license designation as a marriage officiant in a given state.
- If you move, you must notify the issuing office.
- Always keep your license number handy.
- For good standing status, you will need to keep up your association with a sponsoring organization (e.g., church, temple, mosque)
- You are responsible for *filling out and signing the Marriage License* to legalize the marriage.
  - The officiant *witnesses the signing of the license* by the couple, and their witnesses in states that require them.
  - Black ink must be used and no cross-outs or white-outs are permissible on the marriage license.
  - The officiant is responsible for *mailing the license to the Clerk's Office* for verification in the time allotted for filing.

Couple's Legal Requirements:

- *A Marriage License* must be applied for and obtained by the couple marrying, in person, in advance of their wedding day. Each state has its own methodology and time requirements for applying. They are available online or through the local town or County Clerk's Office in the state that the ceremony will take place.
- Couples should inquire *when* the license will be mailed back to them after their wedding.
- *Fees apply* for obtaining a marriage license.
- When applying for a marriage license, this is the information that each marital partner must bring in person to the Clerk's Office:
  - Two pieces of government-issued IDs. The *names* and *addresses* that appear on your government issued IDs will be used on your marriage license application. *All information must match*: the info on your IDs must match the information appearing on your marriage license.
  - Wedding date.
  - Day and evening phone numbers.
  - Full address of the wedding venue, including the zip code.
  - Divorce or death document from a prior marriage, if applicable.
- *Park Permits* must be obtained at the local municipal office by the marrying couple that chooses to hold their ceremony and/or reception in a public space. The size of the gathering determines whether a permit is required or not. *Fees apply.*

Out-of-State Officiant's Legal Requirements:

- An *Out-of-State Officiant Certificate* is sometimes required when marrying a couple out of the state from where the officiant is licensed. As the officiant, you must provide the same information as stated above (in couple's legal requirements) in applying for an in-state marriage license.
  - For out-of-state weddings, you must check if the state requires that you apply for a one-day certificate to officiate a wedding.
  - Some states recognize licenses from other states without the need for a certificate.

- These certificates must be mailed in along with the marriage license. Keep a copy.
- A sample request letter for an out-of-state officiant certificate:

> *The Commonwealth of Massachusetts*
> *Office of the Secretary, Supervisor*
> *Commissions Division, State House*
> *Boston, MA 02133*
>
> *Dear Sir/Madam,*
>
> *I am an ordained Interfaith Minister and have just been hired to perform a wedding ceremony in Boylston, MA on June 28, 2013.*
>
> *I understand that I need to acquire a certificate from the state. Because of the short time I have before this wedding, I am enclosing a copy of my ordination certificate and my letter of good standing. My City of New York Marriage Officiant Registration ID number is _____.*
>
> *Please tell me what else I need to do. All of my contact information is included.*
>
> *Thanking you in advance for any efforts you make to expedite this matter,*
>
> *Reverend Lynn Gladstone Weisman*

For more information on the legal requirements by state go to *northernway.org/marriagelaws.html*. Or search online for *"Out-of-State Officiant."*

Chapter Tips

- When dealing with legal matters related to our ministry, it is essential to dot all of your i's and cross your t's.

39

Odds and Ends and General Tips

Celebrant's Clothing

The couple spends so much time on the aesthetics of their wedding that I feel it is respectful to discuss their choice of what I will wear for the ceremony. It is thoughtful to consider how the couple and I will look in photos and videos that will be with them for a lifetime.

One bride and groom I married, Christina and Fred, are a boating couple. Their wedding theme was thoroughly nautical. For their ceremony, I wore a semi-formal sailor dress.

In addition to robes (some are ministerial while others are more creative), suits and dresses, I have a collection of minister stoles to choose from, some secular and others are religious. Which one I select for a ceremony depends on my conversation with the couple.

Time and Space

Within the ceremony, referencing a nearby calendar event, such as a holiday, adds depth to the ceremony. Also, making mention of the physical surroundings makes the storytelling more memorable to your audience.

Here is an example from one of my ceremonies: "As we look out into this glistening harbor filled with gently rocking boats, we can imagine our lovely couple, Jena and Paul, sailing into their sunny future together."

Pronunciations

Make absolutely certain that you know how to pronounce all names and words in the ceremony. Mark them in your script notes phonetically. This will avoid ill feelings and embarrassment.

Who's on First?

In aiming to be fair, I alternate which partner's name is mentioned first in different sections of the ceremony.

Humor

Humor is a universal language. Though the wedding ceremony is a sacred event, do not be afraid to include a little humor here and there. I promise it goes over easily. One of my favorite mirthful comments is from poet, Ogden Nash: "To keep your marriage brimming with love in the loving cup, whenever you're wrong, admit it; whenever you're right, shut up!"

Punctuality

Simply said, there is no excuse for being late. Rather, it is best to plan for an early arrival.

Payment

Do not leave the wedding without your final payment.

Trust Your Gut

When we interview with potential couples they are evaluating if we are a good fit for them. I pose that there may be clients whom we deem not a good fit for us. It's okay to graciously turn down a couple with whom we feel uncomfortable at the outset.

Rule of Left

I advise that the bride stand to the left of her groom, nearest to his heart.

Which Side?

I recommend that parents sit on the opposite side from where their children are at the altar. This allows them to see their children's faces during the ceremony.

Chapter Tips

- Make absolutely certain that you know how to pronounce all names and words in the ceremony. Mark them in your script notes phonetically. This will avoid ill feelings and embarrassment.
- Do not leave the wedding without your final payment.
- Humor is a universal language.

40

Conclusion

The landscape of American marriage is diversifying. As America's demographic population continues to grow and change ("Modern Immigration," *Pewhispanic.org*), more couples marry outside their faith and racial/ethnic backgrounds (Murphy, *Pewresearch.org*), more couples identify themselves as spiritual and not religious ("U.S. Public Becoming Less Religious," *Pewforum.org*), and marriage is extended to include both heterosexual and homosexual couples (Liptak, *NYTimes.com*). We, as wedding practitioners, must be ready to embrace these diverse marriage-bound couples *as they present themselves to us*. We must listen with an open heart and help guide them on the road to creating the future *they envision,* which may be very different than the ones their parents experienced and imagined for them. Who better to service these couples but an I/I/I officiant? An I/I/I practitioner accepts and embraces without judgment all faith practices and forms of spiritual practice, including agnosticism and atheism. An I/I/I practitioner sees the value in all belief systems and the beauty and commonality that lie within them.

As an officiant, when you listen openly and deeply and share your professional guidance, you are able to fulfill your couples' needs and desires, especially if you regard your couples as *collaborators* in the process of creating the ceremony. These couples are helping to redefine marriage today through the choices they make in selecting partners, the unique values and beliefs they have, and wish to share on their wedding day and in their future together.

Additionally, as I/I/I practitioners, you have been given this incredible opportunity to have access to couples before they make one of their biggest, life-altering decisions. Knowing this, you may be able to engage them in not just working on creating a ceremony, but helping steer them to understand

and appreciate what it means to create a future together. By using the many tools provided in this manual, *The Marriage Mix,* especially the *Custom Wedding Questionnaire* and the *DIYCQ,* you may be able to guide couples to build a foundation for an informed, sharing and mutually understanding relationship and marriage. I hope these tools may pre-empt communication problems before they are united in matrimony. It may also lead some couples to seek the support of marriage counseling. How lucky we are to be doing work that is primarily about love, understanding, family and community!

I feel moved and enlightened being an I/I/I minister. I have the opportunity to meet new people from a variety of backgrounds and help create ceremonies that fulfill their dreams, and I hope to be a stepping-stone to their future together. I feel strongly that the work we do helps society move forward in a positive direction by finding ways to unite people by being inclusive, collaborative, accepting of differences, and seeing and valuing the good in all people. Maybe, in a way, even imagining a grander vision of America: one that is truly a melting pot for all people.

Ultimately, the strength of an I/I/I perspective could possibly provide us with a different lens on how to deal with some of the most challenging conflicts in the world today. One example is the refugee crisis of Syria and the conflicts it has created amongst many countries that have turned from a stance of compassion and collaboration to one of fear regarding helping their fellow human beings in their time of crisis. An I/I/I minister believes that everyone is interconnected, and love, compassion and understanding are the standards that we universally hope to live by. An I/I/I perspective recognizes that all of humanity is woven together, and thereby is able to foster peace in the world even in the most troubling situations. It is when we open our hearts without judgment and remember our universal commonality that we truly stand the strongest as a community, a society and a people.

I hope that my approach in this manual, *The Marriage Mix,* will be helpful to you in your career for many years to come. We are all so fortunate to be in this line of work. At any time, if you wish to contact me, please do so at Lynn@ LynnGladstone.com.

About the Author

Reverend Lynn Gladstone was ordained by the One Spirit Interfaith Seminary in New York City, and recently completed her doctorate through All Faiths Seminary International. This book began as her thesis work. Reverend Lynn is licensed to perform marriages throughout the United States and beyond and provides premarital counseling services. She has a Masters of Social Work from Hunter College. She is certified by CASA, Court Appointed Special Advocates for foster children. Reverend Lynn is certified in Jewish Studies by the Florence Melton School of Hebrew University in Jerusalem and by Disaster Chaplaincy Service to serve as a disaster relief minister, enabling her to help those affected by Hurricane Sandy as well as people recovering from the aftermath of any disaster. In 2015 and 2016, she was selected The Knot Best of Weddings, an award representing the highest-rated wedding professionals.

A strong commitment to community service was significant in Rev. Lynn's upbringing. She has been actively involved in many social justice arenas including: LGBT issues, children, adolescent and elder needs, gender equality, victims of domestic violence, feeding and rights of homeless people, education, religious and spiritual organizations, free health clinics and animal rights.

Rev. Lynn was born and raised in New York and has traveled all over the world. She has two children, one son-in-law, one grandchild and two step-grandchildren. Rev. Lynn is currently living and working in Los Angeles, California with her two small dogs, Diaz and Dora.

Appendices

Appendix 1

The following article was published in *The Knot's* "Ideas + Etiquette," section of *TheKnot.com* (Torgerson, *TheKnot.com*). © Copyright 2016, *TheKnot.com*. Reproduced by Permission. All Rights Reserved. Credit to: *TheKnot.com* and photographers listed at *MichaelMeeksPhotography.com*.

4 Ways to Keep the Peace With Your Religious Parents

More and more couples are describing themselves as "spiritual and not religious," but their families still have some faith-based requirements for the ceremony. Not sure how to reconcile those two opinions? Here's how to deal.

By Rachel Torgerson

MICHAEL MEEKS PHOTOGRAPHY

If you'd describe yourself as "spiritual and not religious," you'll probably find yourself in the majority of couples these days, according to some interfaith premarital counselors and wedding celebrants we talked to recently. It actually seems like most of the time, if couples are discussing religion at all, it's because their parents are more traditional (and oftentimes are the ones footing the bill), and they want to honor them and their upbringing in one of the most

"4 Ways to Keep the Peace with Your Religious Parents"

More and more couples are describing themselves as "spiritual and not religious," but their families still have some faith-based requirements for the ceremony. Not sure how to reconcile those two opinions? Here's how to deal.

By Rachel Torgerson

If you'd describe yourself as "spiritual and not religious," you'll probably find yourself in the majority of couples these days, according to some interfaith premarital counselors and wedding celebrants we talked to recently. It actually seems like most of the time, if couples are discussing religion at all, it's because their parents are more traditional (and oftentimes are the ones footing the bill), and they want to honor them and their upbringing in one of the most important moments in their lives. If that sounds like you, and you find yourself a little at odds in your belief system with your parents, you may be about to enter into a lot of heated discussions with your parents and even your fiancé about what readings are most important to you, and what types of vows you should say, for example. Don't sweat it—we have four pretty foolproof ways to keep the peace and make sure everyone is on the same page when it comes to religion, family and the ceremony that represents you as a couple.

1. Understand your own beliefs as a couple, then find common ground with your parents.

Set the ground rules for your ceremony.

In order to do this, you have to understand what you both want to believe as a couple. There are some simple questions your officiant will give you to help you get to the bottom of this. "The most important conversation the couple needs to have is if God [or any other entity] is 'invited' to the ceremony at all," says Lynn Gladstone, an interfaith officiant and premarital counselor. If not, are you still open to Biblical or other religious passages? Determining what you want to believe as a couple is one of the most important aspects and will form the foundation of your ceremony, not to mention your marriage.

But one thing that's worth noting, as we've mentioned above, is that religion seems to be an issue that concerns your parents more than you two a lot of times. "Many couples are not terribly strict themselves, but have parental or family issues to deal with. I always advise them that while being sensitive to family wishes, it is ultimately their wedding and they must be true to each other and themselves," says David Didio, officiant and premarital counselor. But a good way to make sure things don't blow up just before the wedding, says New York City wedding celebrant Tulis McCall, is to have your officiant chat with your parents to get everything on the table. "Oftentimes I interview the parents also, just to let them know what I'm doing and ask if they have anything in mind for the ceremony," she says. "Most couples really do want to honor their parents."

2. You can customize your ceremony to be inclusive of everyone.

It's easy for your officiant to include important readings, songs and poems from whatever source you deem powerful, whether it's secular or spiritual. Just as you can write your own vows, you can customize your entire ceremony with your officiant to include anything you want—from a meaningful Biblical passage and other religious texts to sonnets, song lyrics or prose. Whatever you imagine is possible, as long as you bring it up in your sessions with your officiant or celebrant. The biggest thing to remember, Gladstone says, is to not intentionally hurt people attending the wedding. "If it's going to devastate a Catholic grandmother if you don't mention scripture at all, is that really worth it?" she asks.

3. Couples are taking bits from both religions and making their own belief systems.

Not only are couples customizing ceremonies, they're mixing and matching the things they like best out of both religions they ascribe to (or any religion at all). "I have found my frame of reference is that the world, in terms of religion, is going through a big shift," Gladstone says. "When people come to me, across the board the issue of being different religions is not very big. I have yet to have a couple who says their families have a problem with the two of them getting married."

But when it comes to adding a bit here and there, it's good to set parameters so you're managing your parents' (and families') expectations. "I think you need to have a discussion with [family members], telling them that you want them to be happy, but it is your day. Tell them to write down the most important things to have in the wedding and pick your top three or five and honor them. It's about setting boundaries, but having respect," Gladstone says.

4. You can have two different ceremonies — if you want.

Parents not budging on what they want? That's really okay. We've seen more than enough dual ceremonies to know it's most certainly a thing. Many couples of different religions choose to have two separate ceremonies, if both faiths are important to them. We have tons of couples in our real weddings who have had two ceremonies — one for one religion and another for the other. If you have the budget to cover it, and you're dead-set on doing a double ceremony, it's definitely not unheard of.

If religion is deeply meaningful to you, then of course you should have a religious ceremony full of the things you find special within your faith. Just make sure you and your partner have discussed how much it means to you. "It's really about communication and compromise," Didio says. "It's important to discuss these issues far in advance of the wedding planning process, so that when the time comes to work with the ceremony officiant, the couple is clear on where they have issues to be resolved, and what they've already worked out."

Appendix 2

Tools: Use Social Media

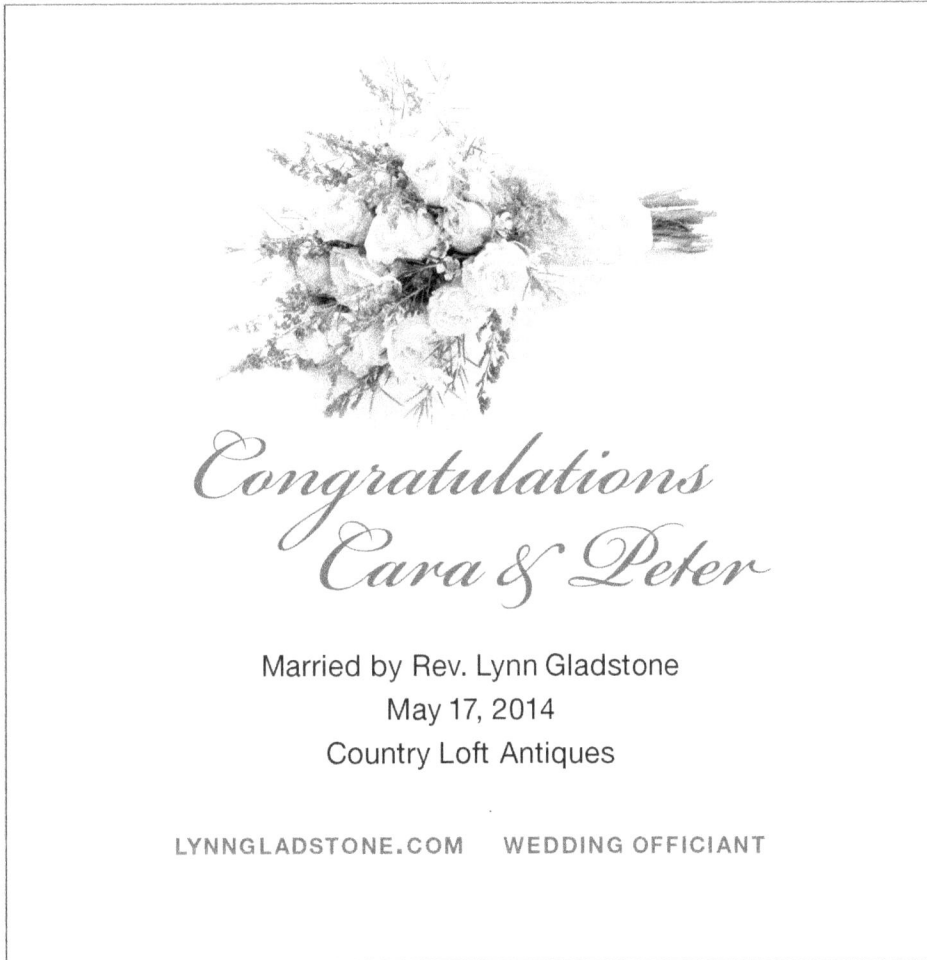

Congratulations
Cara & Peter

Married by Rev. Lynn Gladstone
May 17, 2014
Country Loft Antiques

LYNNGLADSTONE.COM   WEDDING OFFICIANT

Congratulations
Abigail & Akio

Married by Rev. Lynn Gladstone
March 14, 2015
Nobu, Malibu CA

LYNNGLADSTONE.COM   WEDDING OFFICIANT

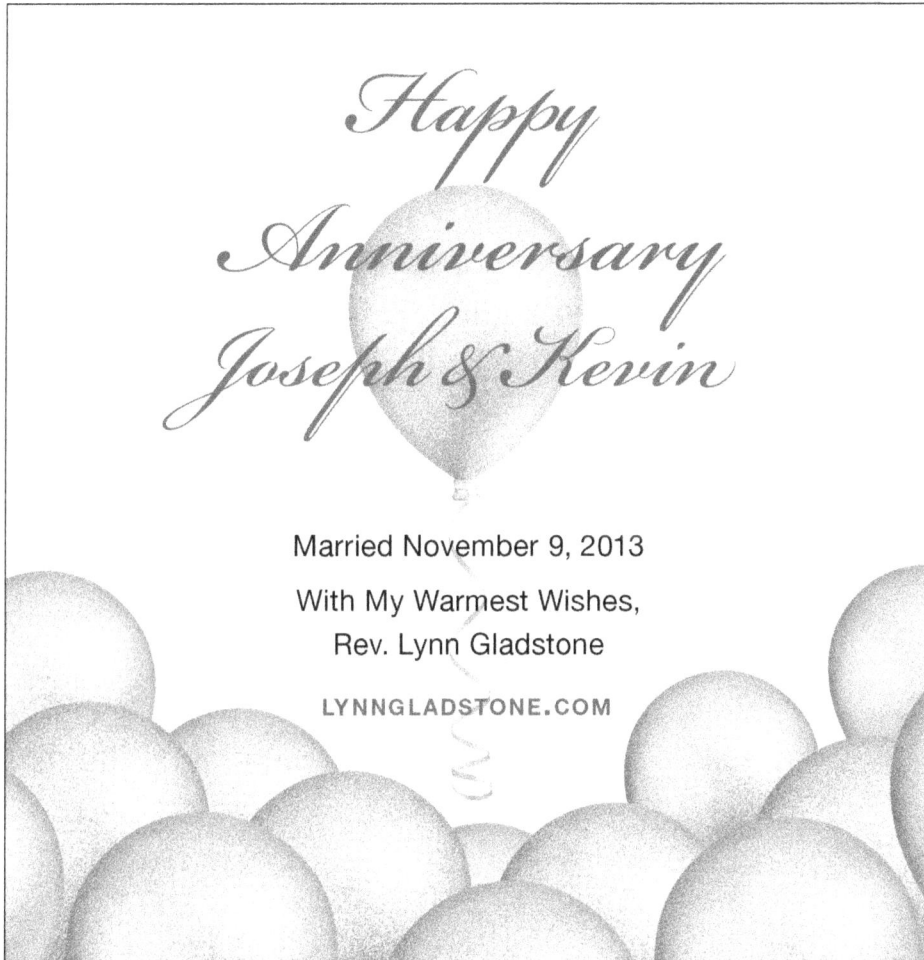

Happy Anniversary Joseph & Kevin

Married November 9, 2013

With My Warmest Wishes,
Rev. Lynn Gladstone

LYNNGLADSTONE.COM

Wedding and happy anniversary digital cards Designed by *IfaatQureshi.com*. All photos/images above are from iStockphoto ©ranplett, iStockphoto ©photoggin and iStockphoto ©malerapaso.

Appendix 3

About Later Love and Marriage

For a celebrant, there is something especially heartwarming about conducting a ceremony for older people. Whether it is a first, second or third marriage, it represents hope and faith. I am including an example of my reflections for my friends' wedding, because I think it speaks to the optimism of marrying later in life.

The blog "Love the Second Time Around" is adapted below having originally been written in 2014 and published on my website, *LynnGladstone.com.* Photography below is from iStockphoto ©IPGGutenbergUKLtd.

Tools: *Love the Second Time Around*

A Practical and Spiritual Approach to "Love the Second Time Around" for the Wedding Ceremony of Pamela and Neil, September 21, 2014 at West Windsor, Vermont.

Marrying for a second time is testimony to *hope* (some say foolishness or insanity). Yet, it is the ones who say, "I do" again that possess the gift of faith in goodness and the ability to learn and grow. There is something rather humbling about marrying again, because that decision begs a myriad of questions. *What happened last time? What went wrong? Where might I have gone off course? Did I sincerely try my very best? What have I learned? Did I learn to tamp down my ego ('Down ego, down!')? Did I learn not to be too defensive, to really listen, and truly hear? Did I learn how to be less possessive and more patient? How to cheer for my partner, and to share the limelight? How to love more gracefully and graciously? Can I do better now?*

We approach remarriage with optimism, and yet leading up to the nuptials there can't help but be a voice whispering inside our ear asking us, "Are you sure about this? Is this time going to be any more successful than the past?"

People who marry in their earlier years are so often faced with unique, all-consuming responsibilities and roles that have to be managed. There could have been the extraordinary effort required to raise and educate children, or to pursue a fledgling career, or to earn that monthly mortgage. When we're older, we hopefully don't have to do all that stuff anymore, and we are freer to focus increasingly on our own needs, desires, and those of our partner.

With second loves, being in different times and spaces in our lives, come fresh opportunities to imagine and navigate our world anew. The deck is dealt differently than before with the face cards looking different—more colorful, more full of perspective and mirth—and hopefully a lot wiser.

So often, people focus on the negatives of those relationships gone by. Yet, what can occur the second time around is two people having the benefit of all that was positive before. Two souls have chosen to synergistically co-create something new and wonderful that is larger than the sum of their pasts. Each brings elements that beget exciting new chances to design an original and sturdy castle in which to reside and flourish.

I trust this couple understands that each of them has come to this juncture having lived a full life of their own and that probably neither mate will change all that much. I sense that this bride and groom have taken hard, honest looks, with hearts and minds, regarding this decision to join their lives. As a twosome, I believe they have come to comprehend that each needs to pursue independent interests, perhaps from a life before they met. That is so fundamental, so essential, for these second time around affairs to thrive.

Dearests, God willing, I wish you the finest opportunity to generously love the one you're with, the one you have been circumspect in choosing to be with from now on.

In closing, I illuminate this theme of the second time around with a quote from Teilhard de Chardin, a French geologist, priest, philosopher and mystic (1881–1955): *"Someday, after mastering the winds, the waves, the tides and gravity, we shall harness for God the energies of love, and then, for a second time in the history of the world, man will have discovered fire."*

And with that fire, oh the places you two will go.

With my deepest loving wishes,

Rev. Lynn

The source for Teilhard de Chardin quote above is goodreads.com.

Appendix 4

Tools: Do-It-Yourself Couple's Questionnaire (DIYCQ) Invitation

When I offer the *Do-It-Yourself Couple's Questionnaire* (DIYCQ) to couples, I send them an invitation inviting them to think about using it. Some welcome it, and yet, others resist. That is their call.

> *Dear Anya and William,*
>
> *I hope you are doing well during this very special time of your lives.*
>
> *I have compiled a self-examining questionnaire for couples who are marrying. I call it the Do-It-Yourself Couple's Questionnaire (DIYCQ). It is for your personal and confidential use alone.*
>
> *Couples like you, who are on their way to a deeper commitment, may find this questionnaire helpful. It will, perhaps, provide an organized way to approach significant areas of knowing one another that you may have not yet explored. Think of it as a gift to yourselves, offering surprises and even greater understanding.*
>
> *I am attaching the table of contents below from this DIYCQ to illustrate the subjects that are covered. If you are interested in receiving a PDF of particular sections or in its entirety, I would be happy to send it to you.*
>
> *With best wishes,*
>
> *Lynn*

Tools: Do-It-Yourself Couple's Questionnaire (DIYCQ)

Increasingly, I have found couples to be interested in seeking counseling. I see this trend to know oneself and one's partner more deeply as an incredibly healthy shift in how people go about making a commitment to one another.

This *DIYCQ is for your private use only.* It is a compilation of other people's hard work and my own professional research and life experiences.

The framework I follow is simply that the better we know ourselves and our beloved, and what we want and what we don't want, the more depth we can bring to our relationship. Even the most intimate couples will eventually come across surprises that could affect their interaction as a twosome. Completing this questionnaire will foster a more understanding, accepting and evolving relationship.

Instructions to the Couple for Filling Out the DIYCQ

The questionnaire is formatted in specific ways. There are twelve sections. Complete the sections mindfully, taking as much time as you need. Be deliberate in formulating your responses and in listening to those of your partner. This is neither homework nor a test. The more you give to it, the more you will gain.

- The questions that are in *regular typeface* are to be answered by each of you *individually* and then shared with one other.
- The questions that are in *italic typeface* are to be discussed and answered *together*.
- There may be questions that will have no relevance to you. Skip those.

Reading the questions alone will have a benefit. Answering the questions will be an invaluable gift that you give to yourselves and your future. New questions may also arise for you.

Congratulations on undertaking this exercise. You both deserve hearty applause for your willingness to work toward further strengthening your current bond. If I can be of any guidance to you, please contact me at any time.

With warmest wishes,

Rev. Lynn Gladstone

I have borrowed material from the following sources in developing this questionnaire, while expanding upon it in considerable detail myself: AAMFT "Marriage Preparation," FOCCUS "Pre-Marriage Inventory," Mid-Manhattan Marriage Counseling Center's "12 Topics and 75 Questions Every Couple Should Explore Before Getting Married" and "Practical Wedding Questions Before (or

After) You Wed," Susan Piver's "The Hard Question," Holly Skinner's "NAWM Premarital Questionnaire," and Sheri and Bob Stritof's "Pre-Marriage Questions List."

Do-It-Yourself Couple's Questionnaire

Table of Contents

Section 1, About You

1. Of all the people you have known, why are you committing to your partner?
2. What attracted you to your partner initially? What about now?
3. What factors have gone into your decision to commit to your partner?
4. Describe what you are committed to being and doing for your partner?
5. In your opinion, what are the most important factors in partnership?
6. What are your expectations of partnership?
7. What do you expect and want from your partner?
8. What do you think your partner expects and wants from you?
9. How do you think you are similar?

10. How do you think you are different?
11. How do your backgrounds and cultures affect your relationship with your partner?
12. How do you think your other personal differences will affect you as a couple?
13. How would you describe yourself?
14. How would you describe your partner?
15. What are your strongest personal characteristics?
16. How important is it to you what people think about you?
17. How confident do you feel about yourself?
18. How comfortable are you in your own skin?
19. How critical or judgmental are you? What about your partner?
20. How patient are you? What about your partner?
21. How compassionate/empathic a person do you consider yourself to be? How so? What about your partner?
22. How responsible do you consider yourself to be? What about your partner?
23. *How ambitious are we individually and how comfortable are we with that?*
24. When it comes to taking care of the tasks at hand, do you procrastinate or hop to it?
25. How comfortable are you with spontaneity? What about your partner?
26. Would you describe yourself as impulsive, acting before you think? What about your partner?
27. How well do you handle compliments?
28. Do you have a tendency to be moody? If so, how frequently does that occur? What gets you down? What makes you feel better?
29. How do you think your partner sees you?
30. What parts of your behavior might you want to improve upon?
31. How do you see yourself in terms of jealousy? What about your partner?
32. What do think are your partner's strongest personal characteristics? Do you feel that your partner is kind and gentle with you? With children, co-workers and family?
33. Describe your love for your partner.
34. Describe your partner's love for you.
35. What are you grateful for? How do you express gratitude?
36. How emotionally honest and truthful are you? What about your partner?

37. How proud of your partner are you?

38. What makes you angry?

39. How angry do you get? Have you ever been violent? Hit someone?

40. Have you ever been arrested or convicted of a crime? Have you ever been a victim of abuse? If yes, how have you dealt with it?

41. Describe if there are trust issues or if you feel insecure in your relationship?

42. What do you envy about your partner?

43. What annoys you about your partner?

44. What habits does your partner have that get on your nerves?

45. Does your partner have sleeping habits that keep you from getting a good night's rest? If yes, how do you deal with it?

46. Are you early to bed/early to rise, late to bed/late to rise, or anything in between? *How do our sleep cycles sync?*

47. When you wake up in the morning, are you slow to converse or are you chatty?

48. If you could adjust something about your partner, what would it be?

49. What do you think might be effective skills in discussing these sensitive matters?

50. How accepting are you that your partner might not change?

51. What are your partner's likes and dislikes?

52. How do these relate to your likes and dislikes?

53. What is your biggest fear about making this monumental commitment?

54. What do you expect and want of a partner in terms of emotional support during: instances of your good fortune? your difficult moments?

55. When you are not feeling well, how much sympathy and attention do you desire?

56. How much sympathy are you willing to give?

57. Do you have any skeletons in your closet (e.g., trauma, addictions, family secrets . . .)?

58. Most people have something(s) private about their lives that they are not proud of How do you feel about discussing such things with your partner? Would you be able to listen to any "confessions" in an open-minded manner? Would you prefer not to know?

59. What routines do you have that your partner might not know about?

60. What was/is the best part of your parents' relationship? What was/is the worst?

61. What do you like and dislike about your partner's parents' relationship?

62. What sorts of things bring you happiness?

63. How do you believe you demonstrate love for your partner? How well do you think your partner appreciates your expression of love?

64. How do you like to be shown love? How good is your partner at expressing love the way you like? How do you show your appreciation for your partner's love?

Section 2, About Your Relationship

1. *Why have we decided to "tie the knot" at this time?*

2. *What do we as a couple want out of life?*

3. *What values do we want to bring from our families into ours?*

4. *How well do you think we listen to one another?*

5. *How do we greet each other: after work, waking up, saying goodbye and goodnight?*

6. *How might we improve our current communication?*

7. *How willing are we to work honestly on our communication skills?*

8. *How do we demonstrate affection for one another?*

9. *Going forward, how do you envision us making decisions together?*

10. *How do we imagine we will relate to: in-laws, opposite-sex friends, an ex-spouse or children from previous relationships?*

11. *Do you think our relationship will change in the future?*

12. *What commitment are we willing to make in order to keep our relationship thriving?*

13. *What will we do if one or both of us feels the relationship is strained or stale?*

14. *Do you or I think we have any significant relationship problems that we need to address?*

15. *Have we both had prior serious relationships? If so, what did we learn about fostering good relationships from those experiences?*

16. *What role will exes have in our lives, especially if there are children involved?*

17. *Can we see ourselves growing old together?*

Section 3, Sex, Intimacy and Romance

1. *How do you feel about discussing our sexual relationship (i.e. our likes and dislikes)?*
2. *What about our sexual fantasies?*
3. *How might lust and/or spirituality play roles in our sexual relationship?*
4. *How do we each feel about our physical and emotional intimacy?*
5. *What are your expectations of our sexual relationship?*
6. *How often does each of you want to make love?*
7. *How will we handle differences in sexual desire, should they arise?*
8. *How does the idea of spontaneous lovemaking sit with you?*
9. *Are there certain sexual activities that are clearly off limits for you?*
10. *What would you like to try that we haven't done or discussed?*
11. *Can we agree to discuss sexual concerns when we are feeling relaxed, not during sex?*
12. *What about seeking therapy if we encounter intimacy issues hard to resolve ourselves?*
13. *How might we want to grow together sexually?*
14. *What is your attitude about monogamy?*
15. *What agreement do we want to have about fidelity?*
16. *How do we feel about sexual affairs as an option?*
17. *What would you do if you felt drawn to someone other than your partner?*
18. *How would an affair of the heart affect our relationship?*
19. *What constitutes romance to you?*

Section 4, Political, Religious and Spiritual Beliefs

1. Describe your political beliefs.
2. With which political party do you identify, if any?
3. *If our political beliefs differ, how do you think it might affect our relationship?*
4. When you were growing up, what role did politics play in your family?
5. When you were growing up, what role did religion have in your life?
6. What role does God have or not have in your life?
7. *What are each of our thoughts about organized religion, spirituality and God?*
8. *Do you think of religion and spirituality as the same or as separate entities?*

9. What role does religion or spirituality play or not play in your life now?
    What role do we imagine religion or spirituality will take in our family life?
    What role do you wish it did or did not have in our life?
10. *Do we share the same faith?*
11. *Do we think it important that we share the same beliefs?*
12. *What differences in customs might we face?*
13. *How will we handle differences?*
14. *What would we each like to teach our children regarding faith?*
15. *If we have different beliefs around faith, how will we worship?*
16. *How might non-traditional or spiritual observance fit into our lives?*
17. *Will we attend a house of worship?*
18. How active do you want to be in some form of religious or spiritual community?
19. How do you feel about playing a part in caring for your community?

Section 5, Your Finances

1. *Are we comfortable talking about money together?*
2. How do you feel about full financial disclosure between the two of us?
3. *What amount of money does each of us need to feel comfortable?*
4. What current debts or ongoing financial obligations do you have?
    (e.g., school loans, credit card debt)
5. What is your credit score?
6. How much money do you earn?
7. How much money do you have in savings?
8. How much money do you hope to save from each paycheck?
9. *What are our combined debts and assets?*
10. *What are our thoughts about having a prenuptial agreement?*
11. Do you expect both of us to support the family financially?
12. What obligations do you have to dependents outside of this relationship?
13. Do you think that will change when children arrive?
14. *What happens if we do not have any money to speak of?*
15. *What if we suddenly get a lot of it?*
16. *Will our money be separate or combined?*

17. *What is our combined annual income goal and target date?*
18. *Will we have a joint checking account, separate accounts or both?*
19. *Will we have a joint safety deposit box and each have a key?*
20. *Can we agree that any borrowing of money will be discussed in advance?*
21. *What do you believe is worth going into debt for?*
22. *What are your thoughts about the use of credit cards?*
23. *How much credit card or home equity loan debt is acceptable for us to have?*
24. *What are our thoughts about having a family budget?*
25. *How will our income be divided among our expenses and savings?*
26. *What will we do with any discretionary money that we attain individually?*
27. *Are you a saver or spender when it comes to money?*
28. *If either of us lost our job, what budget items would we cut?*
29. *Who will pay for what?*
30. *Who is going to be responsible for making sure that bills are paid on time?*
31. *How will we resolve any strong disagreements about spending money?*
32. *What will be our plan for our children's educations?*
33. *What will be our plan for health insurance coverage?*
34. *How do we plan to accumulate savings and retirement funds?*
35. *Are dining out, entertainment and a yearly vacation necessities or luxuries?*
36. *Will we want to use a financial planner?*
37. *Who will do what about paying our taxes and monitoring investments?*
38. What is your philosophy on giving to charitable organizations?

Section 6, Career and Lifestyle

1. What education/training have you received?
2. What jobs have you had?
3. How successful have you been at staying employed?
4. *How might unemployment affect our relationship?*
5. What do you hope to achieve in the near and distant future career-wise?
6. *What life goals for our careers, family, or other personal success do we share?*
7. *What goals are different between us?*
8. *How will we work through any differences we may have about these goals?*
9. Are we comfortable with a salary differential between us?

10. How supportive are you of your partner's career, regardless of income?
11. How comfortable are you with your partner's pursuit of their hobbies?
12. *In what ways might we help each other reach our goals?*
13. How much time do you think is appropriate to give to work?
14. *How much do we value having meals together?*
15. *Is work to be left at the office or can it come home?*
16. *How do we determine if a new career path or job is reason enough to move?*
17. What do you picture your relationship to be like after five years?
18. What about your standard of living?
19. If you had the chance, what would you really like to do?
20. *Do you think we could ever go into business together?*
21. *If one or both of us faces a midlife career "crisis," how might we handle that?*
22. *If we had the opportunity to quit our jobs, what might we do?*
23. *What do you think we will be doing in forty years?*
24. How do you feel about alternative lifestyles?

Section 7, House and Home

1. *Let's discuss what "home" actually means to the two of us.*
2. What sort of home and neighborhood do you hope to live in?
3. What type of amenities would you like in your home?
4. What features would your dream house have?
5. Are there any places where you would refuse to live?
6. *Do you see us renting or owning our home in the future?*
7. *What is our savings plan for our first home?*
8. *How soon do we expect our home to be furnished to our liking?*
9. *How are our home décor preferences similar or different?*
10. What type of bed do you want to sleep in at home?
11. *How will we negotiate differences in sleep environment preferences?*
      (e.g., light, noise, temperature, pajamas)
12. Do you want to keep trading up houses as we can afford it?
13. Do you hope to live in the same house or area for a long time?
14. *How do we each feel about neatness?*
15. Do you hoard or purge when it comes to material possessions?

16. *How close in vicinity would you like to stay to your family or mine?*
17. How do you feel about entertaining at home?
18. How do you react when people drop in unexpectedly?
19. How welcome are pets in the home? If so, what types?
20. How do you feel about having a gun in the house?
21. *How are we going to divide up the household chores (e.g., cleaning, making beds, laundry/ironing, trash, groceries, cooking, dishes, pet care, lawn mowing, gardening, home maintenance and repairs)?*
22. *Will we be hiring any outside help to assist in any of the above?*
23. *What are your dietary preferences?*
     How will we manage any dietary differences?
24. *How often will we cook at home, order in, take-out or dine out?*
25. *How do we feel about tenants, extended family or friends sharing our home?*
     Short-term or long-term?

Section 8, Leisure Time and Social Life

1. *What are each of our expectations about how we will spend our free time?*
2. *What will we do for fun?*
3. *How do we feel about alcoholic beverages and smoking in our home?*
4. *What "recreational activities" will we share?*
5. *What "recreational activities" are acceptable to do separately?*
6. *How will we make sure we have quality time together?*
7. *How important is setting aside time each week to catch up with each other?*
8. Do you believe that we should be doing everything together?
9. What activities do you hope to see us doing as a couple?
10. *Will one or both of us make our social plans?*
11. *Who will be responsible for keeping the family calendar?*
12. *How will we handle scheduling conflicts?*
13. How much personal space and alone time do you need?
14. What leisure activities or sports do you like to engage in?
15. *What hobbies do we have that will affect the other?*
16. *How interested are you in:*
     Spectator sports?

> *Watching TV?*
> *Being on your computer?*
> *Talking/texting on the phone?*
> *Checking your cell phone?*

17. *How much will we be involved in social media?*
18. *Will we be an "official couple" online?*
19. How do you feel about texting/emailing vs. talking on the phone?
20. Regarding a call, email or text, what is an acceptable amount of response time?
21. *When apart, how much communication with one another do we expect?*
22. *What are our thoughts on phone usage while we share private time?*
23. What sorts of humor and comedy appeal to you? What does not?
24. *How will we spend the holidays, birthdays and anniversaries?*
25. How do you feel about long-distance travel?
26. Traveling with other people?
27. What sorts of travel interest you?
28. What types of vacation destinations do you prefer?
    How will we reconcile any differences about vacations?
29. *How do we handle friends from our previous relationships?*
30. How do you feel about your partner interacting with exes?
31. How comfortable are you in social situations? With meeting new people?
32. *How often do we see ourselves hanging out together with friends?*
33. *Will we both have certain times to spend with our own friends?*
34. How would you feel if I want a regular night out with my friends?
35. *How do we feel about spending nights apart for work or fun?*
36. *How might our male/female friendships change in the future?*
37. *What will we do if you dislike one of my friends or family members?*
38. Will you want to join any social clubs?
39. *What is our agreement about discussing private matters with others?*

Section 9, Child and Family Planning

1. What is your attitude towards children?
2. Do you have children from an earlier relationship?

Describe your relationship with them.
What place will they have in our lives?

3. *Do we already have children together?*
   How do we think they feel about us taking the next step in our relationship?

4. *Do we want to have children in the future?*

5. *What if one of us changes our mind?*

6. *When considering pregnancy are there any genetic concerns?*
   If yes, would we pursue genetic testing?

7. *When would we ideally begin having children?*

8. *How many and how far apart?*

9. *What are your feelings/thoughts about birth control?*

10. *What types would you use/not use?*

11. *What are your feelings/thoughts about abortion?*

12. *Will we both be present at pregnancy workshops and birthing?*
    What would we do if we have difficulty conceiving?
    Would we consider pursuing alternative pregnancy methods?
    What if we cannot conceive?

13. *What are your thoughts on adoption?*

14. *How do you foresee the arrival of children affecting our lives?*

15. *How will we handle the child's feeding schedule?*

16. *Will the child be breastfed?*
    For how long?

17. How do you feel about your partner's children from a previous relationship?

18. *What kind of parent do you think you will be in terms of style and philosophy?*

19. What was your childhood like?

20. When growing up, what was your family like?
    (e.g., affectionate and supportive, strict or punishing, close or detached)

21. What 'philosophies' did your parents have about raising children?

22. How do you feel about their parenting approach?

23. What kind of relationship do you expect to have with your children?

24. What kind of relationship do you anticipate they will have with your parents?

25. *How will we divvy up responsibilities regarding our children?*

26. *Will one of us stay home after we have children?*

27. *Will we hire a nanny and/or babysitters or enroll in daycare?*

28. What roles do we see our families playing (or not) in childcare?
29. How do you intend to shape your children's values?
30. How will you share with them what is important to you?
31. *How might we raise children in our chosen religion(s)?*
32. *Will our children go through religious rites of passage?*
33. *What about circumcision?*
34. *Will we send our children to public, private, parochial or home school?*
35. *Will children be expected to attend any religious services or education?*
36. How do you think you will feel if your children chose to embrace your partner's religion or neither of your faiths?
37. *How will we take responsibility for issues at our children's schools?*
38. How much do you want to be involved with your children's school activities? After-school activities?
39. What do you consider your role will be vis-à-vis your children's homework?
40. *When the children get sick, who do we think will stay home with them?*
41. *How will we budget for toys, clothes, camp and extra-curricular activities?*
42. *Will we require our children to do chores?*
43. *What do we think about our children receiving an allowance?*
44. *Will our teenagers have after-school jobs?*
45. How do you think you would discipline our children?
46. What kinds of punishment do you feel are appropriate or inappropriate? For example, today I saw a little kid who cursed and his mom slapped his face. What would you have done?
47. *Can we agree to unite when the children try to play one of us against the other?*
48. *After having children, how will we make time for just the two of us?*

Section 10, Your Families and the Holidays

1. *When you talk about "family," whom do you think of?*
2. *How much time do we need or want to spend with our families?*
3. *What roles do you anticipate our families will have in our lives?*
4. *What will we do if we need to set boundaries?*
5. *What holiday customs will we want to honor?*
6. *How will we celebrate family birthdays?*

7. *If we have different religious beliefs which holidays will we observe?*
8. *What do we think will be the expectations of our families around holidays?*
   How will we manage those expectations?
9. *Do you anticipate problems with your family during the holidays?*
   How might we resolve any such problems?
10. *What do we like and dislike about our own families?*
11. *What do we like and dislike about each other's families?*
12. *Do we think it is okay to talk with our families about our problems?*
13. If you have family problems, what kind of support would you like from your partner?
14. *How might we deal with stress within our extended families?*
15. *How do we deal with family if they experience money crises?*
16. *Do we feel we will need to be nearby our parents now or as they get older?*
17. *What are our parents' plans for their future care, should they need it?*
18. Do you think that you will ever want your parents to move in?
19. What did your parents model for you in terms of who did what in the family?
    Did you feel that was fair or do you expect something different in our family?
20. If either of us are stepparents:
    What role do you see yourself playing or not playing as a stepparent?
    What role you see your partner playing or not playing as a stepparent?
    How do we reconcile any differences in these expectations?
    If either of us have stepchildren:
    How will we include them in family life?
    How do we feel about including exes at holiday celebrations?

Section 11, Physical/Emotional Health and Medical Decisions

1. *How transparent are we about our physical/emotional health and current needs?*
2. *How do we feel about both of our health and fitness regimens?*
   Are there any specific areas of concern?
3. How often, what and how much do you drink?
4. Do you smoke marijuana?
5. Do you use any other drugs?

Which ones?

6. What over-the-counter and prescription medications do you take regularly?
7. Are there any medical or dependency conditions to share with your partner?
8. *Do our family members have any medical conditions or other special needs?*
    How might this affect our life together?
9. *What genetic/medical concerns might come up in the future?*
10. *In case of serious illness, what expectations might we each have for our care?*
    What do we think our support system will be like?
11. What legacy do you hope to leave after you die?
12. How will religious, spiritual or intellectual beliefs affect your medical decisions?
13. *Do we have or do we intend to have:*
    Wills?
    Living Wills/Health Care Proxies?
    Powers of Attorney?
    Do Not Resuscitate requests?
    Life Insurance Policies?
14. What are your thoughts or intentions about organ donation?
15. *Do we know where our health, estate, financial and attorney documents are?*

Section 12, Conflict and Resolution

1. *What do we argue about?*
2. *How do we argue?*
3. What triggers you to become angry?
4. *How willing are we to face any difficult areas of our relationship?*
5. *Do we have a tendency to avoid conflict?*
6. *What strategies will we use to navigate the ups and downs of life and love?*
7. What is your instinctual approach for resolving an argument?
8. How did your parents settle their differences?
    How might that affect your behavior during an argument?
9. What approach does your partner take when there is disagreement?
10. How willing are you to take responsibility for your role in a conflict?
    What is the wisdom of beginning statements with, "I feel _____
    when you do _____." Rather than, "You make me feel _____."

11. Generally, how successful are both of your approaches?

12. *What has worked in the past to resolve disagreements we have had?*

13. *What loving rituals can we develop to indicate the closure of an argument?*

14. *What happens if we cannot agree?*

15. *Can we take a time-out to calm down and be effective in our problem solving?*

16. *Can we agree to not fight dirty and strive for successful resolution strategies (e.g., taking turns speaking and listening)?*

17. *How willing are we to consider that well-placed humor can relieve tension?*

18. How do you act if your partner comes home upset?

19. How hard or easy is it for you to say, "I am sorry" and mean it?

20. How forgiving can you be? Toward others? Toward yourself?

21. What are your most vulnerable issues within the relationship?

22. *How do we feel about seeking professional intervention, if needed?*

23. *Can we agree to counseling if we decide that our partnership is in jeopardy?*

24. *Do we agree that our children's wellbeing is paramount in our lives?*

25. What is your attitude about divorce?

26. *As a couple, what have we learned so far about conflict and resolution?*

27. *Can we agree to try really hard not to go to bed angry?*

Appendix 5

Tools: Special Touches by the Celebrant

I give my couples a small, meaningful wedding gift, and I create an attractive marriage certificate. The original is rather sterile looking.

Appendix 6

Tools: Additional Special Touches by the Celebrant

I give a gift of vintage handkerchiefs to the parents of the couples I marry. With the handkerchiefs, I include this amusing note for their enjoyment.

Vintage Handkerchief Flirtations Circa 1880

Handkerchief signals:

Drawing across the eyes:
I am sorry

Dropping:
We will be friends

Twirling in both hands:
Indifference

Take by the center:
You are too willing

Drawing across the cheek:
I love you

Drawing through the hand:
I hate you

Drawing across the forehead:
We are being watched

Resting on the right cheek:
Yes

Resting on the left cheek:
No

Twisting in the right hand:

I love another

Twisting in the left hand:
I wish to get rid of you

Folding it:
I wish to speak with you

Placed over the shoulder:
Follow me

Opposite corners held in both hands:
Wait for me

Placing on the right eye:
You have changed

Letting remain on the eyes:
You are cruel

Winding around the forefinger:
I am engaged

Winding around the ring finger:
I am married

Placing in the pocket:
No more

Appendix 7

Love and Marriage Readings

Unless otherwise indicated, the sources for these materials are the *Interfaith Seminary* program at *onespiritinterfaith.org*, Susan Turchin's book, *The Interfaith Wedding Manual, Creating Meaningful Wedding Ceremonies: A Guide for Clergy and Couples* (22–59), my eloquent colleagues and my couples. Some materials had no attributed author or source or were defined as public domain material, which may have been further adapted. Material that did have sources, I have credited within this book.

From Judeo-Christian Scripture

Colossians 3
You are the people of God; he loved you and chose you for his own. So then, you must clothe yourselves with compassion, kindness, humility, gentleness, and patience. Be tolerant with one another and forgive one another whenever any of you has a complaint against someone else. You must forgive one another just as the Lord has forgiven you. And to all these qualities add love, which binds all things together in perfect unity.

Ecclesiastes 4
Two are better off than one, because together they can work more effectively. If one of them falls down, the other can help him up. But if someone is alone and falls, it's just too bad, because there is no one to help him. If it is cold, two can sleep together and stay warm, but how can you keep warm by yourself. Two people can resist an attack that would defeat one person alone. A rope made of three cords is hard to break.

Genesis
God said, "It is not good for man to live alone. I will make a companion to help him." So God took some soil from the ground and formed all the animals and all the birds and brought them to the man to see what he would name them: and

that is how they all got their names. So the man named all the birds and all the animals; but not one of them was a suitable companion.

Then God made the man to fall into a deep sleep, and while he was sleeping, God took out one of the man's ribs and closed up the flesh. God formed a woman out of the rib and brought her unto him. Then the man said "At last, here is one of my own kind—bone taken from my bone, and flesh from my flesh, and Woman is her name." But never forget that the Talmud, the oral law of Judaism tells us:

Woman was not created from man's head that he should command her, nor from his feet that she should be his slave, but rather, from his side, that she should ever be near his heart.

I Corinthians 13 (From The First Letter to the Corinthians)

Be ambitious for the higher gifts. And I am going to show you a way that is better than any of them.

If I have all the eloquence of men or of angels, but speak without love, I am simply a gong booming or a cymbal clashing. If I have the gift of prophecy, understanding all the mysteries there are, and knowing everything, and if I have faith in all its fullness, to move mountains, but without love, then I am nothing at all. If I give away all that I possess, piece by piece, and if I even let them take my body to burn it, but am without love, it will do me no good whatever.

Love is always patient and kind; it is never jealous; love is never boastful or conceited; it is never rude or selfish; it does not take offence, and is not resentful.

Love takes no pleasure in other people's sins but delights in the truth; it is always ready to excuse, to trust, to hope, and to endure whatever comes.

Love does not come to an end.

This is the word of the Lord.

John 15

I love you just as the Father loves me; remain in my love.

I have told you this so that my joy may be in you and that your joy may be complete.

My commandment is this: love one another, just as I love you.

Matthew 19

Have you not read that he who made them from the beginning made them male and female, and said, "For this reason a man shall leave his father and mother and be joined to his wife, and the two shall become one?" So they are no longer two but one. What therefore God has joined together, let no man put asunder.

Psalm 1

Blessed are the man and the woman who have grown beyond themselves and have seen through their separations. They delight in the way things are and keep their hearts open, day and night. They are like trees planted near flowing rivers, which bear fruit when they are ready. Their leaves will not fall or wither. Everything they do will succeed.

Psalm 100 (translation: Stephen Mitchell)

Sing to the Lord all creatures!
Worship Him with your joy;
Praise Him with the sound of your laughter.
Know that we all belong to Him,
That He is our source and our home.
Enter His light with thanksgiving;
Fill your hearts with His praise.
For His goodness is beyond comprehension,
And His deep love endures forever.

Romans 12

Let love be without any pretense
Avoid what is evil; Stick to what is good.
In love let your feelings of deep affection for one another
come to expression and regard others as more important than yourself.

Song of Solomon 2

My beloved speaks and says to me;
Arise, my love, my fair one,
and come away;
For lo, the winter is past,
the rain is over and gone.
The flowers appear on the earth,
the time of singing has come,
and the voice of the turtledove
is heard in our land.
The fig tree puts forth its figs,
and the vines are in blossom;
they give forth fragrance.
Arise, my love, my fair one,
and come away.

Song of Songs

I hear my Beloved.
See how he comes
leaping on the mountains,
bounding over the hills.
My Beloved is like a gazelle,
like a young stag.
See where he stands
behind our wall.
He looks in at the window,
he peers through the lattice.

My Beloved lifts up his voice,
he says to me,
'Come then, my love,
my lovely one, come.
My dove, hiding in the clefts of the rock.
In the coverts of the cliff,
show me your face,
let me hear your voice;
for your voice is sweet
and your face is beautiful.'

My beloved is mine and I am his.

Set me like a seal on your heart,
like a seal on your arm.
For love is strong as Death,
jealousy relentless as Shel.
The flash of it is a flash of fire,
a flame of the Lord himself.
Love no flood can quench,
no torrents drown.
This is the word of the Lord.

The Book of Ruth
And Ruth said, Intreat me not to leave thee, or to return from following after thee: for whither thou goest, I will go; and where thou lodgest, I will lodge: thy people shall be my people, and thy God my God.

From Poetry, Literature, Music, Reflections

A Natural History of Love by Diane Ackerman
Love. What a small word we use for an idea so immense and powerful it has altered the flow of history, calmed monsters, kindled works of art, cheered the forlorn, turned tough guys to mush, consoled the enslaved, driven strong women mad, glorified the humble, fueled national scandals, bankrupted robber barons,

and made mincemeat of kings. How can love's spaciousness be conveyed in the narrow confines of one syllable? . . . Love is an ancient delirium, a desire older than civilization, with taproots spreading deep into dark and mysterious days.

The heart is a living museum. In each of its galleries, no matter how narrow or dimly lit, preserved forever like wondrous diatoms, are our moments of loving, and being loved.

The Five People You Meet in Heaven by Mitch Albom

People say they 'find' love, as if it were an object hidden under a rock. But love takes many forms, and it is never the same for any man and woman. What people find then is a *certain* love. And [Name] found a certain love with [Name], a grateful love, a deep but quiet love, one that he knew, above all else, was irreplaceable.

"The Divine Comedy" by Dante Alighieri

The love of God, unutterable and perfect, flows into a pure soul the way that light rushes into a transparent object. The more love that it finds, the more it gives itself, so that as we grow clear and open. The more complete the joy of loving is the more souls who resonate together. The greater the intensity of their love, for, mirror-like, each soul reflects the others.

Apache Wedding Blessing

Now you will feel no storms, for each of you will be shelter to the other. Now you will feel no cold, for each of you will be warmth to the other. Now there is no loneliness, for each of you is companion to the other, you are two persons, but there is one life before you, and one home. Turn together to look at the road you traveled, to reach this - the hour of your happiness. It stretches behind you into the past. Look to the future that lies ahead. A long and winding, adventure-filled road, whose every turn means discovery, new hopes, new joys, new laughter, and a few shared tears. May happiness be your companion, May beauty surround you both in the journey ahead; And through all the years to come. Go this day to your dwelling place and enter into your days together. May your days be good and long upon the earth. Your adventure has just begun!

"O Tell Me the Truth About Love" by W. H. Auden

Some say love's a little boy,
And some say it's a bird,
Some say it makes the world go round,
Some say that's absurd,
And when I asked the man next door,
Who looked as if he knew,
His wife got very cross indeed,
And said it wouldn't do.

Does it look like a pair of pyjamas,
Or the ham in a temperance hotel?
Does its odour remind one of llamas,
Or has it a comforting smell?
Is it prickly to touch as a hedge is,
Or soft as eiderdown fluff?
Is it sharp or quite smooth at the edges?
O tell me the truth about love.

Our history books refer to it
In cryptic little notes,
It's quite a common topic on
The Transatlantic boats;
I've found the subject mentioned in
Accounts of suicides,
And even seen it scribbled on
The backs of railway guides.

Does it howl like a hungry Alsatian,
Or boom like a military band?
Could one give a first-rate imitation
On a saw or a Steinway Grand?
Is its singing at parties a riot?
Does it only like Classical stuff?
Will it stop when one wants to be quiet?
O tell me the truth about love.

I looked inside the summer-house;
It wasn't over there;
I tried the Thames at Maidenhead,
And Brighton's bracing air.
I don't know what the blackbird sang,
Or what the tulip said;
But it wasn't in the chicken-run,
Or underneath the bed.

Can it pull extraordinary faces?
Is it usually sick on a swing?
Does it spend all its time at the races,
or fiddling with pieces of string?
Has it views of its own about money?
Does it think Patriotism enough?
Are its stories vulgar but funny?
O tell me the truth about love.

When it comes, will it come without warning
Just as I'm picking my nose?
Will it knock on my door in the morning,
Or tread in the bus on my toes?
Will it come like a change in the weather?
Will its greeting be courteous or rough?
Will it alter my life altogether?
O tell me the truth about love.

The Bridge Across Forever by Richard Bach
A soul mate is someone who has locks that fit our keys, and keys to fit our locks. When we feel safe enough to open the locks, our truest selves step out and we can be completely and honestly who we are; we can be loved for who we are and not for who we're pretending to be. Each unveils the best part of the other. No matter what else goes wrong around us, with that one person we're safe in our own paradise. Our soul mate is someone who shares our deepest longings, our sense of direction. When we're two balloons, and together our direction is up,

chances are we've found the right person. Our soul mate is the one who makes life come to life.

Interview with Reverend Michael Beckwith

When your life is about change then you find someone who is willing to go on the adventure with you. You assist each other in unfoldment. You have someone who loves you now, and will love and support you as you grow and change . . . .

Marriage is about a way of life that includes being with the right person.

"Friendship" by Judy Bielicki

It is often said that it is love that makes the world go round. However, without doubt, it is friendship which keeps our spinning existence on an even keel. True friendship provides so many of the essentials for a happy life - it is the foundation on which to build an enduring relationship, it is the mortar which bonds us together in harmony, and it is the calm, warm protection we sometimes need when the world outside seems cold and chaotic. True friendship holds a mirror to our foibles and failings, without destroying our sense of worthiness. True friendship nurtures our hopes, supports us in our disappointments, and encourages us to grow to our best potential. Erich and Tara came together as friends. Today, they pledge to each other not only their love, but also the strength, warmth and, most importantly, the fun of true friendship.

"A Marriage" by Michael Blumenthal

You are holding up a ceiling
with both arms. It is very heavy,
but you must hold it up, or else
it will fall down on you. Your arms
are tired, terribly tired,
and, as the day goes on, it feels
as if either your arms or the ceiling
will soon collapse.

But then,
unexpectedly,
something wonderful happens:
Someone,
a man or a woman,
walks into the room
and holds their arms up
to the ceiling beside you.

So you finally get
to take down your arms.
You feel the relief of respite,
the blood flowing back
to your fingers and arms.
And when your partner's arms tire,
you hold up your own
to relieve him again.

And it can go on like this
for many years
without the house falling.

"An Odd Conceit" by Nicholas Breton
Lovely kind, and kindly loving,
Such a mind were worth the moving;
Truly fair, and fairly true-
Where are all these, but in you?

Wisely kind, and kindly wise;
Blessed life, where such love lies!
Wise, and kind, and fair, and true-
Lovely live all these in you.

Sweetly dear, and dearly sweet;
Blessed, where these blessings meet!

Sweet, fair, wise, kind, blessed, true-
Blessed be all these in you!

"How Do I Love Thee?" By Elizabeth Barrett Browning

How do I love thee? Let me count the ways.
I love thee to the depth and breadth and height
My soul can reach, when feeling out of sight
For the ends of being and ideal grace.
I love thee to the level of every day's
Most quiet need, by sun and candle-light.
I love thee freely, as men strive for right.
I love thee purely, as they turn from praise.
I love thee with the passion put to use
In my old griefs, and with my childhood's faith.
I love thee with a love I seemed to lose
With my lost saints. I love thee with the breath,
Smiles, tears, of all my life; and, if God choose,
I shall but love thee better after death.

"Rabbi Ben Ezra" by Robert Browning

Grow old with me! The best is yet to be,
The last of life, for which the first was made:
Our times are in this hand
Who saith, "A whole I planned,
Youth shows but half; trust God: see all, nor be afraid!"

From *The Hungering Dark* by Frederick Buechner

Dostoyevsky describes Alexei Karamazov falling asleep and dreaming about the wedding at Cana, and for him too it is a dream of indescribable joy, but when he wakes from it he does a curious thing. He throws himself down on the earth and embraces it. He kisses the earth and among tears that are in no way sentimental, because they are turned not inward but outward, he forgives the earth and begs its forgiveness and vows to love it forever. And that is the heart of it, after all, and matrimony is called holy because this brave and fateful promise of a man and a woman to love and honor and serve each other through thick and thin looks beyond itself to more fateful promises still and speaks mightily of what human life at its most human and its most alive and most holy must always be.

"A Red, Red Rose" by Robert Burns
O my Luve is like a red, red rose
That's newly sprung in June;
O my Luve is like the melodie
That's sweetly played in tune.
As fair art thou, my bonnie lass,
So deep in luve am I:
And I will luve thee still, my dear,
Till a' the seas gang dry

Till a' the seas gang dry, my dear,
And the rocks melt with the sun:
I will luve thee still, my dear,
While the sands o' life shall run.
And fare thee well, my only Luve

And fare thee well, a while!
And I will come again, my Luve,
Tho' it were ten thousand mile.

Quote by Susan Cain
Opposites attract, and I think temperament is so fundamental that you end up craving someone of the opposite temperament to complete you.

Quote from Joseph Campbell
Love is a friendship set to music.

"The True Meaning of Marriage" by Joseph Campbell

Marriage is not a love affair. A love affair is a totally different thing. A marriage is a commitment to that which you are. That person is literally your other half. And, you and the other are one . . . But a marriage is a life commitment, and a life commitment means the prime concern of your life.

From *Start Where You Are* by Pema Chodron

When you begin to touch your heart or let your heart be touched, you begin to discover that it's bottomless, that it doesn't have any resolution, that this heart is huge, vast and limitless. You begin to discover how much warmth and gentleness is there, as well as how much space. Your world seems less solid, more roomy and spacious. The burden lightens.

"Carrie's Poem" by Cindy Chupack

His hello was the end of her endings.
Her laugh was their first step down the aisle.
His hand would be hers to hold forever.
His forever was as simple as her smile.
An ocean couldn't prevent it.
A New York minute wouldn't let it pass.
Does the universe decide for us
Which love will fade and which will last?
He said she was what was missing.
She said instantly she knew.
She was a question to be answered, and his answer was "I do."

The Alchemist by Paulo Coelho

Because it's not love to be static like the desert, nor is it love to roam the world like the wind. And it's not love to see everything from a distance. Love is the force that transforms and improves the Soul of the World. When I first reached through to it, I thought the Soul of the World was perfect. But later, I could see that it was like other aspects of creation, and had its own passions and wars. It is we who nourish the Soul of the World, and the world we live in will be either better or worse, depending on whether we become better or worse. And, that's where the power of love comes in. Because when we love, we always strive to become better than we are.

Sooner or Later by Anne Cowden

Sooner or later we begin to understand that love is more than verses on valentines, and romance in the movies. We begin to know that love is here and now, real and true, the most important thing in our lives. For love is the creator of our favorite memories and the foundation of our fondest dreams.

Love is a promise that is always kept, a fortune that can never be spent, a seed that can flourish in even the most unlikely of places. And this radiance that never fades, this mysterious and magical joy, is the greatest treasure of all - one known only by those who love.

"Love" by Roy Croft

This is a reading that seems to speak to all couples.
I love you
Not only for what you are,
But for what I am
When I am with you.

I love you,
Not only for what
You have made of yourself,
But for what
You are making of me.

I love you
For the part of me
That you bring out;

I love you
For putting your hand

Into my heaped-up heart
And passing over
All the foolish, weak things
That you can't help
Dimly seeing there,

And for drawing out
Into the light
All the beautiful belongings
That no one else had looked
Quite far enough to find

I love you because you
Are helping me to make
Of the lumber of my life
Not a tavern
But a temple.

Out of the works
Of my every day
Not a reproach
But a song.

I love you
Because you have done
More than any creed
Could have done
To make me good.
And more than any fate
Could have done
To make me happy.

You have done it
Without a touch,
Without a word,
Without a sign.

You have done it
By being yourself.
Perhaps that is what
Being a friend means,
After all.

"i carry your heart with me" by e. e. cummings

i carry your heart with me (i carry it in
my heart) i am never without it (anywhere
i go you go, my dear; and whatever is done
by only me is your doing, my darling)
i fear
no fate (for you are my fate, my sweet) i want
no world (for beautiful, you are my world, my true)
and it's you whatever a moon has always meant
and whatever a sun will always sing is you

here is the deepest secret nobody knows
(here is the root of the root and the bud of the bud
and the sky of the sky of a tree called life; which grows
higher than the soul can hope or mind can hide)
and this is the wonder that's keeping the stars apart

i carry your heart (i carry it in my heart)

"if" by e. e. cummings

if freckles were lovely, and day was night,
and measles were nice and a lie warn't a lie,
life would be delight—
but things couldn't go right
for in such a sad plight
i wouldn't be i.

if earth was heaven and now was hence,
and past was present, and false was true,
there might be some sense
but I'd be in suspense
for on such a pretense
you wouldn't be you.

if fear was plucky, and globes were square,
and dirt was cleanly and tears were glee
things would seem fair,
yet they'd all despair,
for if here was there
we wouldn't be we.

"it is at moments after i have dreamed" by e. e. cummings
it is at moments after i have dreamed
of the rare entertainment of your eyes,
when (being fool to fancy) i have deemed

with your peculiar mouth my heart made wise;
at moments when the glassy darkness holds

the genuine apparition of your smile
(it was through tears always) and silence moulds
such strangeness as was mine a little while;

moments when my once more illustrious arms
are filled with fascination, when my breast
wears the intolerant brightness of your charms:

one pierced moment whiter than the rest

— turning from the tremendous lie of sleep
i watch the roses of the day grow deep

all that is profane becomes sacred again.

Neil deGrasse Tyson

The problem, often not discovered until late in life, is that when you look for things like love, meaning, motivation, it implies they are sitting behind a tree or under a rock. The most successful people recognize that in life they create their own love, they manufacture their own meaning, they generate their own motivation.

"My Sunshine" by Hervé Desbois

When the dawn emerges from the night — it is you I see
When I emerge from the silence of the dark — it is you I see
You are like a river that flows through my dreams
Without you, where would I find light?
When the city veils your smile
It is you I look for
When life batters me and steals my sighs — it is you I look for
You are a fortress that guards and protects me
Without you, where is my shelter, my refuge?
Let me lay down and sleep in the shadow of your eyes
When I am exhausted by the journey of time
As it passes so swiftly and so indifferently
I treasure the sight of the smile on your lips
You are the brilliant light of the sun in my skies
You, my love, my happiness.

Quote by Marguerite de Valois

Love works miracles everyday: such as weakening the strong, and strengthening the weak, making fools of the wise, and wise men of fools; favoring the passions, destroying reason, and, in a word, turning everything topsy-turvy.

Why Marry? By Anita Diamant

Why marry? Because marriage publicly affirms the possibility of moving toward another person without reservation. With that momentum, we are propelled toward the center of the heart, toward the center of the universe, and however far that gets us it's farther than we'd otherwise go alone. Why Marry? Because every wedding enacts a personal connection to the universal story of the human hope for wholeness. Because stepping into the hyperbarically charged space on the altar (in front of the priest, under the canopy), the bride and groom join in a dance that goes all the way back to the beginning of memory.

Getting married is an attempt at turning air into matter, transforming the ineffable workings of the heart into things that are "real:" the invitation, the dress, the ring. The words that constitute a wedding are magical incantations of the highest order. In the presence of witnesses and by a vested authority, two people are pronounced a single unit. Ta-da! Every wedding is an invocation of peace and wholeness and connection and joy. Good wishes flow from family and friends, through history, community, with wings and prayers and everything that might turn out to be holy in the universe.

A Comfortable Couple, from *Nicholas Nickleby* by Charles Dickens

We're too old to be single. Why shouldn't we both be married instead of sitting through the long winter evenings by our solitary fireplaces? Why shouldn't we make one fireplace of it? Come, let's be a comfortable couple and take care of each other! How glad we shall be, that we have somebody we are fond of always, to talk to and sit with. Let's be a comfortable couple. Now do, my dear.

A Reading from *Adam Bede* by George Eliot

What greater thing is there for two human souls than to feel that they are joined for life, to strengthen each other in all labor, to rest on each other in all sorrow, to minister to each other in all pain, to be one with each other in silent unspeakable memories at the moment of the last parting?

Essay "On Love" by Ralph Waldo Emerson

The world rolls; the circumstances vary every hour. The angels that inhabit this temple of the body appear at the windows, and the gnomes and vices also. A man and woman's once flaming regard is sobered by time in either breast, and losing in violence what it gains in extent, it becomes a thorough good understanding.

At last they discover that all which at first drew them together—those once sacred features, that magical play of Charms—was deciduous, had a prospective end, like the scaffolding by which the house was built; and the purification of the intellect and the heart, from year to year, is the real marriage.

Thus are we put in training for a love which knows not sex, nor person, nor partiality, but which seeks virtue and wisdom everywhere? We are by nature observers, and thereby learners. That is our permanent state. But we are often made to feel that our affections are but tents of a night.

There are moments when the affections rule and absorb us, and make our happiness dependent on a person or persons. But the mind is presently seen again – its overarching vault, bright with galaxies of immutable lights, and the warm loves and fears that swept over us as clouds, must lose their finite character and blend with God, to attain their own perfection.

But we need not fear that we can lose any thing by the progress of the soul. The soul may be trusted to the end. That which is so beautiful and attractive, as these relations between lovers must be succeeded and supplanted only by what is more beautiful, and so on forever.

"Everything" by Lifehouse
Find me here, and speak to me
I want to feel you, I need to hear you
You are the light that's leading me to the place
Where I find peace again
You are the strength that keeps me walking
You are the hope that keeps me trusting
You are the life to my soul
You are my purpose
You're everything
And how can I stand here with you
And not be moved by you
Would you tell me how could it be any better than this?

You calm the storms and you give me rest
You hold me in your hands
You won't let me fall
You steal my heart and you take my breath away
Would you take me in, take me deeper now
And how can I stand here with you and not be moved by you
Would you tell me how could it be any better than this
And how can I stand here with you and not be moved by you
Would you tell me how could it be any better than this

Cause you're all I want, you're all I need
You're everything, everything
You're all I want
You're all I need
You're everything, everything
You're all I want
You're all I need
You're everything, everything
You're all I want
You're all I need
Everything, everything

And how can I stand here with you and not be moved by you
Would you tell me how could it be any better than this
And how can I stand here with you and not be moved by you
Would you tell me how could it be any better-any better than this
And how can I stand here with you and not be moved by you
Would you tell me how could it be any better than this
Would you tell me how could it be any better than this

Firefighter's Pledge

I promise concern for others and
a willingness to help all those in need.
I promise courage – courage to face and conquer my fears.

Courage to share and endure the ordeal of those who need me.
I promise strength – strength of heart to bear whatever
Burdens might be placed upon me
Strength of body to deliver to safety all those placed within my care.
I promise the wisdom to lead, the compassion to comfort,
and the love to serve unselfishly whenever I am called.

Blessings for a Marriage by James Dillet Freeman
These are the true vows underlying the words. Wedding vows are not magical oaths. Saying you love, honor and cherish someone doesn't necessarily make it so. Couples have to grow into their vows by intentionally finding ways to turn them into concrete, loving actions. With this commitment to action:

May your marriage bring you all the exquisite excitements a marriage should bring, and may life grant you also patience, tolerance, and understanding. May you always need one another — not so much to fill your emptiness as to help you to know your fullness.

A mountain needs a valley to be complete; the valley does not make the mountain less but more; and the valley is more a valley because it has a mountain towering over it.

So let it be with you and you.

May you need one another, but not out of weakness.
May you want one another, but not out of lack.
May you entice one another, but not compel one another.
May you embrace one another, but not encircle one another.
May you succeed in all important ways with one another,
and not fail in the little graces.
May you look for things to praise, often say, "I love you!"
and take no notice of small faults.

If you have quarrels that push you apart,
May both of you have the good sense enough to take the first step back.

May you enter into the mystery, which is the awareness of one another's presence –
no more physical than spiritual, warm and near when you are side by side,
and warm and near when you are in separate rooms or even distant cities.
May you have happiness, and may you find it making one another happy.
May you have love, and may you find it loving one another!

Thank you, God,
for Your presence here with us
and Your blessing on this marriage.
Amen.

Quote by Robert Frost
Love is the irresistible desire to be irresistibly desired.

All I Ever Really Needed to Know I Learned in Kindergarten by Robert Fulgham
Most of what I really need
To know about how to live
And what to do and how to be
I learned in kindergarten.
Wisdom was not at the top
Of the graduate school mountain,
But there in the sandpile at Sunday school.

These are the things I learned:

Share everything.
Play fair.
Don't hit people.
Put things back where you found them.
Clean up your own mess.
Don't take things that aren't yours.
Say you're sorry when you hurt somebody.
Wash your hands before you eat.
Flush.

Warm cookies and cold milk are good for you.
Live a balanced life—
Learn some and think some
And draw and paint and sing and dance
And play and work everyday some.
Take a nap every afternoon.
When you go out into the world,
Watch out for traffic,
Hold hands and stick together.
Be aware of wonder.

"Let's Call the Whole Thing Off" Song by George and Ira Gershwin
Things have come to a pretty pass
Our romance is growing flat,
For you like this and the other
While I go for this and that, Goodness knows what the end will be
Oh I don't know where I'm at
It looks as if we two will never be one
Something must be done: You say either and I say either,
You say neither and I say neither
Either, either, Neither, neither
Let's call the whole thing off. You like potato and I like potahto
You like tomato and I like tomahto
Potato, potahto, tomato, tomahto.
Let's call the whole thing off. But oh, if we call the whole thing off
Then we must part.
And oh, if we ever part, then that might break my heart. So if you like pajamas
and I like pyjahmas,
I'll wear pajamas and give up pyjamas
For we know we need each other so we
Better call . . . .

Prayer of a Bride and Groom by Clifford Gessler

Let us know how not to ask too much of each other,

Share body and mind and spirit without giving up freedom,

Love without trying to absorb, be kind yet not smother with kindness,

Walk together, but neither retard the others' pace.

I would not lead one who did not choose to follow

Or follow one who demanded that I be led.

That spark of selfhood, that high and precious thing,

Let us not dampen it with scorn or blame;

Each his own master and the two of us richer, dearer because of it,

But neither sunk passively in the other.

That alone is true mating.

From *The Prophet* by Kahlil Gibran

You were born together, and together you shall be forever more.

You shall be together when the white wings of death scatter your days.

Ah, you shall be together even in the silent memory of God.

But let there be spaces in your togetherness,

And let the winds of the heavens dance between you.

Love one another, but make not a bond of love;

Let it rather be a moving sea between the shores of your souls.

Fill each other's cup but drink not from one cup.

Give one another of your bread, but eat not from the same loaf.

Sing and dance together and be joyous, but let each of you be alone,

Even as the strings of a lute are alone, though they quiver with the same music.

Give your hearts, but not into each other's keeping,

For only the hand of Life can contain your hearts.

And stand together, yet not too near together;

For the pillars of the temple stand apart,

And the oak tree and the cypress grow not in each other's shadow.

On Love from *The Prophet* by Kahlil Gibran

When love beckons to you, follow him,
Thought his ways are hard and steep.
And when his wings enfold you yield to him.
Though the sword hidden among his pinions may wound you.
And when he speaks to you believe him,
Though his voice may shatter your dreams as the north
Wind lays waste the garden.
For even as love crowns you so shall he crucify you.
Even as he is for your growth so is he for your pruning.
Even as he ascends to your height and caresses your tender branches that quiver
in the sun, so shall he descend to your roots and shake them in their clinging to
the earth. Like sheaves of corn he gathers you unto himself.

He threshes you to make you naked. He sifts you to free you from your husks.
He grinds you to whiteness. He kneads you until you are pliant;
And then he assigns you to his sacred fire, that you may become sacred bread
for God's sacred feast.
Love gives naught but itself and takes naught but from itself.
Love possesses not nor would it be possessed.
For love is sufficient unto love.

Hawaiian Wedding Song from an Ancient Marriage Prayer

Before we met, you and I were halves unjoined except in the wide rivers of
our minds. We were each other's distant shores, the opposite wings of a bird,
the other half of a seashell. We did not know the other then, did not know our
determination to keep alive the cry of one riverbank to the other. We were apart,
yet connected in our ignorance of each other, like two apples sharing a common
tree. Remember?

I knew you existed long before you understood my desire to join my freedom to
yours. Our paths collided long enough for our indecision to be swallowed up by
the greater need of love. When you came to me, the sun surged towards the earth
and moon escaped from darkness to bless the union of two spirits, so alike that
the creator had designed them for life's endless circle.

Beloved partner, keeper of my heart's odd secrets, clothed in summer blossoms, so the icy hand of winter will never touch us. I thank your patience. Our joining is like a tree to earth, a cloud to sky and even more. We are the reason the world can laugh on its battlefields and rise from the ashes of its selfishness to hear me say, in this time, this place, this way – I loved you best of all.

Quote by Hermann Hesse
Our mind is capable of passing beyond the dividing line we have drawn for it. Beyond the pairs of opposites of which the world consists, other, new insights begin.

Foundations of Marriage by Regina Hill
Love, trust, and forgiveness are the foundations of marriage. In marriage, many days will bring happiness, while other days may be sad. But together, two hearts can overcome everything . . . In marriage, all of the moments won't be exciting or romantic, and sometimes worries and anxiety will be overwhelming. But together, two hearts that accept will find comfort together. Recollections of past joys, pains, and shared feelings will be the glue that holds everything together during even the worst and most insecure moments. Reaching out to each other as a friend, and becoming the confidant and companion that the other one needs, is the true magic and beauty of any two people together. It's inspiring in each other a dream or a feeling, and having faith in each other and not giving up . . . even when all the odds say to quit. It's allowing each other to be vulnerable, to be himself or herself, even when the opinions or thoughts aren't in total agreement or exactly what you'd like them to be. It's getting involved and showing interest in each other, really listening and being available, the way any best friend should be. Exactly three things need to be remembered in a marriage if it is to be a mutual bond of sharing, caring, and loving throughout life: love, trust, and forgiveness.

"Summer Poem" by Heather Holden
I will bring you flowers
Every morning for your breakfast
And you will kiss me
With flowers in your mouth

And you will bring me flowers
Every morning when you wake
And look at me with flowers in your eyes

"A Poem for a Sister" by Larry Howland

I think of all the things we shared when we were small children.
I close my eyes and travel back and still can see it all.
Although, it was so long ago. It seems like yesterday.
I sometimes wish those childhood days had never gone away.
The closeness only sisters know is etched in both our hearts.
And may your hopes and dreams come true as your new marriage starts.

Loving Tenderly by Rosemary Hyde

I've called you, dear,
Loved you since the world took shape –
Loved your exotic bloom, your heady fragrance and spirit essence.
You are my special blossom,
That I've nurtured, held gently within my heart;
I've known you unutterably beautiful – so sweet, so tender,
An extravagantly blooming love,
All fragrant petals, wondrous shapes and colors unbeknown to others
Before they fell in love with you.
I want to see you loved by all, radiating Spirit essence all around you where you're planted.
Last night was time.
I took you with me, cherished you, blew into you my Spirit,
Guided you in transformation, creating from you a whole garden.
I called you as my gardener.
I bade you walk into the world, to cultivate and love
All flowers that you meet, making other gardens for my glory.

Irish Blessings

May the road rise to meet you.
May the wind be always at your back.

May the sun shine warm upon your face, and the rains fall soft upon your field.
May the light of friendship guide your paths together.
May the laughter of children grace the halls of your home.

May the joy of living for one another trip a smile from your lips, a twinkle from your eyes.
And, when eternity beckons, at the end of a life heaped high with love,
May the good Lord embrace you with the arms that have nurtured you the whole length of your
joy-filled days.
May the gracious God hold you both in the palm of his hand.
And today may the spirit of love find a dwelling place in your hearts.

May flowers always line your path and sunshine light your day
May song birds serenade you every step along the way.
May a rainbow run beside you in a sky that's always blue,
And may happiness fill your heart each day, your whole life through.

Quote by Franklin P. Jones
Love doesn't make the world go round. Love is what makes the ride worthwhile.

The Committed Marriage by Esther Jungreis
Under the *chuppah* (marriage canopy) we pronounce a special blessing that renders the couple loving, kind friends, always at each other's side, always encouraging each other, and when necessary, criticizing and gently showing where the other erred. God has endowed each of us with unique gifts. When our mates become our best friends, we pool our spiritual resources and strengthen each other. In such a relationship, life's trials become less threatening, and even the most formidable challenges become manageable. "Two are better than one" is the wise teaching of King Solomon. If one falls, the other is there to pick him/her up. If one is attacked, the other is there to rescue him; if one is depressed, the other is there to buoy her spirits.

Quote by Sonam Kapoor

Opposites generally create intense chemistry. There are more chances of fireworks when different people are together than similar personalities.

Love is a Great Thing by Thomas A Kempis

Love is a great thing, a great good in every way; it alone lightens what is heavy, and leads smoothly over all roughness. For it carries a burden without being burdened. And makes every bitter thing sweet and tasty. Love wants to be lifted up, not held back by anything low. Love wants to be free, and far from all worldly desires, so that its inner vision may not be dimmed and good fortune bind it or misfortune cast it down. Nothing is sweeter than love; nothing stronger, nothing higher, nothing wider; nothing happier, nothing fuller, nothing better in heaven and earth; for love is born of God . . . .

Love keeps watch and is never unaware, even when it sleeps; tired, it is never exhausted; hindered, it is never defeated; alarmed, it is never afraid; but like a living flame and a burning torch it bursts upward and blazes forth . . . Love is quick, sincere, dutiful, joyous, and pleasant; brave, patient, faithful, prudent, serene, and vigorous; and it never seeks itself. For whenever we seek ourselves, we fall away from love. Love is watchful, humble, and upright; not weak, or frivolous, or directed toward vain things; temperate, pure, steady, calm, and alert in all the senses. Love is devoted and thankful to God, always trusting and hoping in him, even when it doesn't taste his sweetness, for without pain no one can live in love.

Quote from House of Aegea by Diana Lanham

The universe maintained a balance, moving first one way and then the other in a forever equalizing of opposites.

From *The Irrational Season* by Madeleine L'Engle

Ultimately there comes a time when a decision must be made. Ultimately two people who love each other must ask themselves how much they hope for as their love grows and deepens, and how much risk they are willing to take. It is indeed a fearful gamble. Because it is the nature of love to create, a marriage itself is something, which has to be created. To marry is the biggest risk in human relations that a person can take. If we commit ourselves to one person for life this is not, as many people think, a rejection of freedom; rather it demands the courage to move into all the risks of freedom, and the risk of love which is permanent; into that love which is not possession, but participation. It takes a lifetime to learn about another person. When love is not possession, but participation, then it is part of that co-creation which is our human calling.

Gift from the Sea by Anne Morrow Lindbergh

When you love someone you do not love them all the time, in exactly the same way, from moment to moment. It is impossibility. It is even a lie to pretend to. And, yet this is exactly what most of us demand. We have so little faith in the ebb and flow of life, of love, of relationships. We leap at the flow of the tide and resist in terror its ebb. We are afraid it will never return. We insist on permanency, on duration, on continuity; when the only continuity possible, in life as in love, is in growth, in fluidity – in freedom, in the sense that the dancers are free, barely touching as they pass, but partners in the same pattern. The only real security is not in owning or possessing, not in demanding or expecting, not in hoping, even. Security in a relationship lies neither in looking back to what was in nostalgia, nor forward to what it might be in dread or anticipation, but living in present relationship and accepting it as it is now.

For relationships, too, must be like islands, one must accept them for what they are here and now, within their limits — islands surrounded by and interrupted by the sea, and continually visited and abandoned by the tides. One must accept the security of the winged life, of intermittency.

Gift from the Sea by Anne Morrow Lindbergh

A good relationship has a pattern like dance. The partners do not need to hold on tightly, because they move confidently in the same pattern, intricate, but swift and free. There is no place here for the possessive clutch, the clinging arm, the heavy hand. Because they know they are partners, moving to the same rhythm, creating a pattern together, and being invisibly nourished by it. The joy of such a pattern is not only the joy of creation, or the joy of participation, it is also the joy of living in the moment. One cannot dance well unless one is completely in time with the music, not leaning back to the last step, or pressing forward to the next one, but poised directly on the present step as it comes. But how does one learn this technique of the dance?

Why is it so difficult? What makes us hesitate and stumble? It is fear, I think, that makes one cling nostalgically to the last moment, or clutch greedily toward the next. Fear can only be exorcised by its opposite . . . love. When the heart is flooded with love there is no room in it for fear, for doubt, for hesitation. And it is this lack of fear that makes for the dance. The partners only know that they love, and are moving to its music.

Lutheran Thought
The union of two persons in heart, body, and mind is intended by God for their mutual (good), for the help and comfort given one another in prosperity and adversity; and that their love may be a blessing to all whom they encounter. This solemn covenant is not to be entered into unadvisedly or lightly, but reverently, deliberately, and with commitment to seek God's will for their lives.

A Lasting Marriage by Michael C. Mack
A close relationship is based on friendship.
A caring relationship is based on sharing and understanding.
A romantic relationship is based on giving freely and on the ability to receive gratefully and graciously.
An intimate relationship is based on openness and honesty.
An affectionate relationship is based on patience and acceptance.
A secure relationship is based not on promise, but rather on trust, respect, faithfulness, and the ability to forgive.
A lasting marriage is based on all of these, bound together by love.

Quote by Marc Maihueird
Love is what we call the situation, which occurs when two people who are sexually compatible discover that they can also tolerate one another in various other circumstances.

"Outwitted" by Edwin Markham

Excerpt

He drew a circle that shut me out –
Heretic, rebel, a thing to flout.
But love and I had the wit to win
We drew a circle and took him in!

"The Passionate Shepherd to His Love" by Christopher Marlowe

Come live with me and be my love,
And we will all the pleasures prove,
That valleys, groves, hills, and fields,
Woods, or steepy mountain yields.
And we will sit upon the rocks,
Seeing the shepherds feed their flocks,
By shallow rivers, to whose falls
Melodious birds sing madrigals.

And I will make thee beds of roses,
And a thousand fragrant posies,
A cap of flowers and a kirtle
Embroidered all with leaves of myrtle:
A gown made of the finest wool,
Which from our pretty lambs we pull;
Fair lined slippers for the cold,
With buckles of the purest gold:
A belt of straw and ivy buds,
With coral clasps and amber studs;
And if these pleasures may thee move,
Come live with me and be my love.
The shepherd swains shall dance and sing
For thy delight each May morning;
If these delights thy mind may move,
Then live with me and be my love.

I can walk with you beside;
Furthermore, I tell you what,
I sit and sulk where you are not.
Visitors remark my frown
When you're upstairs and I am down,
Yes, and I'm afraid I pout
When I'm indoors and you are out.
In fact I care not where you be,
Just as long as it's with me.
In all your absence I glimpse
Fire and flood and trolls and imps.
Is your train a minute slothful?
I goad the stationmaster wrathful.
When with friends to bridge you drive I never know if you're alive,
And when you linger late in shops
I long to telephone the cops. Yet how worth the waiting for,
To see you coming through the door.
Somehow, I can be complacent
Never but with you adjacent.
Near and far, near and far,
I am happy where you are;
Likewise, I have never learnt
How to be it where you aren't.
Then grudge me not for fond endeavor,
To hold you in my sight forever;
Let none, not even you, disparage
Such valid reason for a marriage

Another Excerpt from the Decision: MA Chief Justice Margaret H. Marshall
Marriage also bestows enormous private and social advantages on those who choose to marry. Civil marriage is at once a deeply personal commitment to another human being and a highly public celebration of the ideals of mutuality,

companionship, intimacy, fidelity, and family. "It is an association that promotes a way of life, not causes; a harmony in living, not political faiths; a bilateral loyalty, not commercial or social projects." Griswold v. Connecticut, 381 U.S. 479, 486 (1965). Because it fulfills yearnings for security, safe haven, and connection that express our common humanity, civil marriage is an esteemed institution, and the decision whether and whom to marry is among life's momentous acts of self-definition . . . Love is the 'why' of life: why we are functioning at all, what we want to be efficient for . . . I am convinced it [love] is the fundamental energy of the human spirit, the fuel on which we run, the wellspring of our vitality. And grace, which is the flowing, creative activity of love itself, is what makes all goodness possible. Love should come first; it should be the beginning of and the reason for everything.

Massachusetts Court Decision - 11/2003: MA Chief Justice Margaret H. Marshall

Marriage is a vital social institution. The exclusive commitment of two individuals to each other nurtures love and mutual support; it brings stability to our society. Marriage provides an abundance of legal, financial, and social benefits. In return it imposes weighty legal, financial, and social obligations . . . A civil marriage enhances the "welfare of the community." It is a social institution of the highest importance . . . Civil marriage is at once a deeply personal commitment to another human being and a highly public celebration of the ideals of mutuality, companionship, intimacy, fidelity, and family . . . The decision whether and whom to marry is among life's momentous acts of self-definition.

The Awakened Heart by Gerald G. May

There is a desire within each of us, in the deep center of ourselves that we call our heart. We were born with it, it is never completely satisfied, and it never dies. We are often unaware of it, but it is always awake. It is the human desire for love. Every person on this earth yearns to love, to be loved, to know love. Our true identity, our reason for being, is to be found in this desire. . . .

Quote by Tracy McMillan

I think of masculine and feminine energy like two sides to a battery. There's a plus side and a minus side, and in order to make something turn on, you need to have opposites touching. It's the same in relationships.

Quote by Henry Louis Mencken

Love is the triumph of imagination over intelligence.
Love isn't perfect, love is just love.

"Two Trees" by Janet Miles

A couple that lives in the countryside chose this reading.
A portion of your soul has been entwined with mine.
A gentle kind of togetherness, while, separate we stand.
As two trees deeply rooted in separate plots of ground,
While their topmost branches come together,
Forming a miracle of lace against the heavens.

Quote by Ram Mohan

Two people of similar nature can never get along; it takes two opposites to harmonize.

A Lovely Love Story by Edward Monkton

The fierce Dinosaur was trapped inside his cage of ice. Although it was cold he was happy in there. It was, after all, his cage. Then along came the Lovely Other Dinosaur. The Lovely Other Dinosaur melted the Dinosaur's cage with kind words and loving thoughts. I like this Dinosaur thought the Lovely Other Dinosaur. Although he is fierce he is also tender and he is funny. He is also quite clever though I will not tell him this for now. I like this Lovely Other Dinosaur, thought the Dinosaur. She is beautiful and she is different and she smells so nice. She is also a free spirit, which is a quality I much admire in a dinosaur. But he can be so distant and so peculiar at times, thought the Lovely Other Dinosaur. He is also overly fond of things. Are all Dinosaurs so overly fond of things? But her mind skips from here to there so quickly thought the Dinosaur.

She is also uncommonly keen on shopping. Are all Lovely Other Dinosaurs so uncommonly keen on shopping? I will forgive his peculiarity and his concern for things, thought the Lovely Other Dinosaur. For they are part of what makes him a richly charactered individual.

I will forgive her skipping mind and her fondness for shopping, thought the Dinosaur for she fills our life with beautiful thoughts and wonderful surprises. Besides, I am not unkeen on shopping either. Now the Dinosaur and the Lovely Other Dinosaur are old. Look at them. Together they stand on the hill telling each other stories and feeling the warmth of the sun on their backs. And that, my friends, is how it is with love. Let us all be Dinosaurs and Lovely Other Dinosaurs together. For the sun is warm. And the world is a beautiful place

"The Elric Saga Part I" by Michael Moorcock

Elric knew that everything that existed had its opposite. In danger he might find peace. And yet, of course, in peace there was danger. Being an imperfect creature in an imperfect world he would always know paradox. And that was why in paradox there was always a kind of truth. That was why philosophers and soothsayers flourished. In a perfect world there would be no place for them. In an imperfect world the mysteries were always without solution and that was why there was always a great choice of solutions.

"The Confirmation" by Edwin Muir

Yes, yours, my love, is the right human face.
I, in my mind, had waited for this long,
Seeing the false and searching for the true,
Then found you as a traveler finds a place
Of welcome suddenly amid the wrong
Valleys and rocks and twisting roads.
But you, what shall I call you? A fountain in a waste,
A well of water in a country dry,
Or anything that's honest and good, an eye
That makes the whole world bright. Your open heart, Simple with giving, gives
   the primal deed,

The first good world, the blossom, the blowing seed, The hearth, the steadfast land, the wandering sea. Not beautiful or rare in every part.

"Tin Wedding Whistle" by Ogden Nash
Though you know it anyhow
Listen to, darling, now,
Proving what I need not prove
How I know
I love you, love. Near and far, near and far,
I am happy where you are;

Likewise I have never learnt
How to be where you aren't. Far and wide, far and wide,

And overhead, a plane
Sing songs coming down.
Nothing is changed, except
There was a moment when
The wolf, the mongering wolf
Who stands outside the self
Lay lightly down, and slept.

Native American Water Blessing
God in heaven above
please protect the ones we love.
We honor all you created as we pledge
our hearts and lives together.
We honor mother-earth
We honor water to clean and soothe our relationship
that it may never thirst for love.

Navajo, "I Walk with Beauty"
With your feet I walk
I walk with your limbs

I carry forth your body
For me your mind thinks
Your voice speaks for me
Beauty is before me
And beauty is behind me
Above and below me hovers the beautiful
I am surrounded by it
I am immersed in it
In my youth I am aware of it
And in old age I shall walk quietly
The beautiful trail.

"In My Sky at Twilight" by Pablo Neruda
You are taken in the net of my music, my love and my nets of music are as wide as the sky.

My soul is born on the shore of your eyes of mourning. In your eyes of mourning the land of dreams begins.

Quote from Pablo Neruda
To feel the love of people whom we love is a fire that feeds our life.

"Sonnet XII" by Pablo Neruda
Loving is a journey with water and with stars,
With smothered air and abrupt storms of flour:
Loving is a clash of lightning bolts
And two bodies defeated by a single drop of honey.
Kiss by kiss move across your small infinity,
Your borders, your rivers, your tiny villages,
And the gentile fire transformed into delight
Runs through the narrow pathways of the blood
Until it plunges, like a dark carnation,
Until it is and is no more than a flash in the night.

"Sonnet XVII" by Pablo Neruda

I don't love you as if you were the salt-rose, topaz or arrow of carnations that
propagate fire:
I love you as certain dark things are loved, secretly, between the shadow and the
soul.

I love you as the plant that doesn't bloom and carries hidden within itself the
light of those flowers,
and thanks to your love, darkly in my body
lives the dense fragrance that rises from the earth.
I love you without knowing how, or when, or from where, I love you simply,
without problems or pride:
I love you in this way because I know no other way of loving but this, in which
there is no I or you,
so intimate that your hand upon my chest is my hand,
so intimate that when I fall asleep it is your eyes that close.

"Sonnet XLVIII" by Pablo Neruda

Two happy lovers make one single bread,
One single drop of moonlight in the grass.
When they walk, the leave two shadows that merge,
And they leave one single sun blazing in their bed.

"Why Marriage?" By Mari Nichols-Hailing

Because to the depths of me, I long to love one person,
With all my heart, my soul, my mind my body . . .
Because I need a forever friend to trust with the intimacies of me,
Who won't hold them against me, who loves me when I'm unlikable,
Who sees the small child in me, and who looks for the divine potential of me ...
Because I need to cuddle in the warmth of the night
With someone who thanks God for me,
With someone I feel blessed to hold . . .
Because marriage means opportunity to grow in love and friendship . . .

Because marriage is a discipline to be added to a list of achievements . . .
Because marriages do not fail, people fail
When they enter into marriage expecting another to make them whole . . .
Because knowing this, I promise myself to take full responsibility
For my spiritual, mental and physical wholeness,
I create me; I take half of the responsibility for my marriage
Together we create our marriage . . .
Because with this understanding the possibilities are limitless

"Creating a Home Together" by Henri Nouwen

Many human relationships are like the interlocking fingers of two hands . . . Human relationships are meant to be like two hands folded together. They can move away from each other while still touching with the fingertips. They can create space between themselves, a little tent, a home, a safe place to be . . . True relationships among people point to God. They are like prayers in the world. Sometimes the hands that pray are fully touching, sometimes there is distance between them. They always move to and from each other, but they never lose touch. They keep praying to the One who brought them together.

Anam Cara: A Book of Celtic Wisdom by John O'Donohue

Love allows understanding to dawn, and understanding is precious. Where you are understood, you are at home. Understanding nourishes belonging. When you really feel understood, you feel free to release yourself into the trust and shelter of the other person's soul.

Annam Cara: A Book of Celtic Wisdom by John O'Donohue

When love awakens in your life, in the night of your heart, it is like the dawn breaking within you. Where before there was anonymity, now there is intimacy; where before there was fear, now there is courage; where before in your life there was awkwardness, now there is a rhythm of grace and gracefulness; where before you used to be jagged, now you are elegant and in rhythm with your self. When love awakens in your life, it is like a rebirth, a new beginning.

"For Marriage," from *To Bless the Space Between Us* by John O'Donohue
As spring unfolds the dream of the earth,
May you bring each other's hearts to birth.

As the ocean finds calm in the view of land
May you love the gaze of each other's mind.

As the wind arises free and wild,
May nothing negative control your lives.

As kindly as moonlight might search the dark,
So gentle may you be when light grows scarce.

As surprised as the silence that music opens,
May your words for each other be touched with reverence.

As warmly as the air draws in the light,
May you welcome each other's every gift.

As elegant as dreams absorbing the night,
May sleep find you clear of anger and hurt.

And as twilight harvests the day's colors,
May love bring you home to each other.

"Of Love" by Mary Oliver
I have been in love more times than one,
thank the Lord. Sometimes it was lasting
whether active or not. Sometimes
it was all but ephemeral, maybe only
an afternoon, but not less real for that.
They stay in my mind, these beautiful people,
or anyway beautiful people to me, of which
there are so many. You, and you, and you,
whom I had the fortune to meet, or maybe
missed. Love, love, love, it was the
core of my life, from which, of course, comes

the word for the heart. And, oh, have I mentioned
that some of them were men and some were women
and some—now carry my revelation with you—
were trees. Or places. Or music flying above
the names of their makers. Or clouds, or the sun
which was the first, and the best, the most
loyal for certain, who looked so faithfully into
my eyes, every morning. So I imagine
such love of the world—its fervency, its shining,
its innocence and hunger to give of itself—I imagine
this is how it began.

"On Your Wedding Day," Author Unknown
Today is the day you will always remember,
The greatest in anyone's life.
You'll start off the day just two people in love
And end it as husband and wife.
It's a brand new beginning, the start of a journey,
With moments to cherish and treasure.
And although there'll be times when you both disagree,
These will surely be outweighed by pleasure.
You'll have heard many words of advice in the past,
When the secrets of marriage were spoken,
But you know that the answers lie hidden inside,
Where the bond of true love lies unbroken.
So live happy forever, as lovers and friends,
It's the dawn of a new life for you,
As you stand there together with love in your eyes,
From the moment you whisper "I do".
And with luck, all your hopes and your dreams can be real,
May success find its way to your hearts.
Tomorrow can bring you the greatest of joys,
But today is the day it all starts.

"Marriage Joins Two People in the Circle of Its Love" by Edmund O'Neill

Marriage is a commitment to life, the best that two people can find and bring out in each other. It offers opportunities for sharing and growth that no other relationship can equal. It is a physical and an emotional joining that is promised for a lifetime.

Within the circle of its love, marriage encompasses all of life's most important relationships. A wife and a husband are each other's best friend, confidant, lover, teacher, listener, and critic. And there may come times when one partner is heartbroken or ailing, and the love of the other may resemble the tender caring of a parent for a child.

Marriage deepens and enriches every facet of life. Happiness is fuller, memories are fresher, commitment is stronger, even anger is felt more strongly, and passes away more quickly. Marriage understands and forgives the mistakes life is unable to avoid. It encourages and nurtures new life, new experiences, and new ways of expressing a love that is deeper than life.

When two people pledge their love and care for each other in marriage, they create a spirit unique unto themselves, which binds them closer than any spoken or written words. Marriage is a promise, a potential made in the hearts of two people who love each other and takes a lifetime to fulfill.

"A Prayer for a Wedding" by Joel Oppenheimer

Because everyone knows exactly what's good for another
Because very few see
Because a man and a woman may just possibly look at each other
Because a man or a woman can do anything he or she pleases
Because you can reach any point in your life saying: now, I want this
Because eventually it occurs we want each other,
we want to know each other, even stupidly, even ugly
Because there is at best a simple need in two people to try and reach some
simple ground
Because that simple ground is not so simple
Because we are human beings gathered together whether we like it or not

Because we are human beings reaching out to touch
Because sometimes we grow
We ask a blessing on this marriage
We ask that some simplicity be allowed
We ask their happiness
We ask that this couple be known for what it is and that the light shine upon it.
We ask a blessing for their marriage.

"The Art of a Good Marriage" by Wilfred Arlan Peterson
Happiness in marriage is not something that just happens.
A good marriage must be created.
In the art of marriage the little things are the big things . . . .
It is never being too old to hold hands.
It is remembering to say "I love you" at least once a day.
It is never going to sleep angry.
It is at no time taking the other for granted;
the courtship should not end with the honeymoon,
it should continue through all the years.
It is having a mutual sense of values and common objectives.
It is standing together facing the world.
It is forming a circle of love that gathers in the whole family.

It is doing things for each other, not in the attitude
of duty or sacrifice, but in the spirit of joy.
It is speaking words of appreciation
and demonstrating gratitude in thoughtful ways.
It is not looking for perfection in each other.
It is cultivating flexibility, patience,
understanding and a sense of humor.
It is having the capacity to forgive and forget.
It is giving each other an atmosphere in which each can grow.
It is finding room for the things of the spirit.
It is a common search for the good and the beautiful.
It is establishing a relationship in which the independence is equal,

dependence is mutual and the obligation is reciprocal.

It is not only marrying the right partner; it is being the right partner.

It is discovering what marriage can be, at its best.

Letter to His Wife by Tim Pratt

Adapted

If starship travel from our Earth to some far star and back again at velocities approaching the speed of light made you younger than me due to the relativistic effects of time dilation, I'd show up on your doorstep hoping you'd developed a thing for older men, and I'd ask you to show me everything you learned to pass the time out there in the endless void of night.

If I had a time machine, I'd go back to the days of your youth to see how you became the someone I love so much today, and then I'd return to the moment we first met at (Mead Hall) just so I could see my own face when I saw your face for the first time. If I became lost in the multiverse, exploring infinite parallel dimensions, my only criterion for settling down somewhere would be whether or not I could find you, and once I did, I'd stay there even if it was a world ruled by Rodents Of Unusual Size (ROUSs), or one where killer robots won the Civil War, or even a world where sandwiches were never invented, because you'd make it the best of all possible worlds anyway, and plus we could get rich off inventing sandwiches.

If the Singularity comes and we upload our minds into a vast computer simulation of near-infinite complexity and perfect resolution, and become capable of experiencing any fantasy, exploring worlds bound only by our enhanced imaginations, I'd still spend at least 1021 processing cycles a month just sitting on a virtual couch with you, watching virtual TV (*30 Rock* and virtual *Simpsons*), eating virtual sandwiches, holding virtual hands, and wishing for the real thing.

"Wedding Poem" by Steven Ratiner

Yes is at the heart of it —
no matter the words you say or how you say them;
no matter the sign you make —
cross, star, crescent moon, candle flame —
sprinkled over bowed heads

or angled into eyes turned skyward,
it is Yes all the same, even if
he simply holds her hand in silence.

It is Yes when they walk down a line
between family and friends,
the nervous fathers breathing slowly,
the mothers' glossy eyes flying backward through time
to their own solemn aisles.

Yes, the wedding clasp, the braided fingers,
the trust beyond the grasp of reason,
the lover's voice more familiar each day.
Yes, to his secret smile, watching her in the morning as she sleeps.
And Yes to that touch of protection
when she takes his arm and tells him with her eyes,
"Yes, always Yes."

When the guests have gone,
when the family and friends have traveled to their homes
and the clamor of celebration has become
the crystal of quiet days,
when the husband and wife stop to look back —
one or ten or fifty years after today —
and still find in each other's look
the beginning of home, knowing
someone else's life as you know your own —

we won't be surprised if they remember this gathering,
this single arching assent we lifted up about us all,
An unbound unspoken praying.

And Yes, Yes, for the promise, for the word —
said, not because we have to,
but because we take such lasting pleasure
in the saying.

"That's How Strong My Love Is" by Otis Redding

If I was the sun way up there
I'd go with love most everywhere
I'll be the moon when the sun goes down
Just to let you know that I'm still around

That's how strong my love is, oh
That's how strong my love is,
That's how strong my love is, baby, baby,
That's how strong my love is.

I'll be the weeping willow drowning in my tears
You can go swimming when you're here
I'll be the rainbow when the sun is gone
Wrap you in my colors and keep you warm

That's how strong my love is, darling,
That's how strong my love is, baby,
That's how strong my love is, oooh,
That's how strong my love is.

I'll be the ocean so deep and wide
I'll get out the tears whenever you cry,
I'll be the breeze after the storm is gone
To dry your eyes and love you warm

That's how strong my love is, baby,
That's how strong my love is,
That's how strong my love is, darling,
That's how strong my love is,

That's how strong my love is, so deep in,
Well, that's how strong my love is
So much love, yes so much love, oooh,
Yes so much love, yes so much love,
Anything that I can do, I'll be good for you,
Any kind of love you want, I'll be with you . . . .

Rainer Maria Rilke

Understand, I'll slip quietly away from the noisy crowd
When I see the pale stars rising, blooming over the oaks.
I'll pursue solitary pathways through the pale twilit meadows,
With only this one dream:
You come too.

Quote by Rainer Maria Rilke

Love consists in this, that two solitudes protect and border and salute each other.

From *Letters to a Young Poet* by Rainer Maria Rilke

Marriage is in many ways a simplification of life, and it naturally combines the strengths and wills of two young people so that, together, they seem to reach farther into the future than they did before. Above all, marriage is a new task and a new seriousness – a new demand on the strength and generosity of each partner.

The point of marriage is not to create a quick commonality by tearing down all boundaries; on the contrary, a good marriage is one in which each partner appoints the other to be the guardian of their solitude, and thus they show each other the greatest possible trust. A merging of two people is an impossibility, and where it seems to exist, it is a hemming-in, a mutual consent that robs one party or both parties of their fullest freedom and development. But once the realization is accepted that even between the closest people infinite distances exist, a marvelous living side by side can grow up for them, if they succeed in loving the expanse between them, which gives them the possibility of always seeing each other as a whole and before an immense sky.

Life is self-transformation, and human relationships, which are an extract of life, are the most changeable of all, they rise and fall from minute to minute, and lovers are those for whom no moment is like any another. People between whom nothing habitual ever takes place, nothing that has already existed, but just what is new, unexpected, unprecedented. There are such connections, which must be a very great, an almost unbearable happiness, but they can occur only between very rich beings, between those who have become, each for his own sake, rich, calm, and concentrated; only if two worlds are wide and deep and individual can they be combined.

From *Letters to a Young Poet* by Rainer Maria Rilke
For one human being to love another human being: that is perhaps the most difficult task that has ever been entrusted to us, the ultimate task, the final test and proof, the work for which all other work is merely preparation . . . Loving does not at first mean merging, surrendering, and uniting with another person . . . it is a high inducement for the individual to ripen, to become something in himself, to become world, to become world in himself for the sake of another person; it is a great, demanding claim on him, something that chooses him and calls him to vast distances.

"A Birthday" by Christina Rossetti
My heart is like a singing bird
    Whose nest is in a water'd shoot;
My heart is like an apple-tree
    Whose boughs are bent with thickset fruit;
My heart is like a rainbow shell
    That paddles in a halcyon sea;
My heart is gladder than all these
    Because my love is come to me.

Raise me a dais of silk and down;
    Hang it with vair and purple dyes;
Carve it in doves and pomegranates,
    And peacocks with a hundred eyes;
Work it in gold and silver grapes,
    In leaves and silver fleurs-de-lys;
Because the birthday of my life
    Is come, my love is come to me.

"I Love my Friends" by Jalaluddin Rumi
I love my friends neither with

my heart nor with my mind.
Just in case heart might stop, mind can forget.
I love them with my soul. Soul never stops or forgets.

"O Love" by Jalaluddin Rumi (translation: Coleman Barks)
O love, O pure deep love, be here, be now,
Be all—worlds dissolve into your stainless endless radiance,
Frail living leaves burn with you brighter than cold stars—
Make me your servant, your breath, your core.

The minute I heard my first love story
I started looking for you, not knowing
how blind that was.
Lovers don't finally meet somewhere.
They're in each other all along.

When I am with you, we stay up all night.
When you're not here, I can't go to sleep.
Praise God for these two insomnias!
And the difference between them.

"O Love" by Jalaluddin Rumi (translation: Coleman Barks)
This is an appealing reading to highly romantic couples that prefer fewer words.

The minute I heard my first love story
I started looking for you, not knowing
how blind that was.
Lovers don't finally meet somewhere.
They're in each other all along.

"Faithful Star" by Sabri
Once I looked up to the sky
in the night and I saw
bright star sparkling there
in the darkness of the night

and I said who are you?
what are you doing over there
tell me please,
tell me who put you over there
she looked down at me
with a smile on her face
like a rose in the shadow of the bush
little one don't you know?
why it is that I am standing over here?
it is Allah who made me
and made you and the earth
then I said pretty one
tell me please tell me how
how to be just like you
very pure, very high, very nice
once again pretty face shined again
little one listen well
little one take good care . . . .

"Come to the Heart" by Alaya Samadhi
Come to the Heart
In simple light
come to the heart.
We have walked in eons of seemingness . . .
Come to the heart

We have huddled, weaving our philosophies
Come to the Heart
We tracked the beast and named it love
Come to the Heart
The heart is all and you come in simple light.
And there you always were, and never other than that
Come to the Heart

And you come when all else has departed
When hail and farewell dissolve in abiding love
Come to the Heart
Come to where you always were
from where you never left
Come to the Heart

Though the path has seemed endless
Not one real step, has moved along its way
Come to Heart
Journeys without end only seemed so
And you and I are the journey
That only seemed so
Come to Heart

I Heart You, You Haunt Me by Lisa Schroder

When you meet someone so different from yourself, in a good way, you don't even have to kiss to have fireworks go off. It's like fireworks in your heart all the time. I always wondered, do opposites really attract? Now I know for sure they do. I'd grown up going to the library as often as most people go to the grocery store. Jackson didn't need to read about exciting people or places. He went out and found them, or created excitement himself if there wasn't any to be found. The things I like are pretty simple.

Burning CDs around themes, like Songs to Get Your Groove On and Tunes to Fix a Broken Heart; watching movies; baking cookies; and swimming. It's like I was a salad with a light vinaigrette, and Jackson was a platter of seafood Cajun pasta. Alone, we were good. Together, we were fantastic.

"Love Is" by Susan Polis Schutz

Love is
    being happy for the other person
    when that person is happy
    being sad for the other person

when that person is sad
being together in good times
and being together in bad times
Love is the source of strength

Love is
being honest with yourself at all times
being honest with the other person at all times
telling, listening, respecting the truth
and never pretending
Love is the source of reality

Love is
an understanding that is so complete that
you feel as if you are a part
of the other person
accepting the other person
just the way he or she is
and not trying to change each other
to be something else
Love is the source of unity

Love is
the freedom to pursue your own desires
while sharing your experiences
with the other person
the growth of one individual alongside of
and together with the growth
of another individual
Love is the source of success

Love is
the excitement of planning things together
the excitement of doing things together
Love is the source of the future

Love is
> the fury of the storm
> the calm in the rainbow

Love is the source of passion

Love is
> giving and taking in a daily situation
> being patient with each other's
> needs and desires

Love is the source of sharing

Love is
> knowing that the other person
> will always be with you
> regardless of what happens
> missing the other person when he or she is away
> but remaining near in heart at all times

Love is the source of security

Love is the source of life

Sonnet 18 by William Shakespeare

Shall I compare thee to a summer's day?
Thou art more lovely and more temperate:
Rough winds do shake the darling buds of May,
And summer's lease hath all too short a date:
Sometime too hot the eye of heaven shines,
And often is his gold complexion dimm'd;
And every fair from fair sometime declines,
By chance, or nature's changing course, untrimm'd;
But thy eternal summer shall not fade,
Nor lose possession of that fair thou ow'st;
Nor shall death brag thou wander'st in his shade,
When in eternal lines to time thou grow'st;
So long as men can breathe or eyes can see,
So long lives this, and this gives life to thee.

Sonnet 47 by William Shakespeare
Betwixt mine eye and heart a league is took,
And each doth good turns now unto the other:
When that mine eye is famish'd for a look,
Or heart in love with sighs himself doth smother,
With my love's picture then my eye doth feast,
And to the painted banquet bids my heart;
Another time mine eye is my heart's guest
And in his thoughts of love doth share a part:
So, either by thy picture or my love,
Thyself away art resent still with me;
For thou not farther than my thoughts canst move,
And I am still with them and they with thee;
Or, if they sleep, thy picture in my sight,
Awakes my heart to heart's and eye's delight.

Sonnet 116 by William Shakespeare
Let me not to the marriage of true minds
Admit impediments. Love is not love
Which alters when it alteration finds,
Or bends with the remover to remove.
O no; it is an ever-fixed mark,
That looks on tempests, and is never shaken;
It is the star to every wand'ring bark,
Whose worth's unknown, although his height be taken.
Love's not Time's fool, though rosy lips and cheeks
Within his bending sickle's compass come;
Love alters not with his brief hours and weeks,
But bears it out even to the edge of doom.
If this be error and upon me prov'd,
I never writ, nor no man ever loved.

Quote by William Shakespeare
Love looks not with the eye, but with the mind, and therefore is winged Cupid painted blind.

"Love's Philosophy" by Percy Bysshe Shelley
The fountains mingle with the river
And the rivers with the ocean,
The winds of heaven mix forever
With a sweet emotion;
Nothing in the world is single;
All things by a law divine
In one spirit meet and mingle.
Why not I with thine?—
See the mountains kiss high heaven
And the waves clasp one another;
No sister-flower would be forgiven
If it disdained its brother,
And the sunlight clasps the earth
And the moonbeams kiss the sea:
What is all this sweet work worth
If thou kiss not me?

"The Gift" by Hafiz Shirazi
Our union is like this:
You feel cold so I reach for a blanket to cover our shivering feet.
A hunger comes into your body so I run to my garden and start digging potatoes.
You ask for a few words of comfort and guidance,
I quickly kneel at your side offering you a whole book as a gift.
You ache with loneliness one night
So much you weep
and I say, "Here's a rope, tie it around me,
I will be your companion for life.

"A Point in One's Life Becomes Two" by Krishan Singh

There comes a point in one's life, where we are drawn inward.
A unique experience to each of us.
A quest to understand who we truly are.
Along this journey inward, we discover new light upon ourselves.
Yet this light was always there.
Then we find that in order for this light to shine forth with more brilliance,
we must share this light with another.
At just the proper moment the other will appear,
but not until a certain amount of work on the self is complete.
And thus a point in one's life becomes two.
Discovery of who we are together becomes the journey.
Marriage is a foundational key.
It unlocks the hearts of two, and unifies.
Love permeates the foundation and builds the journey of togetherness.

Quote by Nicholas Sparks

Every couple needs to argue now and then—just to prove that the relationship is strong enough to survive. Long-term relationships, the ones that matter, are all about weathering the peaks and the valleys.

Quote by Theodore Spencer

Words were his delight;
Hers, a gay gracefulness
Of dancing and moving.
But when to the place
Of deep loving
(Starlight at midnight)
At last they came,
Their full communion
And consummation,
Their complete sphere,
Was stillness for her,
Silence for him.

Sonnet by Edna St. Vincent Millay

Love is not all: It is not meat nor drink
Nor slumber nor a roof against the rain,
Nor yet a floating spar to men that sink
and rise and sink and rise and sink again.
Love cannot fill the thickened lung with breath
Nor clean the blood, nor set the fractured bone;
Yet many a man is making friends with death
even as I speak, for lack of love alone.
It well may be that in a difficult hour,
pinned down by need and moaning for release
or nagged by want past resolutions power,
I might be driven to sell you love for peace,
Or trade the memory of this night for food.
It may well be. I do not think I would.

Quote by Han Suyin

Love from one being to another can only be that two people come nearer, recognize and protect and comfort each other.

"Words of Wisdom" by Bill Swetmon

It is never being too old to hold hands.

It is remembering to say, "I love you" at least once a day.

It is at no time taking the other for granted.

It is having a mutual sense of values and common objectives. It is standing together facing life.

It is forming a circle of love that gathers in the whole family.

It is doing things for each other not in the attitude of duty or sacrifice, but in the spirit of joy. It is speaking words of appreciation and demonstrating gratitude.

It is not looking for perfection in each other.

It is cultivating flexibility, patience, understanding, and a sense of humor. It is having the capacity to forgive and forget.

It is giving each other an atmosphere in which each can grow. It is finding room for the things of the spirit.

It is a common search for the good and the beautiful.

It is establishing a relationship in which independence is equal, dependence is mutual, and obligation is reciprocal. It is not marrying the right partner; it is being the right partner.

"For the Union of You and Me" by Rabindranath Tagore

It is for the union of you and me that there is light in the sky.

It is for the union of you and me that the earth is decked in dusky green.

It is for the union of you and me that the night sits motionless with the world in her arms; Dawn appears opening the eastern door with sweet murmurs in her voice.

The boat of hope sails along the currents of eternity toward that union; flowers of the ages are being gathered together for its welcoming ritual.

It is for the union of you and me that this heart of mine, in the garb of a bride,

Has proceeded from birth to birth upon the surface of this ever-turning world to choose the beloved.

"Peace" by Sara Teasdale

Peace flows into me as the tide to the pool by the shore; It is mine forevermore, it will not ebb like the sea.

I am the pool of blue that worships the vivid sky;

My hopes were heaven-high, they are all fulfilled in you,

I am the pool of gold when sunset burns and dies – you are my deepening skies;

Give me your stars to hold.

Hymn of the Universe by Pierre Teilhard de Chardin

Only love can bring individual beings to their perfect completion, as individuals, by uniting them one with another, because only love takes possession of them and unites them by what lies deepest within them. This is simply a fact of our everyday experience. For indeed at what moment do lovers come into the most complete possession of themselves if not when they say that they are lost in one another? And is not love all the time achieving—in couples, in teams, all around us—the magical and reputedly contradictory feat of personalizing through totalizing? And why should not what is thus daily achieved on a small scale be repeated one day on worldwide dimensions? Humanity, the spirit of the earth, the synthesis of individuals and peoples, the paradoxical conciliation of the element with the whole, of the one with the many: all these are regarded as utopian fantasies, yet they are biologically necessary; and if we would see them made flesh in the world what more need we do than imagine our power to love growing and broadening, till it can embrace the totality of human beings and of the earth?

Quote by Henry David Thoreau
There is no remedy for love but to love more.

"Bargain," A song by Pete Townshend of *The Who*
Here is a lyric familiar to anyone of my generation, or who listens to classic rock radio — "Bargain," by The Who. When one realizes that Pete Townsend was a devoted disciple of Meher Baba, and primarily writes about the search for connection to God, the lyrics take on new clarity:

I'd gladly lose me to find you
I'd gladly give up all I had
To find you I'd suffer anything and be glad

I'd pay any price just to get you
I'd work all my life and I will
To win you I'd stand naked, stoned and stabbed
I'd call that a bargain
The best I ever had
I'd gladly lose me to find you
I'd gladly give up all I got
To catch you I'm gonna run and never stop
I'd pay any price just to win you
Surrender my good life for bad

To find you I'm gonna drown an unsung man
I'd call that a bargain
The best I ever had

I sit looking 'round
I look at my face in the mirror
I know I'm worth nothing without you
In life one and one don't make two
One and one make one
And I'm looking for that free ride to me
I'm looking for you
I'd gladly lose me to find you
I'd gladly give up all I got
To catch you I'm gonna run and never stop

I'd pay any price just to win you
Surrender my good life for bad
To find you I'm gonna drown an unsung man
I'd call that a bargain
The best I ever had

The Best Relationship from the *Tumblr.com*
The best relationship is when you two can act like lovers and best friends at the same time. It's when you have more playful moments than serious moments. It's when you can joke around, have unexpected hugs, and random stolen kisses. It's when you two give each other that specific stare and just smile. It's when you'll rather chill inside to watch movies, eat junk food, and cuddle than go out all the time. It's when you'll stay up all night just to settle your arguments and problems. It's when you can completely act yourself and they can still love you for who you are.

"These I Can Promise" by Mark Twain
I cannot promise you a life of sunshine;
I cannot promise riches, wealth or gold;

I cannot promise you an easy pathway
That leads away from change or growing old.

But I can promise all my hearts devotion;
A smile to chase away your tears of sorrow;
A love that's ever true and ever growing;
A hand to hold in yours through each tomorrow.

From a Letter to his Brother Theo by Vincent Van Gogh

I want to paint men and women with that something of the eternal which the halo used to symbolize . . . express the love of two lovers by a wedding of two complementary colors, their mingling and opposition, the mysterious vibration of kindred tones. To express the thought of a brow by the radiance of a light tone against a somber background. To express hope by some star, the eagerness of a soul by a sunset radiance.

Quote by Gottfried Wilhelm von Leibnitz

To love is to place our happiness in the happiness of another.

"If Life Is to Have Meaning" by Martin M. Weitz

If life has meaning to us at all, it possesses it because of love. It is that which enshrines and ennobles our human experience. It is the basis for the peace of family and the peace of the peoples of the earth. The greatest gift bestowed upon humans is the gift not of demanding, but of giving love between two persons.

"Love Song" by William Carlos Williams

Sweep the house clean, hang fresh curtains in the windows put on a new dress and come with me! The elm is scattering its little loaves of sweet smells from a white sky!
Who shall hear of us in the time to come?
Let him say there was a burst of fragrance from black branches.

"To His Wife Mary" by William Wordsworth

Every day every hour every moment makes me feel more deeply how blessed we are in each other, how purely how faithfully how ardently, and how tenderly we love each other; I put this last word last because, though I am persuaded that a deep affection is not uncommon in married life, yet I am confident that a lively, gushing, thought-employing, spirit-stirring, passion of love is very rare even among good people . . . O, I love you with a passion of love which grows till I tremble to think of its strength.

"He Wishes for the Cloths of Heaven" by William Butler Yeats

Had I the heavens' embroidered cloths,
Enwrought with golden and silver light,
The blue and the dim and the dark cloths
Of night and light and the half-light,
I would spread the cloths under your feet:
But I, being poor, have only my dreams;
I have spread my dreams under your feet;
Tread softly because you tread on my dreams.

Appendix 8

For much of this chapter, I have collected the *Vows* from a variety of wedding- and marriage-related resources found on the Internet. Many vows had no attributed author or source or were defined as public domain material, which may have been further adapted. Vows and material that did have sources I have credited within this book. Finally, some of the vows are from my writings or from my eloquent colleagues in *Interfaith Seminary* program at *onespiritinterfaith. org, myweddingvows.com* and *TheKnot.com.*

Tools: Examples of Traditional Vows

I, (name), take you, (name), to be my beloved wife/husband, to have and to hold you, to honor you, to treasure you, to be at your side in sorrow and in joy, in the good times, and in the bad, and to love and cherish you always. I promise you this from my heart, for all the days of my life.

I, (name), take thee, (name), to be my lawfully wedded wife/husband to love and to comfort, from this day forward. I promise to be true to you in good times and in bad, in plenty and in want, in joy and in sorrow, in sickness and in health. I will love you and honor you all the days of my life.

(Name), you are my husband and in the witness of family and friends I vow to cherish you, always trying deeply to understand who you are and offer whatever you may need from me.

I, (name), in the witness of our dear guests, take you, (name), fully as you are to be my lawful wife/husband . . . To have and to hold, to honor and treasure, to be at your side in happiness and in sorrow, as we build the life we dream of together. I promise you my devotion and to love you as I do this moment and for all the days of my life.

In the witness of our dear family and friends I, (name), take you (name), to be my lawful husband/wife. I vow to cherish you, to best understand you and to offer my support as you need it. I am joyful about spending our lives as loyal partners, through good times and challenging ones, with the intention of building a most meaningful present and future together. I love you now and will always love you.

Appendix 9

Tools: Examples of Personal Vows

Groom:

"Susannah, you are my wife and in the witness of family and friends I vow to cherish you, always trying deeply to understand who you are and offer whatever you may need from me. I look forward to spending our lives as husband and wife, through good times and challenging ones, with the intention of building a most meaningful present and future within our loving marriage and friendship."

Bride:

"Peter, there is not a day that goes by that I don't thank God that I met you. I am no longer lost in life, as I have found my purpose in you. I vow to keep you happy for all eternity. To make you laugh and smile every day. If you fall from the clouds, I will find a way to bring you back up. I vow to shelter you and provide you with the life you have always wanted and dreamed of. I promise to never let you down. I will be there for you to get you through the hardest days and will also be there to enjoy the happy life we have worked so hard to build. We are now a family, a family that cannot be broken. You are now a part of me and I am a better person because of it. Thank you for seeing and loving the true me.

"It goes beyond those two spectacular sentences that you say to me regularly . . . 'Where are we going to watch the game today? And, they have to have good wings.'

"I wanted to share how you make me feel. All the obvious descriptions came to mind: Loved, Happy, Special, but, for me, the description that just exists in every thought is 'Absolutely Delighted.' I am truly delighted every day.

"I promise to become better at dining with one hand, so one can always be entwined with yours.

I promise that seeing you smile will always be the criteria for a successful day.

I promise that jumping in the car with you, with no destination in mind, will continue to be all that I need for a great plan.

I promise a warm embrace at the end of each day.

I promise to love and laugh.

And I promise that when you are looking at two roads that diverge in a wood, I will come too."

Appendix 10

I have collected the *Ring Exchange Vows* from a variety of wedding- and marriage-related resources found on the Internet. Many vows had no attributed author or source or were defined as public domain material, which may have been further adapted. Vows and material that did have sources I have credited within this book. Finally, some of the vows are from my writings and from my eloquent colleagues in *Interfaith Seminary* program at *onespiritinterfaith.org*, *myweddingvows.com* and *TheKnot.com*.

Tools: Ring Exchange Vows

With this ring, as a symbol of my forever love and affection, I thee wed.

I give you this ring as a symbol of my love and faithfulness. As I place it on your finger, I commit my heart and soul to you. I ask you to wear this ring as a reminder of the vows we have spoken today, our wedding day.

I give you this ring to wear with love and joy. As a ring has no end, neither shall my love for you. I choose you to be my wife/husband this day and forevermore.

This ring I give to you as a token of my love and devotion to you. I pledge to you all that I am and all that I will ever be as your husband/wife. With this ring, I gladly marry you and join my life to yours.

I give this ring as my gift to you. Wear it and think of me and know that I love you.

I give you this ring as a visible and constant symbol of my promise to be with you as long as I live.

I give you this ring as a symbol of my love for you. Let it be a reminder that I am always by your side and that I will always be a faithful partner to you.

I give you this ring as a symbol of my love, my faith in our strength together, and my covenant to learn and grow with you.

With this ring, I thee wed, and with it, I bestow upon thee all the treasures of my mind, heart, and hands.

(Name), I give you this ring as a symbol of my love. As it encircles your finger, may it remind you always that you are surrounded by my enduring love.

Response: I will wear it gladly. Whenever I look at it, I will remember this joyous day and the vows we've made.

I have for you a golden ring. The most precious metal symbolizes that your love is the most precious element in my life. The ring has no beginning and no ending, which symbolizes that the love between us will never cease. I place it on your finger as a visible sign of the vows which have made us husband and wife.

Because this ring is perfectly symmetrical, it signifies the perfection of true love. As I place it on your finger, I give you all that I am and ever hope to be.

Response: Because this ring has no end or beginning, it signifies the continuation of true love. As I place it on your finger, I give you all that I am and ever hope to be.

Appendix 11

Tools: Announcements

Example 4:
Celebrant says:

"The wedding couple has asked me to kindly tell you, and I quote, 'During the ceremony we'd prefer to see everyone's faces in their professional photographs rather than a bunch of phones.' Now we're ready for the wedding to begin."

Example 5:
Celebrant says:

"Welcome everyone. I am Reverend Lynn Gladstone, and I am honored to be here to perform the marriage ceremony of this mischievous and music-loving couple. I cherish the opportunity to partake in this exhilarating wedding ceremony, and I invite you to do the same.

To begin, the wedding couple is requesting that you kindly put your phones on silent, but feel free to take photos.

To get us started, please turn to someone you do not know, shake their hand and say hello.

Okay, please clap or holler to show me that you are ready to have some serious fun! Thank you. Let's begin."

Appendix 12

Tools: Celebrant's Introductory Remarks

For much of this chapter, I have collected the *Introductory Remarks* from a variety of wedding- and marriage-related resources found on the Internet. Many materials had no attributed author or source or were defined as public domain material, which may have been further adapted. Material that did have sources for I have credited within this book. Finally, an additional source for these materials is the *Interfaith Seminary* program at *onespiritinterfaith.org*.

Baal Shem Tov
From every human being there rises a light that reaches straight to heaven that is designed to be together, to find each other, their streams of light flow brighter, light goes forth from their united being.

Words by Bob Dylan
Ever since you walked right in, the circle's been complete
I've said goodbye to haunted rooms and faces in the street
To the courtyard of the jester which is hidden from the sun
I love you more than ever and I haven't yet begun.

Words by Kahlil Gibran
Love gives naught but itself and takes naught but from itself.
Love possesses not nor would be possessed. For love is sufficient unto love.

John 15
. . . my joy may be in you and that your joy may be complete.
My commandment is this: Love one another as I love you.
Therefore now they are no longer two, but one flesh.
What therefore God has joined together, let no man put asunder.

Matthew 19
Let us be grateful to the people who make us happy; they are the charming gardeners who make our souls blossom.

Medieval Christian Vow
You cannot possess me for I belong to myself
But while we both wish it, I give you what is mine to give

1 Corinthians
Love is patient; love is kind; it rejoices in the truth,
Hopes all things, endures all things . . . .
Love is eternal. Love never ends.

1 John 4
Love comes from God. Everyone who truly loves is a child of God.

Psalms 1
Blessed are the man and the woman who have grown beyond themselves and have seen through their separations. They delight in the way things are and keep their hearts open, day and night. They are like trees planted near flowing rivers, which bear fruit when they are ready. Their leaves will not fall or wither. Everything they do will succeed.

Romans 12
Let love be without any pretense. In love, let your feelings of deep affection for one another come to expression and regard others as more important than yourself.

Words by William Shakespeare
What made me love thee?
Let that persuade thee there's something extraordinary in thee.
I cannot but I love thee, none but thee, and thou deservest it.

Words by Robert Francis Smith

Weddings are the one celebration where all the streams of life run together into the human ocean. Bereft of ecstatic bridal couples, nuptial bliss and happy families, who could endure life?

Song of Songs

I hear my
Beloved
My Beloved lifts up his voice, (he) [my beloved] says to me,
"Come then, my love, my lovely one, come.
 . . . your face is beautiful."

Words from Ancient Sanskrit

Be like two sweet-singing birds
Perched upon the highest branches of the tree of life.
Filling the air with songs of love and rapture.

Appendix 13

Tools: Celebrant's Invocations for I/I/I Ceremonies

The following are my original invocations:

Spiritual:

Celebrant's says:

"Dear Spirit, please take notice of this beloved pair and bestow your loving consideration upon them always. Please protect them with your kind benevolence."

Spiritual:

Celebrant's says:

"And now we gladly greet the Universal Spirit of life and love, of all beliefs, and ask that every form of blessing be given to you two as you move forward in your lives and adventures together."

Spiritual:

Celebrant's says:

"With all the good will present and the grace surrounding us, we may sense that this is a reverent time and space. So, we ask the Spirit of life and the Spirit of love to please shine their glorious generosity upon this gathering. Those creative forces of love and kindness underlie everything that is good in our lives. We call upon you, benevolent spirit, to shower magnanimous blessings for Jessica and Carson's marriage ceremony."

Spiritual:

Celebrant's says:

"And, we have one more important welcoming. We invite the Spirit of love to shine its glorious light here today. We ask love to shower its magnanimous blessings on Jeanine and Beau at this sacred celebration of their union."

Spiritual:

Celebrant's says:

"Great Spirit, we ask that you bless this wedding couple with your guidance through this ceremony for their deep commitment to each other with all of your heart. May you reveal to this special couple, Rachel and David, an ancient secret about surrendering to love and the ways to share this precious love with the rest of the world."

Spiritual:

Celebrant's says:

"And we have one more important welcome. We invite the spirit of life and love to shine its glorious presence here. Yes, those creative forces of love and kindness underlying everything that is good in our lives. We call upon this spirit to shower magnanimous blessings for Patricia and Didier's marriage ceremony.

"At this time, let us take a moment of silence in reverence to that invocation on behalf of this beloved pair."

Religious:

Celebrant's says:

"We are joined here by the unfailing love of The Father, The Son and The Holy Spirit. Dear God, we are here tonight for the marriage of Bea and Drew, and I am confident in your abiding presence to witness this ceremony alongside all of us. Please be generous with this dear twosome by inspiring and sustaining them in their love for all the days of their life together into eternity."

Religious:

Celebrant's says:

"We are joined here by the unfailing and loving presence of The Father, The Son and The Holy Spirit. At this time, we faithfully invoke God's love and support.

"Deborah and Seth, may every form of blessing be given to you. Dear God, please be generous with this couple offering your wise guidance to them.

"Inspire and sustain them in their love for all the days of their lives. We ask you, O Universal Spirit, to also regard their family and friends. Please bestow upon them your caring consideration, providing them all with good health and healing. Let us be grateful for God's listening heart.

"And we say Amen."

Religious:

Celebrant's says:

"Dear God, we are here tonight to witness the wedding of Nora and Ted. I trust in your presence and ask you to bless this marriage ceremony. Please be generous with this precious couple by inspiring and sustaining them in their love and commitment, always.

"In this moment and place, we can take a speck of silent time to recognize our appreciation for the creative forces of God's love that are the foundation of everything that is good in our lives. Let us be grateful for God's listening heart.

"And we say, 'Amen'."

Appendix 14

Tools: Blessings by the Celebrant

The following are examples of my original blessings:

Example 4:
Celebrant says:
"My hands on them
Ye vah recha Adonai ve yish me recha — May God bless you and keep you.
Remember that when you look into each other's eyes,
You are looking into the eyes of a spirit that connects all of humanity."

Example 5:
Celebrant says:
"May the Force of Devotion bless you both and keep you always.
As we near the end of the ceremony, I would like to read a Hawaiian
wedding blessing, which speaks of it all so beautifully."

Example 6:
Celebrant says:
"May your faith in your beloveds, in yourselves and in God forever bring you
the stability and discernment that will guide you through all your days together.
May joy, peace, wisdom and good humor abound in your marriage and in the
world. For the very first time, I present you these newlyweds Mr. and Mrs. Emily
and John Price. And now you may kiss!"

Example 7:
Celebrant joins their left hands.
Celebrant says:
"May the Universal Spirits of life and of love bless you both and be gracious to
you in your marriage. May your faith in one another and in yourselves forever
bring you the stability and discernment that will guide you through all your days

together. May joy, peace, wisdom and good humor abound in your marriage and in the *world*. Please remember that when you look into each other's eyes, you are looking into the eyes of a force that connects all of humanity. May the powers above bless you and keep you."

Example 8:

Celebrant says:

"As we are gathered to share the meaning of this most heartfelt, significant moment in these newlyweds' lives, let me ask you all to go silently within and fill yourselves with the best of wishes for them as they walk into the light of their future together. And, may we consider that when looking into another's eyes, we are looking into the light of all of humanity."

Blessings by Other I/I/I Ministers

By Rev. Diane Finlayson

May you be patient with each other as you each find your way.

May you support each other in times of need.

May you fly together in times of joy.

And may you be open to the blessings of all the communities who hold you dear, however those blessings may appear.

By Rev. Mary Gracely

Married love is woven into a pattern of living. It contains the elements of understanding and the passionate kindness of two people toward each other. It is rich in the many-sided joys of life, because each person is more concerned with giving joy than receiving it. As you know, joys are most truly experienced when they are most fully shared. May your marriage bring you the exquisite excitements a marriage should bring, and may your life together grant you patience, tolerance, and understanding. May you enter into the mystery, which is the awareness of one another's presence—both physical and spiritual—a presence warm and near when you are side-by-side, and warm and near when you are in separate rooms or even different cities. May you have happiness and may you find it by making one another happy. May you have love, and may you find it by loving one another.

By Rosemary Hyde
May you find deep happiness and fulfillment as you join lives, knowing that the essence of love is to walk forward together tuned into the well-being of the other — and that over time, as ego dissolves into ever greater love, joy overtakes anxiety and fear.

By Grenetta Briggs Mason
May your love continue to inform you of how to be with each other authentically.

May the Spirit continue to bless and enfold you.

You are loved!

By Kindle Perry
Ever may you see each other tenderly, with mutual reverence.
Ever may you listen to each other carefully, with mutual reverence.
Ever may you speak to each other truthfully, with mutual reverence.
Ever may you think of each other faithfully, with mutual reverence.
Ever may you act towards each other honorably, with mutual reverence.
Ever may you embrace each other passionately, with mutual reverence.
Mutual reverence,
Mutual reverence,
Mutual reverence.

By Marama Winder
May your union bring remembrance that you are twin souls
created from the same essence, one for the other.
May you discover the deepest secrets of love —
May you be blessed with the understanding that there is
no separation between true beloveds —
that you are never apart in your spirits.
-As written in the Legend of Solomon and Sheba

Appendix 15

Tools: Blessings from World Cultures

I have collected the *World Culture Blessings* from a variety of wedding- and marriage-related resources found on the Internet. Many materials had no attributed author or source or were defined as public domain material, which may have been further adapted. Material that did have sources I have credited within this book. Finally, additional sources for these materials are Susan Turchin's book, *The Interfaith Wedding Manual, Creating Meaningful Wedding Ceremonies: A Guide for Clergy and Couples* (22–62), professional colleagues from the *Interfaith Seminary* program at *onespiritinterfaith.org* and *weddingdells.com.au*.

Cherokee
May you each be like the air that inhabits the other.

Gaelic
May couples live to grow together in your love under their own vine and fig tree and seeing their children's children.

Great Plains Indian
Above you are the stars, below you are the stones
As time does pass, remember,
Like a star should your love be constant,
Like a stone should your love be firm.

Hawaiian
Here all seeking is over
The lost has been found
A mate has been found
To share the chills of winter
Now love ask
That you be united
Here is a place to rest

A place to sleep, a place in heaven.
Now two are becoming one, the black night is scattered.
The Eastern sky grows bright; at last the great day has come.

Irish

In homage to all of the Irish presence in this room, please turn to your programs and join me in offering this delightful blessing to Mathew and Callie:

May flowers always line your path and sunshine light your day;
May song birds serenade you every step along the way.
May a rainbow run beside you in a sky that's always blue,
And may happiness fill your heart each day, your whole life through.
May you always have walls for the winds, a roof for the rain, tea beside the
    fire, laughter to cheer you, those you love near you, and all your heart might
    desire.
May the road rise to meet you,
May the wind be always at your back,
May the sun shine warm upon your face, The rains fall soft upon your fields,
    and, Until we meet again,
May God hold you in the palm of His hand.
May you have: A world of wishes at your command. God and his angels close
    to hand. Friends and family their love impart, and Irish blessings in your
    heart!
May you always walk in sunshine.
May you never want for more.
May Irish angels rest their wings right beside your door.
May the embers of the open hearth warm your hands.
May the sun's rays from the Irish sky warm your face.
May the children's bright smiles warm your heart.
May the everlasting love you receive warm your soul.
May joy and peace surround you, Contentment latch your door, And happiness
    be with you now, And bless you evermore.
May brooks and trees and singing hills join in the chorus, too.
And every gentle wind that blows send happiness to you.

May the raindrops fall lightly on your brow.

May the soft winds freshen your spirit.

May the sunshine brighten your heart. And may God enfold you in the mantle of His love.

May the sound of happy music, And the lilt of Irish laughter, fill your heart with gladness, that stays forever after.

Jewish: The Seven Blessings

וְפגה ירפ ארוב ,םלועה ךלמ וניהלא 'ה התא ךורב.

Baruch ata Adonai Eloheinu melech ha'olam, bo'rei p'ri hagafen.

Blessed are You, our God, sovereign of the universe,
who creates the fruit of the vine.

ודובכל ארב לכהש ,םלועה ךלמ וניהלא 'ה התא ךורב.

Baruch ata Adonai Eloheinu melech ha'olam shehakol bara lich'vodo.

Blessed are You, our God, sovereign of the universe,
who created everything for God's Glory.

םדאה רצוי ,םלועה ךלמ וניהלא 'ה התא ךורב.

Baruch ata Adonai Eloheinu melech ha'olam, yotzeir ha'adam.

Blessed are You, our God, sovereign of the universe, who creates human
beings.

ונממ ול ןיקתהו ,ותינבת תומד םלצב ,ומלצב םדאה תא רצי רשא ,םלועה ךלמ וניהלא 'ה התא ךורב
םדאה רצוי ,'ה התא ךורב .דע ידע ןיינב

Baruch ata Adonai Eloheinu melech ha'olam, asher yatzar et ha'adam b'tzalmo,
b'tzelem d'mut tavnito, v'hitkin lo mimenu binyan adei ad. Baruch atah Adonai,
yotzeir ha'adam.

Blessed are You, our God, sovereign of the universe, who creates man in your
image, fashioning perpetuated life. Blessed are You, creator of human beings.

הינבב ןויצ חמשמ ,'ה התא ךורב. החמשב הכותל הינב ץוביקב ,הרקעה ולגתו שישת שוש.

Sos tasis v'tageil ha'akara b'kibutz baneha l'tocha b'simcha. Baruch ata Adonai, m'sameach Tziyon b'vaneha.

May parents be glad as their children are joyfully gathered to them. Blessed are You, who gladden Zion with Children.

הלכו ןתח חמשמ 'ה התא ךורב. םדקמ ןדע ןגב ךרדירצי'ך ךחמשכ םיבוהאה םיער חמשת חמש.

Sameiach tesamach reiim ha-ahuvim k'sameichacha y'tzircha b'gan eden mikedem. Baruch ata Adonai, m'sameiach chatan v'chalah.

Grant perfect joy to these loving companions, as you did your creations in the Garden of Eden. Blessed are You, who grants the joy of loving couples.

הוודחו הציד ,הניר הליג ,הלכו ןתח ,החמשו ןושש ארב רשא ,םלועה ךלמ וניהלא 'ה התא ךורב ,תוער שושו לוק ,םילשורי תוצוחבו הדוהי ירעב עמשי וניקלא 'ה הרהמ. תוערו םולשו ושלש ,םתאיחו הבהא 'ה התא ךורב. םתניגנ התשממ םירענו. םתפוחמ םינתח תולהצמ לוק ,הלכ לוקו ןתח לוק ,החמש הלכה םע ןתח חמשמ

Baruch ata Adonai Eloheinu melech ha'olam, asher bara sason v'simcha chatan v'kallah, gilah rinah ditzah v'chedvah, ahavah v'achavah v'shalom v're'ut. M'hera Adonai Eloheinu yishamah b'arei Yehudah uv-chutzot Yerushalayim kol sason v'kol simcha, kol chatan v'kol kalah, kol mitzhalot chatanim mechupatam un'arim mimishte n'ginatam. Baruch ata Adonai, m'sameach chatan im hakalah.

Blessed are You, our God, sovereign of the universe, who created joy and gladness, loving companions, mirth, song, delight and rejoicing, love and harmony and peace and companionship.

Soon, God, may there ever be heard in the cities of Judah and in the streets of Jerusalem voices of joy and gladness, voices of loving couples, the jubilant voices of those joined in marriage under the canopy, the voices of young people feasting and singing. Blessed are You, who causes couples to rejoice with one another.

Jewish: The Priestly Blessing

דְּכְרְבְּ הֹוֹהִי דְּרֶמְשָׁיו.

Y'varekh-chah Adonai v'yish-m'rechah

May God bless you and watch over you.

ראֵיַ הֹוֹהִי וינָפֿ דִּילֵא :דְּנֶחָיוְדְנֶחָיו.

Ya'er Adonai panav eilechah vi-chunekah.

May God's face shine upon you and be gracious to you.

אשֵׁי הֹוֹהִי וינָפֿ דִּילֵא מֹשֵׁיַו דְּל מֹולֹשֵׁ.

Yisah Adonai panav eilechah v'yasem lechah shalom.

May God smile upon you and grant you peace.

Keres Indian

Now you will feel no rain, for each of you will be shelter for the other.

Now you will feel no cold for each of you will be warmth to the other.

Now you will feel no loneliness for each of you will be companion to the other.

Now you are two persons but there is only one life before you.

May beauty surround you both in the journey ahead and through all the years.

May happiness be your companion and your days together be good and long
    upon the earth.

Sufi

May the blessing of God rest upon you,

May his peace abide with you,

May his presence illuminate your heart

Now and forevermore.

Appendix 16

Tools: Celebrant's Meal Blessings

I have collected the *Meal Blessings* from a variety of wedding- and marriage-related resources found on the Internet. Many materials had no attributed author or source or were defined as public domain material, which may have been further adapted. Material that did have sources I have credited within this book. Finally, an additional source for these materials is *indifferentlanguages.com*.

Birkat Hazan, Torah

בָּרוּךְ אַתָּה יְיָ, אֱלֹהֵנוּ מֶלֶךְ הָעוֹלָם, הַמּוֹצִיא לֶחֶם מִן הָאֶרֶץ.

Baruch ata Adonai, Eloheinu melech ha'olam, hamotzilechem min ha'artez.
Blessed are you, Lord, our God, Ruler of the universe,
Who brings forth bread from the earth.

Christian
For good food and those who prepare it, for good friends with whom to share it, we thank you God.

Christian
Dear God, we give thanks for the pleasure of gathering together for this occasion. We give thanks for this food prepared by loving hands. We give thanks for life, the freedom to enjoy it all, and all other blessings.

Ecclesiastes
Go, eat your bread with joy,
And drink your wine with a merry heart.

By Reverend Diane Finlayson
Creator of the Universe,
Thank you for the bounty of your gifts.

Thank you for the fresh fields in which this food grew.

We ask that you bless the workers who labored long and hard to raise and harvest it.

And, the cooks who placed their loving energy into cooking this meal.

May we remember all that has happened to bring us to this moment and send blessings to all who have contributed to this meal that we may be nourished and sustained.

And Beloved Creator, we thank you for the fellowship we share that nourishes our spirits in the same manner that this food nourishes our bodies.

Your goodness blesses us richly each day.

We send our good will and our hearts to those who have not had these benefits and pray that we may be shown ways, in our refreshed state, that we may be a blessing to others in our community as well. We ask this in your Gracious name, Amen.

Saint Francis of Assisi

Praised be my Lord for our Mother the Earth,

Which sustains us and keeps us and brings forth diverse fruits,

And, flowers of many colors.

Hindu

Bless this food.

Make it holy.

Let no impurity or greed defile it.

The food comes from thee.

It is for thy temple.

By Walter Rauschenbrusch

Thanks be to Thee for friendship shared,

Thanks be to Thee for food prepared,

Bless Thou the cup; bless Thou the bread;

Thy blessing rest upon each head.

By Reverend Angie Siegler
A circle of friends is a blessed thing.
Sweet is the breaking of bread with friends.
For the honor of their presence at our board.
We are deeply grateful, God.

By Reverend Angie Siegler
Heavenly Father/Mother, you have gathered us together to break bread, to receive the gifts of Mother Earth, and we are grateful. We acknowledge the many beings whose loving hands brought this food from its origins to this table and we thank the food itself for the nourishment it provides us. We are nourished not only by the food before us but the companionship between and amongst us. For food, friendship, and fun we thank you. Amen.

Traditional
For what we are about to receive, the Lord makes us truly thankful, for Christ's sake. Amen.
What we are about to receive, may the Trinity and the Unity bless. Amen.

Traditional
Our Dear Heavenly Father, we thank Thee for this food. Feed our souls on the bread of life and help us to do our part in kind words and loving deeds. We ask in Jesus' name.

Appendix 17

Tools: Ceremony Toasts from World Cultures

For much of this chapter, I have collected the *Ceremony Toasts* from a variety of wedding- and marriage-related resources found on the Internet. Many materials had no attributed author or source or were defined as public domain material, which may have been further adapted. Material that did have sources I have credited within this book. Finally, an additional source for these materials is *TheKnot.com*. © Copyright 2016, *TheKnot.com*. Reproduced by Permission. All Rights Reserved. Credit to: *TheKnot.com*.

African
May your love be like the misty rain, gentle coming in, but flooding going to the river.

Armenian
May you grow old on one pillow.

Chinese
Ten thousand things bright
Ten thousand miles, no dust
Water and sky one color
Houses shining along your road.

Greek
The heart that loves is always young.

Hawaiian
Ka mau ki aha.
May you never thirst again.

Latin

Ad multos annos!
To many years!

Old English

May your joys be as sweet as spring flowers that grow.
As bright as a fire when winter winds blow,
As countless as leaves that float down in the fall,
As serene as the love that keeps watch over us all.

Traditional

A toast to love, and laughter, and happily ever after.

Traditional

Let us toast the health of the bride;
Let us toast the health of the groom;
Let us toast the person that tied;
Let us toast every guest in the room.

Appendix 18

Tools: Historical Quotes as Toasts

For much of this chapter, I have collected the *historical toasts* from a variety of wedding- and marriage-related resources found on the Internet. Many materials had no attributed author or source or were defined as public domain material, which may have been further adapted. Material that did have sources I have credited within this book. Finally, an additional source for these materials is *TheKnot.com.* © Copyright 2016, *TheKnot.com.* Reproduced by Permission. All Rights Reserved. Credit to *TheKnot.com.*

Dante Alighieri
A great flame follows a little spark.

St. Augustine
Insomuch as love grows you, so beauty grows. For love is the beauty of the soul.

Plato
All love should be simply stepping-stones to the love of God . . . .
Blessed be His name for His great goodness and mercy.

King Henry V by Shakespeare
God, the best maker of all marriages,
Combine your hearts in one.

Romeo and Juliet by Shakespeare
A flock of blessings light upon thy back.

The Merchant of Venice by Shakespeare
Fair thought and happy hours attend you.

Timon of Athens by Shakespeare

The best of happiness, honor, and fortunes keeps with you.

"Venus and Adonis" by Shakespeare

Love comforteth like sunshine after rain . . . .

Appendix 19

Tools: Additional Quotes as Toasts

The following toasts were published in the "Ideas + Etiquette" section of *The Knot* in an article titled "30 Inspiring Quotes for Wedding Toasts. Use these top tips to make a memorable moment at the reception" *("30 Inspiring," TheKnot.com).* © Copyright 2016, *TheKnot.com*. Reproduced by Permission. All Rights Reserved. Credit to: *TheKnot.com*.

By Joseph Campbell
Love is friendship set to music.

By Julie Wittey
Love is a moment that lasts forever.

From *Toasts for Every Occasion* edited by Jennifer Rahel Conover
May your dreams ride on the wings of angels who know their way home to the skies.

By Emily Bronte
Whatever our souls are made of, his and mine are the same.

Gwendolyn Brooks
We are each other's harvest; we are each other's business; we are each other's magnitude and bond.

By Marc Chagall
In our life there is a single color, as on an artist's palette, which provides the meaning of life and art. It is the color of love.

By Antoine de Saint-Exupéry
Love does not consist in gazing at each other, but in looking outward together in the same direction.

Lope de Vega
Without love, the world itself would not survive.

By Emily Dickinson
That love is all there is
Is all we know of love.

By Kahlil Gibran
Marriage is like a golden ring in a chain, whose beginning is a glance and whose ending is eternity.

By Nikki Giovanni
We love because it's the only true adventure.

By Langston Hughes
When people care for you and cry for you, they can straighten out your soul.

Indian Proverb
When love reigns, the impossible may be attained.

By John Keating, in *Dead Poets Society*
We don't read and write poetry because it's cute. We read and write poetry because we are members of the human race. And the human race is filled with passion. And medicine, law, business, engineering, these are noble pursuits and necessary to sustain life. But poetry, beauty, romance, love, these are what we stay alive for.

By John Lennon and Paul McCartney

Love is all you need.

By Pablo Neruda

Love is a fire that feeds our life.

By Plato

At the touch of love everyone becomes a poet.

By Cole Porter

Night and day you are the one,
Only you, beneath the moon and under the sun.

By Walter Rauschenbusch

We never live so intensely as when we love strongly.

We never realize ourselves so vividly as when we are in full glow of love for others.

By Rainer Maria Rilke

A good marriage is that in which each appoints the other guardian of his solitude.

By George Sand

There is only one happiness in life: to love and be loved.

By William Shakespeare

They do not love that do not show their love.

By Sophocles

One word
Frees us of all the weight and pain of life:
That word is love.

By Leo Tolstoy
Love is life.

By Lao Tzu
To love someone deeply gives you strength. Being loved by someone deeply gives you courage.

By Voltaire
Love is a canvas furnished by nature and embroidered by imagination.

By Walt Whitman
The strongest and sweetest songs
yet remain to be sung.

Works Cited

1. Berke, Diane. *Interfaith Minister's Training and Reference Manual, Second Year Training Program.* New York: Diane Berke and One Spirit Learning Alliance, 2005. Print.

2. Blum, Marcy. *Wedding Planning for Dummies.* 3rd ed. New Jersey: John Wiley & Sons, Inc., 2013. Print.

3. Culliford, Larry. "Spiritual Care and Psychiatric Treatment: An Introduction." *Psychology Today, Advances in Psychiatric Treatment,* Vol. 8, (2002): 249–261. Sussex Publishers. Web. Jan. 12, 2016. <http://www.psychologytoday.com/sites/default/files/attachments/52072/apt-2002-spirituality-introduction.pdf>.

4. Gladstone, Lynn. *LynnGladstone.com.* Lynn Gladstone, 2012. Web. 25 Mar. 2016.

5. Head, Tom. "Interracial Marriage Laws: A Short Timeline History." *About.* n.p. 16 Dec. 2014. Web. 5 Jan. 2016. <http://civilliberty.about.com/od/raceequalopportunity/tp/Interracial-Marriage-Laws-History-Timeline.htm>.

6. "Intermarriage." *Dictionary.com Unabridged.* Random House, Inc. Web. 25 Mar. 2016. <http://www.dictionary.com/browse/intermarriage>.

7. Kahlenberg Rebecca R. "The I Do's and Don'ts of Intercultural Marriage." *Interfaith Family.* Edmund Case, March 2003. Web. 5 Jan. 2016. <http://www.interfaithfamily.com/relationships/marriage_and_relationships/The_I_Dos_and_Donts_of_Intercultural_Marriage.shtml>.

8. Liptak, Adam. "Supreme Court Ruling Makes Same-Sex Marriage a Right Nationwide. *The New York Times.* The New York Times Company, 26 June 2015. Web. 5 Jan. 2016. <http://www.nytimes.com/2015/06/27/us/supreme-court-same-sex-marriage.html>.

9. "Marriage." *Merriam-Webster.* Merriam-Webster, Inc. n.d. Web. 5 Jan. 2016. <http://www.merriam-webster.com/dictionary/marriage>.

10. Miller, Claire Cain and Quoctrung Bui. "Equality in Marriages Grows, and So Does Class Divide." *The New York Times.* The New York Times Company, 27 Feb. 2016. Web. 28 Feb. 2016. <http://www.nytimes.com/2016/02/23/upshot/rise-in-marriages-of-equals-and-in-division-by-class.html>.

11. "Modern Immigration Wave Brings 59 Million to U.S., Driving Population Growth and Change Through 2065. Views of Immigration's Impact on U.S. Society Mixed." *Pew Research Center.* The Pew Charitable Trusts, 28 Sept. 2015. Web. 15 March. 2016. <http://www.pewhispanic.org/2015/09/28/modern-immigration-wave-brings-59-million-to-u-s-driving-population-growth-and-change-through-2065/>.

12. "Muhyiddin Ibn 'Arabi: The Treasure of Compassion." *The Muhyiddin Ibn 'Arabi Society.* n.p. Web. 13 Jan. 2016. <http://www.ibnarabisociety.org/articles/treasureofcompassion.html>.

13. Murphy, Caryle. "Interfaith Marriage is Common in U.S., Particularly Among the Recently Wed." *Pew Research Center.* The Pew Charitable Trusts, 2 Jun. 2015. Web. 7 Jan. 2016. <http://www.pewresearch.org/fact-tank/2015/06/02/interfaith-marriage/>.

14. "October 9 - Philip Simmons." *Onespiritinterfaith.org.* One Spirit Learning Alliance, 9 Oct. 2012. Web. 25 March 2016. <http://onespiritinterfaith.org/october-9-philip-simmons/>.

15. *Onespiritinterfaith.org.* One Spirit Learning Alliance, 2012. Web. 25 March 2016.

16. Pollinger, Maureen Burwell. *Yes! I Will! I Do! Your Step-by-Step Guide to Creating a Wedding Ceremony as Unique as You Are.* New York: Purple Plume, a division of Inkwell, Ltd., 2011. Print.

17. Seamon, Erika B. *Interfaith Marriage in America, The Transformation of Religion and Christianity.* New York: Palgrave MacMillan, 2012. Print.

18. "Spirituality." *Psychology Today.* Sussex Publishers. n.d. Web. 12 Jan. 2016. <https://www.psychologytoday.com/basics/spirituality>.

19. "30 Inspiring Quotes for Wedding Toasts. Use These Top Tips to Make a Memorable Moment at the Reception." *The Knot.* XO Group, 1997–2016. Web. 6 Mar. 2015. <https://www.theknot.com/content/wedding-toast-tips-30-inspiring-quotes>.

20. Torgerson , Rachel. "4 Ways to Keep the Peace with Your Religious Parents." *The Knot.* XO Group, 1997–2016. Web. 16 Feb. 2016. <https://www.theknot.com/content/religion-isnt-a-marriage-deal-breaker>.

21. Turchin, Susan, ed. *The Interfaith Wedding Manual: Creating Meaningful Wedding Ceremonies: A Guide for Clergy and Couples.* 3rd ed. New York: Suespirit Publishers, 2009. Print.

22. "Union by Robert Fulghum — A wedding reading." *English-wedding.* The English Wedding Blog, 25 June 2013. Web. 1 March 2016. <https://english-wedding.com/2013/06/union-by-robert-fulghum-a-wedding-reading/>.

23. "U.S. Public Becoming Less Religious: Modest Drop in Overall Rates of Belief and Practice, but Religiously Affiliated Americans Are as Observant as Before." *Pew Research Center.* The Pew Charitable Trusts, 3 Nov. 2015. Web. 15 March 2016. <http://www.pewforum.org/2015/11/03/u-s-public-becoming-less-religious/>.

24. Wright, Matthew. "Reshaping Religion: Interspirituality and Multiple Religious Belonging." *Interspirituality, The Interspiritual Network.* n.p. 30 Oct. 2014. Web. 5 Jan. 2016. <http://interspirituality.com/729/>.

25. Yinger, Milton J. "On the Definition of Interfaith Marriage." *Jstor, Journal for the Scientific Study of Religion,* Vol. 7, No. 1, (Spring 1968): 104–107. Wiley. Web. 5 Jan. 2016. <http://www.jstor.org/stable/1385115>.

* 9 7 8 1 9 4 5 4 4 6 3 1 3 *